Pro SharePoint with jQuery

Phill Duffy

Apress®

Pro SharePoint with jQuery

Copyright © 2011 by Phill Duffy

ISBN-13 (pbk): 978-1-4302-4098-3

ISBN-13 (electronic): 978-1-4302-4099-0

President and Publisher: Paul Manning
Lead Editor: Kate Blackham
Technical Reviewer: Anthony Pounder
Editorial Board: Steve Anglin, Mark Beckner, Ewan Buckingham, Gary Cornell, Jonathan Gennick, Jonathan Hassell, Michelle Lowman, James Markham, Matthew Moodie, Jeff Olson, Jeffrey Pepper, Douglas Pundick, Ben Renow-Clarke, Dominic Shakeshaft, Matt Wade, Tom Welsh
Coordinating Editor: Rebecca Freed
Copy Editor: Kim Wimpsett
Production Support: Patrick Cunningham
Indexer: SPi Global
Artist: SPi Global
Cover Designer: Anna Ishchenko

Distributed to the book trade worldwide by Springer Science+Business Media, LLC., 233 Spring Street, 6th Floor, New York, NY 10013. Phone 1-800-SPRINGER, fax (201) 348-4505, e-mail orders-ny@springer-sbm.com, or visit www.springeronline.com.

For information on translations, please e-mail rights@apress.com, or visit www.apress.com.

Apress and friends of ED books may be purchased in bulk for academic, corporate, or promotional use. eBook versions and licenses are also available for most titles. For more information, reference our Special Bulk Sales–eBook Licensing web page at www.apress.com/bulk-sales.

The source code for this book is available to readers at www.apress.com. You will need to answer questions pertaining to this book in order to successfully download the code.

Dedicated to Pip, my family, and all those who go out of their way to help others.

Contents at a Glance

Contents

About the Author

Phill Duffy is a product manager at Lightning Tools, Ltd., who lives in the amazing city of Bristol, England, with his gorgeous partner, Pip, and wonder-dog, Billy. Phill's passion for speaking has allowed him to talk at conferences in London, Boston, San Diego, and San Francisco on SharePoint, jQuery, and the SharePoint BCS. He runs the South West England SharePoint User Group and has a Microsoft Community Contributor Award, as well as an MCTS: Application Development for SharePoint 2007 and 2010 certification.

About the Technical Reviewer

Tony Pounder is a director of Intelligent Decisioning Ltd., a SharePoint-focused solutions provider based in Nottingham, England. He has worked in a development-focused role for his whole career and holds numerous Microsoft certifications, including the recently launched SharePoint Beta 2010. He has been involved with SharePoint since 2004, working on many SharePoint projects for both public- and private-sector companies.

Tony is a keen runner and has completed numerous half-marathons and the London Marathon twice, and he enjoys other running events such as the P Coy challenge: 10 miles in military boots wearing a 35-pound pack and traversing "challenging" ground! He is usually found organizing or taking part in #sprunners events wherever SharePoint people get together. Contact Tony at `www.id-live.com`, `www.twitter.com/WorTony`, or `www.anthonypounder.com`.

Acknowledgments

My loving fiancée, Pip, was so patient with my late nights, early starts, busy weekends, and all the time I spent in the study that I feel she should be thanked first. Pip has encouraged and supported me all the way through writing this book; she made sure I was looked after as I whiled away the hours with my laptop. Pip took the dog out, fed me, and simply gave me the reason to succeed. She's the perfect partner in crime for writing a book—I couldn't wish for anyone better. To my loving family, I have to say, "Look, I've written a book!" because I know how proud they are—and how proud of them I am too.

Being able to work with two of the best people you could wish for has been a great honor and has really helped with writing this book. To Brett and Nick, I want to say a massive thank-you for the advice and support and for encouraging me constantly to achieve. Their support has helped me do so many things that a younger me could have only dreamed of, such as talking at conferences and writing this book. I would also like to thank the rest of the guys at Lightning Tools who all have been amazing inspirations to succeed.

There are people you meet along the way that really make a difference. I consider myself to be lucky to have met three such people who have given me so much of their time, wisdom, and drive. Mr. Brown taught so much more than the lessons he delivered: he urged me to fulfill my potential and inspired me. In hindsight I'm very happy to have been given that gift. Mr. Brown is also the person who first suggested that I purchase Visual Studio 6 when I was 16—one of the best suggestions ever.

In my first job as a data entry bod, I had the great pleasure of working with a great friend of mine, Stephen Bouchereau. Stephen spent countless hours listening to me talk about what I wanted to do with my career. Stephen is one of those people who oozes ability, and to have him mentor me was a real boost. He even took to learning MySQL with me, just so I'd have someone to help me through it. A nicer person would be hard to find.

At that same data entry job, I was also lucky enough to meet another great friend of mine, Rob Funnell. I later went off to work with Rob as a second/third-line support engineer, and since Rob knew I wanted to become a developer, he gave me every possible opportunity to learn more development skills. Without him, my first step into the world of programming would have been a much tougher one, so I want to give him a big thank-you. He is also a great person to know…and to have beer with.

A great big thank-you to Tony Pounder for doing an excellent job as the technical reviewer for this book. Tony is a first-class guy, and I am grateful to him for being part of the team.

This book has been such a positive challenge for me, since I've only ever contributed to books before. I wasn't aware of everything that goes into making a book possible. I would like to thank Apress for giving me the opportunity to put my thoughts and experiences down into this book and also all of the editors and backstage hands involved in turning my ditherings into the book you're looking at. A big thank-you to Jonathan Hassell for seeing the potential in my conference talk. Becca Freed has been a true legend; she has been an absolute joy to work with as the project manager of the book, and as much as I have deviated from the schedule, Becca has been there to reassess and help me get back (nearly) on track.

Finally, I want to thank the both the SharePoint and jQuery communities, which are constantly helping, sharing, and pushing forward everyone's knowledge. The people who really put themselves out there in the community are truly superstars, and I thank you for all of your hard work in making both technologies a great place to be

Introduction

In 2009, Lightning Tools decided to take one of its best-selling products, a desktop application, and put it into the browser as an application page in SharePoint—which turned out to be quite a challenge. When we were looking at technologies to use, jQuery stood out as something that could be really helpful.

We spent a lot of time trying to understand how to make SharePoint and jQuery work together initially, and then we started to learn what jQuery actually could do. Finding the information we needed was often a struggle (not as many blogs on the topic were available at the time), but ultimately we successfully created our product.

I learned so much about jQuery that I jumped at the chance to talk about SharePoint and jQuery when the opportunity arose to speak about them at SPTechCon. I knew that so many people have needed, and will continue to need, to create a client-side solution in SharePoint using jQuery, and I wanted to share the benefit of my experience. In my talk I tried to communicate where to start and how to explore what SharePoint with jQuery can do—and the feedback from the full room at SPTechCon was positive.

When I was approached by Jonathan Hassell to write this book at SPTechCon in Boston in 2011, I leapt at the chance. I wanted to write the book that I really could have used when I first started. I hope your experience with this book is like learning to ride a bike: taking you from your first time in the seat and getting acquainted with the controls to doing a lap around the neighborhood without training wheels.

Who This Book Is For

This book is primarily written for SharePoint developers who are looking to expand their knowledge into working with jQuery. SharePoint and jQuery is for intermediate programmers interested in building rich, interactive web parts, application pages, and more using the combined power of jQuery and SharePoint. jQuery is one of those technologies that has been around for a few years, and the kind of functionality it offers is really quite amazing. Many of the "slick" web sites these days have a splash of jQuery in their mix; if you want to bring this kind of dazzle to SharePoint, then this book is for you.

How This Book Is Structured

Pro SharePoint and jQuery will introduce to you some of the basics of jQuery, starting with what jQuery is and looking at some of the advantages it offers over writing pure JavaScript. Then you will see some of the different ways that jQuery can be deployed to your SharePoint environment. Activating jQuery to make the library available on the page to your jQuery-consuming solutions is another task that can be done in a multitude of ways; with this book, you will be able to compare them and figure out which one suits your requirements. If you're like me, wading into some examples and seeing how they work is a great way to learn. That's why there are lots of tasks to work through: from simply viewing information in SharePoint with jQuery to building a complete Task Viewer application that demonstrates some key principles of working with SharePoint and jQuery. Once you have learned the fundamentals, you will learn how to work with plug-ins such as the jQuery UI library, and then you'll go on to create your own.

Coding Conventions

When writing production-standard code, you should always make sure that you handle exceptions correctly and log errors when required. This book omits these steps for brevity.

The examples in this book are complete and will allow you to get a functional result that you can use for further experimentation.

Prerequisites

You should be familiar with concepts such as SharePoint solutions, features, the SharePoint root, lists, and libraries. You should also have some knowledge of working with JavaScript. C# developers will see that jQuery is not too different from C#, but it is worth knowing where the differences are. Readers will also need to have some experience working with Visual Studio, because it is used for most of the development work.

Downloading the Code

The source code is available on the Apress web site (`www.apress.com`). Simply navigate to the book and click the Source Code/Downloads tab.

Contacting the Author

If you have any questions regarding this book's source code, are in need of clarification for a given example, or simply want to offer your thoughts regarding SharePoint with jQuery, feel free to drop me a line at `mail@phillduffy.com`, Skype me at `phill.duffy`, or even follow me on Twitter at `http://twitter.com/phillduffy`. I'll do my very best to get back to you as soon as possible; I'll let you know that I've received your message, but it may take a little time for me to respond in full. Finally, thank you for buying this book. I hope you enjoy reading it and putting your newfound knowledge to good use.

CHAPTER 1

Introduction

Since you've picked up this book about SharePoint and jQuery I am going to assume you know a little about SharePoint and have an idea of what jQuery is and what it does. This book will also assume that you have done some client-side programming with JavaScript and are familiar with using methods such as getElementById(). jQuery is one of those buzzwords that has been around for a little while now but with Microsoft's decision to make it part of the official development platform more people are taking a serious look at what it can do for them.

This book is not looking to teach you everything about SharePoint: there are many books on that topic. The aim of *Pro SharePoint with jQuery* is to take you all the way from understanding why SharePoint and jQuery are good partners and how to get them to play nicely and on to giving you enough information, examples, and desire to explore what can be achieved.

In your daily life on the Internet you would be hard-pressed not to come across a site that makes use of jQuery. According to one web site (http://trends.builtwith.com/javascript/JQuery), there are 25 million sites using jQuery, and almost a quarter of the top 1 million sites use it. What can be achieved using this relatively small file is frankly very impressive and you will get to explore what it is about this library that makes it so very popular.

A Bit About SharePoint

SharePoint has been around since 2001, when it was known as SharePoint Server 2001. It has matured from SharePoint Portal Server 2003 and Microsoft Office SharePoint Server 2007 (MOSS and WSS) through to its current incarnation of SharePoint Server 2010 (Foundation and Server) and Office 365. In this book, we will be looking at solutions that can work with 2007, 2010 and Office 365. The great thing about jQuery is that it works with any HTML, which is what SharePoint boils down to on the browser. If you can access the jQuery library in the HTML, then you can make use of its power within SharePoint. SharePoint is a huge development platform based on the ASP.NET Framework with a large array of facets to it. We'll take a look at some of those areas now so you can see where you can use jQuery.

Web Parts

Web parts provide a unit of functionality to the end user, and their purpose can be whatever the business requires or the developer can dream up. Web parts can range from simple tools for viewing text, data from a SharePoint list, or even data from an external system to interactive maps, a video player, or even a game.

Office 365

Office 365 has offered companies a new way of being able to work with SharePoint. With hosted SharePoint however it means that you're no longer in charge of the "box" and it means that some of the artifacts you can create for an on-premise installation are not available. Some of the restrictions are that you can't put any dynamic link libraries (DLLs) into the Global Assembly Cache (GAC), and that deploying files to the SharePoint filesystem location (known as the SharePoint *root* in 2010 or the *12 hive* in 2007) is not permitted.

Application Pages

When a web application was required in the past, the options usually were limited to either buying an off-the-shelf piece of software or creating it in-house. These kinds of applications were traditionally written in ASP.NET and mostly had to be written from scratch, taking into consideration how you were going to handle user authentication, data storage, and the look and feel.

As well as creating web part pages in SharePoint 2007 and 2010, it is also possible to create application pages. Application pages provide the ability to create web applications that are consistent with the look and feel of SharePoint: the advantage is that you can make use of SharePoint's security, its list storage functionality, and its user interface. SharePoint has a powerful API that the developer can code against, which provides much of the functionality that most business applications require. Consequently, it saves time, money, and resources.

Framework

One of the concepts that developers sometimes take a while to understand is of thinking of SharePoint as a framework. If you're a traditional ASP.NET developer, it can be tricky to think of SharePoint as your friend, instead seeing it as a block to your creativity. If you're used to having complete control over the exact behavior of your applications and all of a sudden it needs to "work with SharePoint," it can be daunting and occasionally frustrating. The frustration stops as soon as you realize that the framework is there to help you. Microsoft has put a lot of time and effort into ensuring that it all works in harmony, so if you realize that the application can make use of the SharePoint API, then you can avoid a lot of the pain points in traditional development.

Scalability is another key area where Microsoft has worked hard, and it's a point that is sometimes missed by custom solutions. If you work following the best practices, then the solutions you write can grow with your business.

SharePoint Lists

Ah, SharePoint Lists, the backbone of SharePoint. In my opinion, they're great. So what do they do? SharePoint Lists are SharePoint's main mechanism for storing data. As a developer, they're a life-saver: most of the applications that developers are asked to write are of the simple variety: "I need to store some data. I want some people to be able to see it, and some not. I want to be able to see that data. I want to be able to edit that data…and so on." SharePoint Lists give you this functionality out of the box. You can configure a list, either by using the SharePoint UI, by using a declarative means such as a Feature, or by using the API. You can even do a combination and use a feature to perform some API calls!

What's very useful with SharePoint Lists is that the UI is handled by SharePoint; it's generated for you as you create the List. However great this is, it will take you only so far. It will take 90 percent of the requirements asked of developers all the way, but for the remaining 10 percent there are lots of ways you can work with the underlying data through the API or Web Services.

Web Services

Microsoft has kindly opened up a lot of the SharePoint functionality via its Web Services, and you will use these later on in the book to provide your Ajax functionality. You can easily pull the data out from a SharePoint List and display it in whatever way you want. With the API and Web Services being so easy to use, you are not constrained by the UI when working with your data.

Self-Service

The concept of allowing end users to manage their own content and sites was exciting, especially for developers who would often find their days filled with updating small pieces of text here and there to keep pages updated and preventing them from going stale. The end users also would be frustrated by what seemed like a fairly simple task taking longer than they thought it should (but that's just users for you and who can blame them?).

The modern Internet has also changed the way that end users perceive their own intranet or extranet sites. Web sites such as Twitter, Tumblr, Facebook, and so on all give users control over a page or area where they can manage the content. Coming back from the World Wide Web to a static intranet site where the content needs to be managed by another department seems impractical and old-fashioned.

jQuery: The "Write Less, Do More JavaScript Library"

I have to admit that the jQuery tag line is genius; I am not sure who would read that and think "Nah, I don't think that's for me!" The best way to introduce jQuery is in its own words:

> jQuery is a fast and concise JavaScript Library that simplifies HTML document traversing, event handling, animating, and Ajax interactions for rapid web development. jQuery is designed to change the way that you write JavaScript.

jQuery is a library that aims to make writing JavaScript a magnitude easier than it has ever been before. It was originally released at the beginning of 2006 which makes it even more incredible to think it is now part of more than 25 million web sites.

It's important to realize early on that jQuery is not a language; it's an abstraction of JavaScript. jQuery has been written to make web developers' lives a whole lot easier and that is its only purpose in life. If you take a look at the jQuery library, you will see that it is written in JavaScript and through some clever JavaScript programming the authors have given consumers a greatly simplified way of performing tasks. The best way to think of it is like what the .NET Framework gave to us. As well as providing a huge array of functions for you to make use of, jQuery is also highly extensible through its plug-in capabilities. As a developer, this is a huge plus as you can create reusable artifacts as well as use ever-growing pool of plug-ins available on the Internet.

Let's take a look now at some of the key points to get you excited about using jQuery:

- It's open source, and the project is licensed under an MIT and a GNU General Public License (GPL).

- The documentation for jQuery is superb with "live" examples and inline code demonstrations.

- It's small and gzipped; at the time of writing, the file sizes were 31 KB minified and 229 KB uncompressed, respectively.

- It normalizes the differences between web browsers so that you don't have to.

- There are a vast range plug-ins for it.

- It's designed for rapid web development.

jQuery is written in JavaScript, and you will be required to understand how to write JavaScript to use it. Although it is possible to deploy and load jQuery to your SharePoint page and then use the plethora of plug-ins available, you will still need to understand what's going on, as well as know how to configure them correctly.

It is very important that you understand what jQuery is and the impact it can have on your end user experience. The last thing you want to do is create a fancy new application page with all of the bells and whistles and have it run slow.

With writing any code, it is important, arguably more important than coding, that you know how to debug the code to find out why things may not be working the way you would have hoped. Later in the book you will learn the invaluable tricks of how to look under the hood and understand how to resolve any issues you come across.

Where Do You Get jQuery From?

The following sections explain where you can get jQuery.

Download and Host It Yourself

You can download jQuery from the jQuery web site (`www.jquery.com`), and it comes in two different flavors:

- jQuery minified: For production

- jQuery regular: For development and testing

The two versions work exactly the same, and if you were writing your code against the library, you wouldn't be able to tell the difference. The difference becomes apparent when you want to see what jQuery is like "under the hood." The regular version is understandable, as you can see in Figure 1-1.

```
hide: function( speed, easing, callback ) {
        if ( speed || speed === 0 ) {
                return this.animate( genFx("hide", 3), speed, easing, callback);

        } else {
                var elem, display,
                        i = 0,
                        j = this.length;

                for ( ; i < j; i++ ) {
                        elem = this[i];
                        if ( elem.style ) {
                                display = jQuery.css( elem, "display" );

                                if ( display !== "none" && !jQuery._data( elem, "olddisplay" ) ) {
                                        jQuery._data( elem, "olddisplay", display );
                                }
                        }
                }

                // Set the display of the elements in a second loop
                // to avoid the constant reflow
                for ( i = 0; i < j; i++ ) {
                        if ( this[i].style ) {
                                this[i].style.display = "none";
                        }
                }

                return this;
        }
},
```

Figure 1-1. jQuery regular

If you now take a look at the jQuery minified version (Figure 1-2), you will notice that it's not quite as easy to understand.

```
hide:function(a,b,c){if(a||a===0)return this.animate(cw("hide",3),a,b,c);var d,e,g=0,h=this.length;for
(;g<h;g++)d=this[g],d.style&&(e=f.css(d,"display"),e!=="none"&&!f._data(d,"olddisplay")&&f._data
(d,"olddisplay",e));for (g=0;g<h;g++)this[g].style&&(this[g].style.display="none");return this}
```

Figure 1-2. jQuery minified

There is method to this madness. There are considerable savings to be had by "minifying" the library. For instance, it doesn't need to be understandable in production, and the file size is reduced to just 10 percent of its original size by removing unnecessary whitespace and changing the variables to something as small as possible. On the other hand, while developing against jQuery, it makes sense to be able to step through the code and be able to understand what is going on, which is why there is the regular version too. Another very valid point of this shrinking down of the jQuery file is that with all web pages, you want to reduce the amount of data needing to be transferred. So if you think that every visitor to your site requires the file to be downloaded, you should make the file as small as possible. The size issue benefits both the visitor, who has to wait for a page to load, as well as the server, which is dishing out the files.

Content Delivery Network

Another way you can get access to the jQuery library is by using a content delivery network, more commonly known as a CDN. A CDN-hosted version is basically a copy of the library hosted by a large organization such as:

- Google Ajax API CDN:
  `http://ajax.googleapis.com/ajax/libs/jquery/1.6.2/jquery.min.js`

- Microsoft CDN: `http://ajax.aspnetcdn.com/ajax/jQuery/jquery-1.6.2.min.js`

- jQuery CDN: `http://code.jquery.com/jquery-1.6.2.min.js`

For the two different methods of getting access to the jQuery library there are some pros and cons to consider. If your site is Internet-facing, it is a good way to off-load the task of delivering the jQuery library to your visitors. The CDN will be making use of caching, large amounts of bandwidth, redundancy, and lower latency. The main thing you will lose with this option is control of the library. Although it is possible to point to a specific version of the library, you need to rely on the third party to deliver that to your users. Otherwise, they won't get the jQuery experience you were hoping for. It is possible to add some clever jQuery to your solutions that can check for a missing library on the CDN and then fall back to your in-house version (we'll explain how to do this later in the book). By hosting the library yourself, you are able to be in control of which version is available in your environment; it is also the only option to use if you are working where access to the external CDN is not possible.

To sum up the options available, you need to consider whether the slight speed increase you may get from using the external version is worth the risk of the reference disappearing, being replaced by hijacked code, or somehow getting a bug that knocks out your pages. Otherwise, I recommend keeping it in-house.

Summary

In this chapter we covered a brief history of SharePoint and its key features for our purposes in this book. We also introduced jQuery, talked about downloading and hosting jQuery yourself, and explained how to access jQuery via a CDN. In the next chapter, you'll learn more detail on how to integrate jQuery into SharePoint.

CHAPTER 2

Integrating jQuery into SharePoint

This chapter covers how SharePoint and jQuery can meet and work in harmony.

Integrating SharePoint and jQuery requires three tasks. The first task is putting the jQuery library in a location where it can be accessed in your SharePoint environment. The second task is loading the jQuery library in the SharePoint page, and the final task is creating an artifact that uses jQuery, such as an application page or a web part on a web part page.

We'll describe each of these tasks in its own section. This chapter will show you how to deploy and make jQuery available, and in the next chapter, you will learn how to use it. You should be aware that it's entirely possible to deploy, activate, and deploy a jQuery-enabled web part from within one solution. Separating these components, however, makes each a lot easier to manage. By using feature dependencies, you can make sure one feature has been deployed before the next is able to do so.

Deploying jQuery to SharePoint

In this section, you will discover the different ways you can make jQuery available within SharePoint. As you saw in the first chapter, there are two ways to get your hands on the jQuery library: downloading and hosting it yourself or accessing a hosted version on a CDN. (If you are using the latter, you can skip this section.)

When deploying to SharePoint, there are a few issues to consider, such as whether you are deploying to a sandboxed solution. If you're not sure what a sandboxed solution is, here is a little introduction.

A *sandboxed solution* runs in its own secure little bubble where the solution has only limited access to part of your SharePoint environment. Because the service that runs the sandboxed solution is on a different worker process than the standard W3WP.exe, it can be tightly secured and easily monitored. One of the key benefits is that site collection administrators can deploy sandboxed solutions without requiring a farm administrator to deploy them. Site collection administrators can monitor the solutions to check how many resources are being consumed, and, if need be, a solution can be automatically deactivated if it becomes too resource heavy. A solution uses *resource points* for performing certain actions, and a farm administrator can set a limit on the number of points that can be used. A sandboxed solution will not be able to deploy jQuery to the Layouts folder because it does not have access to the filesystem. In addition, using jQuery does not involve deploying any assemblies, which is perfect for your sandboxed solutions.

You also need to consider what happens when there is a new version of jQuery or somebody wants to use a specific version of jQuery for their plug-in. Do you need to ensure there is just one version of jQuery for everyone to use, or will you make all versions available and manage them centrally? Do you want to allow site collection administrators to manage their own libraries by creating a document library to store the version that they need? As mentioned in the previous chapter, jQuery is also greatly enhanced by using plug-ins, so it's worth thinking about how you want to manage their deployment too.

Let's look at these questions in turn to figure out which deployment method would suit each scenario.

To centrally manage the deployment of jQuery libraries, adding them to the Layouts folder is the most suitable option. You can use the solution in Central Administration to deploy the necessary files to the filesystem, and if another version comes along, you can update the solution, and the files can again be deployed where necessary. When you deploy using this method, you have just one location where the files reside, and they can be put there only by people with the correct permissions. The flip side of this is that if someone retracts this solution, then jQuery will be unavailable across your business. It's also important to note that, like many libraries, just because there is a new version released doesn't mean it should be rolled out freely across your organization without forethought and testing.

Allowing site collection administrators to manage jQuery libraries can be a good way of allowing freer reign of which jQuery version to use and which plug-ins to make available. To work with this method, you *can* use a simple document library to house the jQuery files and allow administrators to upload the libraries as they wish. There is a huge trust required here because you need to be happy that your support queue won't go through the roof with the wrong libraries showing up or being deleted, or similar. This is a very simple way of enabling jQuery; all it takes is some code in a Content Editor web part, and away you go!

The more controlled way of giving site-collection administrators control is if you provide the libraries as features, scoped at either the web or site level, and then allow the administrator to enable the features for the libraries they require. By putting an activation dependency on your web parts, you can ensure that the correct libraries are available when you activate a web part.

It's also worth planning how the library will be made available on the page; we will be going into this in more detail in the "Making jQuery Available to the SharePoint Page" section.

Deploying Using a WSP (SharePoint Solution Package)

In this section, you will see some of the different options you have available for deploying the jQuery library. There are pros and cons for each, so it is worth looking at each to figure out which is suitable for your own scenario.

Deploying to the Layouts Folder

When deploying to the Layouts folder, the library will be available to artifacts such as a web part that load the script directly:

```
<script type="text/javascript" src="http://sharepoint/_layouts/jquery/jquery-1.6.js"></script>
```

But if an artifact is just using the jQuery JavaScript code, and not referencing the script, this won't work because the library will not have been loaded in the SharePoint page. This is where the "Making jQuery Available to the SharePoint Page" section is relevant, because you can choose how and when to load the jQuery library.

When using the Layouts folder deployment option, the solution gets activated in Central Administration, and the library gets deployed to the SharePoint filesystem. The advantage of deploying to the filesystem is that the jQuery library will be available throughout your whole SharePoint environment. This is because the Layouts folder works as a virtual directory meaning that any page will be able to load the file at any site or subsite:

- `http://sharepoint/_layouts/jquery/jquery-1.6.js`

- `http://sharepoint/subsite/_layouts/jquery/jquery-1.6.js`

If you're familiar with SharePoint, you should be familiar with the `SharePointRoot` folder, which is the core SharePoint installation directory and which contains a large proportion of the files SharePoint needs to run. In the SharePoint root, you'll find the folders that contain site definitions, list definitions, features, logs, DLLs, application pages, and so on as shown in Figure 2-1.

The SharePoint files typically live in the following directory, based on the version you're using:

- *SP2007 "12 hive"*: `C:\Program Files\Common Files\Microsoft Shared\Web Server Extensions\12SP2010`

- *SP2010 "SharePoint root"*: `C:\Program Files\Common Files\Microsoft Shared\ Web Server Extensions\14`

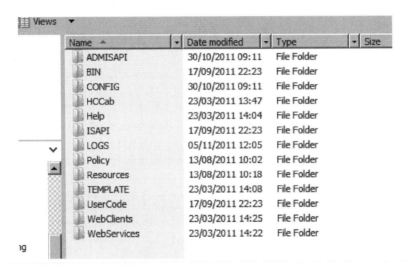

Figure 2-1. *SharePoint files on the filesystem*

Within the `SharePointRoot` folder you'll find a subfolder called `TEMPLATE\LAYOUTS`; this is where you will deploy the jQuery library, in its own folder.

This gives you a tiny speed advantage because it means that the jQuery library will be loading from the filesystem rather than the SharePoint database, as we will be doing with some of the other solutions.

Creating a Solution for Deploying to the Layouts Folder

The following example uses Visual Studio 2010 to deploy to a SharePoint 2010 environment; however, the really nice thing about working with jQuery is that it doesn't matter what the host is. Visual Studio 2010 has vastly improved the development process by including a rich set of SharePoint projects and project items, as well as automatic feature, solution, and deployment generation. If you want to follow the examples using SharePoint 2007 and Visual Studio 2008, you will need to manually create your folder structure and write your own DDF files to build the necessary WSP. A tool such as WSPBuilder (`http://wspbuilder.codeplex.com/`) can improve this development workflow in Visual Studio 2008. Deployment and attaching the debugger are also manual processes.

1. Open Visual Studio 2010, and choose File ➤ New Project.

2. Select SharePoint ➤ 2010 ➤ Empty SharePoint Project. Name the project jQueryDeploymentProject, and click OK as shown in Figure 2-2.

Figure 2-2. *Creating an empty SharePoint project in Visual Studio 2010*

3. In the next dialog, enter a valid URL where you want to deploy your solution (see Figure 2-3). Once you've entered the URL, click Validate to check that it's OK. You will also be asked whether you want to deploy this as a sandbox or farm solution. Select the farm solution because you will be deploying a file to the SharePoint root, which is not possible in a sandboxed solution.

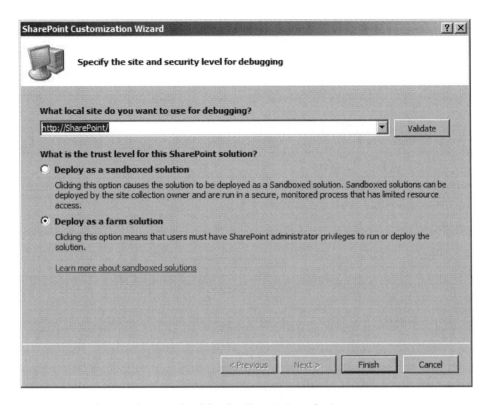

Figure 2-3. Selecting the trust level for the SharePoint solution

4. Once the project is loaded, you will need to add a mapped folder to Solution Explorer. This tells SharePoint where to unpack the files once this solution is deployed. To add a mapped folder, you need to right-click the project in the Solution Explorer and select Add ➤ SharePoint "Layouts" Mapped Folder (see Figure 2-4 for the location of the menu item).

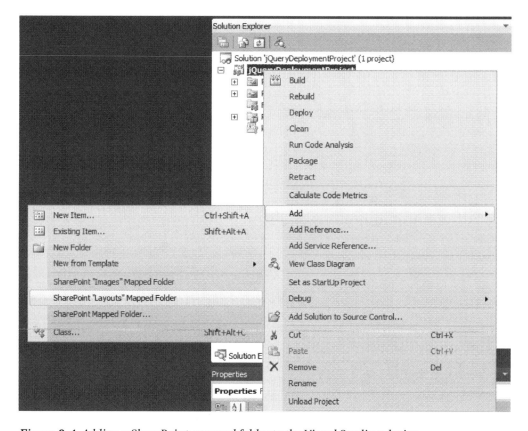

Figure 2-4. Adding a SharePoint-mapped folder to the Visual Studio solution

The Layouts folder will be added to your Solution Explorer and will contain a folder with the same name as your Visual Studio project. Rename the folder to jQuery. The reason it adds the extra folder is to try to keep the Layouts folder tidy as well as making sure you are not overwriting existing files when you deploy your solution. Although it is possible to deploy directly to the Layouts directory, it is best practice to put your own deployment files into their own folder. A best practice for ensuring you have no conflicts with other files is to adopt a syntax such as naming your solution's deployment folders like [CompanyName]\jQuery.

1. Add your jQuery file to the folder; you can either drag and drop the file or right-click and choose Add ➤ Existing Item….

2. This is all you need to do for this solution. When the solution is deployed, it will place the file on the filesystem for this server.

3. To test this solution, you can either press F5 to deploy and activate the solution (as well as open the browser to the URL specified in step 3) or right-click the project (as highlighted in Figure 2-5) and click Deploy. It's worth noting that if you use the first method when you close the browser, the solution will be retracted, whereas in the second method it won't be.

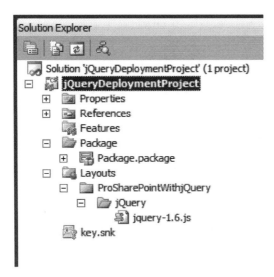

Figure 2-5. Solution Explorer with the jQuery library added to a jQuery folder

4. After you have deployed the solution, you can check that it has been successful in two ways; the first is to navigate to the filesystem and see whether the folder and JS file exist:

```
C:\Program Files\Common Files\Microsoft Shared\Web Server
Extensions\14\TEMPLATE\LAYOUTS\ProSharePointWithjQuery\jQuery
```

The other method is to navigate to a SharePoint site and append the _layouts path to see whether you can view the JS file:

```
http://sharepoint/_layouts/ProSharePointWithjQuery/jQuery/jquery-1.6.js
```

This completes the deployment to the Layouts folder. If you need to deploy a new version of the jQuery library, you can add it to the jQuery folder in Visual Studio's Solution Explorer and upgrade the solution, which will redeploy the new changes to your environment.

Deploying jQuery to a Restricted SharePoint Library

The restricted SharePoint Library method of deployment is great if you want to put the library only on certain site collections or webs. There is not a specific requirement to use a restricted library, as you will see in the next example, but it does offer some protection from the library being accidentally changed. By using a jQuery feature, it's possible for a site collection administrator to activate or deactivate the availability of jQuery. This will, however, mean that there will be lots of copies of the jQuery library throughout your environment, but if a certain area needs a later release, it can be updated without affecting other areas.

Creating a Solution to Deploy to a Restricted SharePoint Library

Follow these steps:

1. Open Visual Studio 2010, and choose File ➤ New Project.

2. Select SharePoint ➤ 2010 ➤ Module. Name the project jQueryLibraryDeploymentProject, and click OK.

3. In the next dialog, enter a valid URL where you want to deploy your solution. Once you've entered the URL, click Validate to check that it's OK. Select "Deploy as a sandboxed solution" from the two options.

4. You will see in the Solution Explorer that you have a module containing an Elements.xml file and also a Sample.txt file, as shown in Figure 2-6.

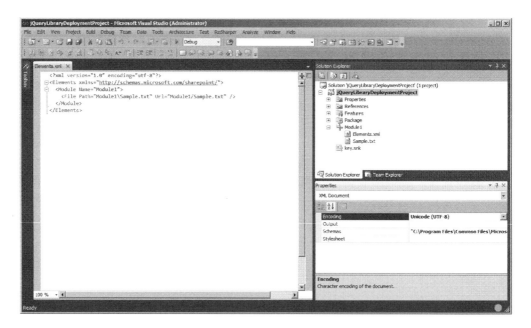

Figure 2-6. *Module added to the project*

5. Rename the Module1 module to Assets, and delete the Sample.txt file. If you have the Elements.xml file open while doing this, you will see it automatically update to reflect these changes.

   Add your jQuery file to the Assets module; you can either drag and drop the file or right-click and choose Add ➤ Existing Item….

   Again, as in Figure 2-7, you will see the Elements.xml file update with these changes.

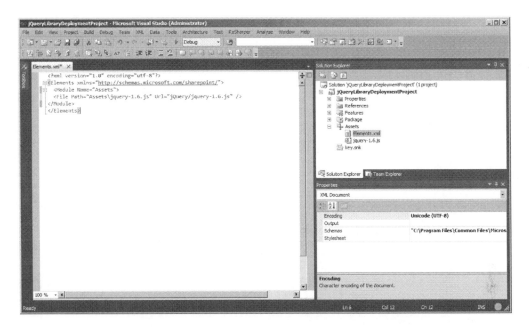

Figure 2-7. Module updated to deploy the jQuery library to the Assets library

6. Add a Url attribute to the Module element to tell SharePoint to deploy this module to the SiteAssets library. It should look like this:

```
<?xml version="1.0" encoding="utf-8"?>
<Elements xmlns="http://schemas.microsoft.com/sharepoint/">
  <Module Name="Assets" Url="SiteAssets">
  <File Path="Assets\jquery-1.6.js" Url="jQuery/jquery-1.6.js" />
</Module>
</Elements>
```

You could deploy now, but we will be good citizens and name the feature more appropriately for its use.

7. Expand the Feature node in Solution Explorer, and then rename Feature1 to jQuerySiteAssetsFeature, and then double-click the file to open the configuration screen. In this screen (see Figure 2-8), you can change which items are deployed by the feature as well as the title, description, and scope. Change the following values to give the feature more meaning to those who will be deploying it from within SharePoint, for example:

Title: Deploy jQuery to Site Assets Feature

Description: Feature to deploy jQuery to the Site Assets library

We are targeting the Site Assets library at the site collection here, which means the feature will appear under Site Collection Features, and once activated, the jQuery library will be available to all sites in the site collection.

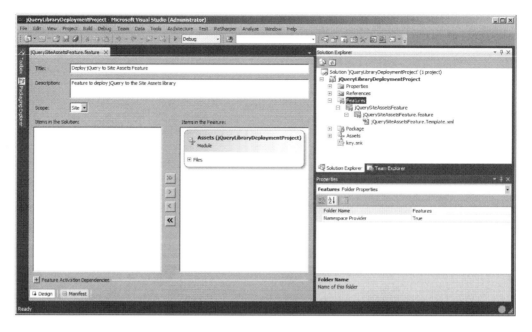

Figure 2-8. Configuring a friendly title and description for the feature

8. Press F5 to deploy and activate this solution and its feature. If you want to be able to deploy this solution manually, you can build and package the solution and navigate to the `bin` directory and then deploy like you would any other WSP.

9. You can test the deployment by navigating to the following location:

```
http://sharepoint/SiteAssets/jQuery/jquery-1.6.js
```

Deploying jQuery Directly to a Document Library

This method basically involves relinquishing control to your site collection administrators; it's possible to just upload the jQuery library to a document library. With this scenario, it's more difficult tell SharePoint how to load the library because it could be in any document library and could be called anything. In this section, you will see how it is possible to get SharePoint to load the jQuery from a document in the next section. This method has a couple of benefits: the first being that it can be managed by "non-IT" users, which means they can upload new versions if they desire or even add extra plug-ins. By using versioning, it's possible to keep multiple versions of the libraries available. Again, as when using a secure library, there will be a slight performance hit because of the file not being loaded directly from the filesystem.

If you want to prevent your users from uploading JavaScript files, it is possible to block them. You can find more information about this in the TechNet article "Manage blocked file types (SharePoint Server 2010)" at `http://technet.microsoft.com/en-us/library/cc262496.aspx`.

Making jQuery Available to the SharePoint Page

Just like the deployment methods, you can make jQuery available to your SharePoint pages in a number of ways:

- Content Editor web part
- Using custom actions
- `AdditionalPageHead` delegate control
- Adding the script to the master page
- Directly from an artifact
- Dynamically through code

These steps will assume that you have followed one of the previous steps to put the jQuery library into a location available to use, or that you are using a CDN and you know the path to the library.

You need to make sure the library is loaded before any JavaScript code tries to run. If it hasn't loaded yet, you will encounter numerous errors. The head section of the HTML page is typically where scripts are loaded to the page, and you will see the different ways you can achieve this. Some methods, however, load the script in a more ad hoc method, which may lead to issues where the JavaScript tries to execute some code without the library having loaded.

Let's take a look at these in turn.

Using the Content Editor web part (CEWP)

Using the Content Editor web part (CEWP) is by far the simplest option available. This method will enable jQuery on the same page where the Content Editor web part is added; it will not affect any other pages and can be used in a sandboxed environment. Although this method is easy to get working with jQuery, it also comes at a high risk, because anybody who has permissions to edit the page could either remove or edit the web part and knock out the jQuery functionality.

Configuring Content Editor Web Part with the script Element

Follow these steps:

1. Navigate to a SharePoint web part page where you want to load jQuery.

2. Click Site Actions ➤ Edit, and then click the Add a Web Part link in one of the web part zones.

3. Select the Content Editor web part from the Media and Content category and click Add (Figure 2-9).

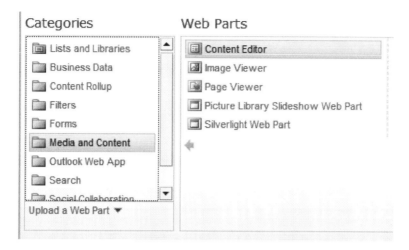

Figure 2-9. Adding a Content Editor web part

4. Click "Click here to add new content" to edit the contents of the web part.

5. In the Ribbon, go to the Format Text section, select HTML in the Markup group, and choose HTML Source. Figure 2-10 shows the location of the menu item.

Figure 2-10. Editing the HTML from the HTML Markup section

6. Add the following, making sure you replace the src so it points to the location of your jQuery library:

    ```
    <script type="text/javascript" src="http://sharepoint/_layouts/jquery/jquery-
    1.6.js"></script>
    ```

    You could also use the CDN URL here or the path to the Site Assets folder if the library has been deployed there.

7. Exit edit mode. You may get a warning like that shown in Figure 2-11; this is because sometimes when the HTML has been edited, SharePoint makes some further changes. This is not something you need to worry about here.

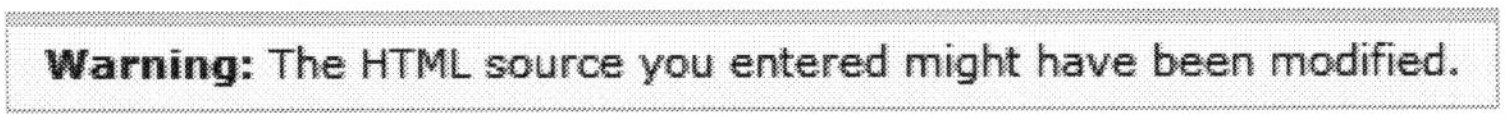

Warning: The HTML source you entered might have been modified.

Figure 2-11. Warning notification after editing the HTML

8. At the moment, all this web part does is load the jQuery library; it is not using it in any way. You can check that it's loaded by pressing F12 in Internet Explorer and looking at which scripts have loaded. Go to the Script tab, and from the drop-down list, you should be able to select jQuery-1.6.js. You can see that the library has been loaded successfully, as shown in Figure 2-12.

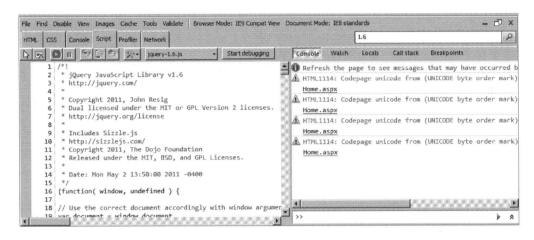

Figure 2-12. Using the IE Developer Tools to check the library has loaded

Using a Custom Action

Using custom actions is a great way to be able to load the jQuery library if you are using it in a sandboxed environment.

Creating a Custom Action Using Visual Studio

Follow these steps:

1. Open Visual Studio 2010, and choose File ➤ New Project. Select SharePoint ➤ 2010 ➤ Empty SharePoint Project. Name the project jQueryCustomActionProject, and click OK.

2. In the next dialog, enter a valid URL where you want to deploy your solution. Once you've entered the URL, click Validate to check that it's OK, and select "Deploy as a sandboxed solution" from the two options.

3. Right-click the project in the Solution Explorer and choose Add ➤ New Item. Select Empty Element, and call it jQueryCustomActionElement.

4. Open the Elements.xml file, which sits in the jQueryCustomActionElement folder, as shown in Figure 2-13.

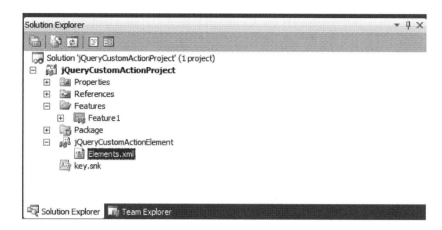

Figure 2-13. *Visual Studio Project with a custom action added*

5. Add the following between the element's tags:

```
<CustomAction
    ScriptSrc="~SiteCollection/SiteAssets/jQuery/jquery-1.6.js"
        Location="ScriptLink"
        Sequence="100">
    </CustomAction>
```

ScriptSrc is the relative path to the jQuery library; here we are using the ~SiteCollection token, which SharePoint will replace with the current site collection URL. It is possible to load the library from the Layouts folder using the ScriptSrc attribute of jQuery/jquery-1.6.js, although this would not work in a sandboxed solution because it is accessing a file on the filesystem. There is no need to include the _layouts part of the URL because it is automatically prepended. It is not possible to use a CDN URL with this method. The Location attribute tells SharePoint to load the library in the head element of the page.

The full elements.xml file looks like this:

```
<?xml version="1.0" encoding="utf-8"?>
    <Elements xmlns="http://schemas.microsoft.com/sharepoint/">
        <CustomAction
            ScriptSrc="~SiteCollection/SiteAssets/jQuery/jquery-1.6.js"
            Location="ScriptLink"
            Sequence="100">
        </CustomAction>
    </Elements>
```

6. Deploy the solution.

7. All the custom action does is just load the jQuery library; it is not using it in any way. You can check that it's loaded by pressing F12 in Internet Explorer, or you can use the tools for your browser and look at which scripts have loaded. Go to the Script tab, and from the drop-down list you should be able to select jQuery-1.6.js loading from the Site Assets library.

Using the AdditionalPageHead Delegate Control

Provided that the master page you are using has the AdditionalPageHead control on, you can use an ASCX file to reference the jQuery library.

Creating a Delegate Control Using Visual Studio

Follow these steps:

1. Open Visual Studio 2010, and choose File ➤ New Project. Select SharePoint ➤ 2010 ➤ Empty SharePoint Project. Name the project jQueryDelegateControlProject, and click OK.

2. Because an ASCX control is needed for this technique, the solution will need to be deployed as a farm solution. This is because the ASCX file is put in the ControlTemplates folder within the SharePoint root, and this cannot be done with a sandboxed solution.

3. Next you need to add a mapped folder to tell SharePoint where to deploy the user control. Add a SharePoint-mapped folder by clicking the project in Solution Explorer and selecting Add ➤ SharePoint Mapped Folder.... In the dialog that pops up (see Figure 2-14), you need to navigate to Template ➤ ControlTemplates and click OK.

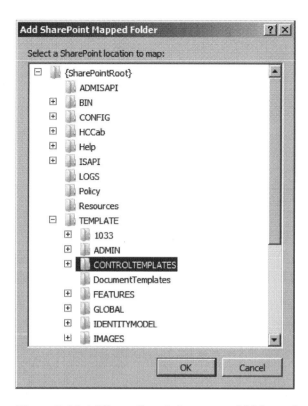

Figure 2-14. Adding a SharePoint-mapped folder to the Control Templates folder

4. Inside the mapped folder, add a new folder called jQuery. This is to keep your code and solutions separate in the ControlTemplates directory. You now need to add the ASCX control to the jQuery folder you added, so right-click it, go to Add ➤ New Item, and add a new User Control control called jQueryDelegateControl.

5. If you expand the ASCX file in Solution Explorer, you will see two more files nested underneath it; one is called jQueryDelegateControl.ascx.cs, and the other is called jQueryDelegateControl.designer.ascx. Delete these files because you're only using the ASCX control to load the jQuery library. Usually when you create an ASCX control, you want to put code behind to perform certain server-side actions. Because all this control is doing is adding some HTML, it is not required. Once you're done, your project structure should look like Figure 2-15.

Figure 2-15. ASCX control added to the mapped folder

6. Double-click the User Control to edit its contents. Because all this file is doing is referencing the jQuery library, the code inside is very simple:

```
<%@ Control Language="C#" %>
<script type="text/javascript" src="http://sharepoint/_layouts/jQuery/jquery-↵
1.6.js"></script>
```

The src attribute can point to any location where jQuery is available, whether it is from the Layouts directory as it is in this example, a SharePoint library, or an external CDN.

7. With the User Control configured, you need to add a SharePoint element to tell SharePoint that this control should be used in the AdditionalPageHead delegate control. Right-click the project in Solution Explorer again, and add a new empty element. Call this new element jQueryDelegateControlElement. With the element added, open the Elements.xml file and add the following snippet between the element tags:

```
<Control Id="AdditionalPageHead" ↵
ControlSrc="~/_controltemplates/jQuery/jQueryDelegateControl.ascx" />
```

Here Id represents the delegate control you want to use, and ControlSrc is the path to the User Control control that should be used. You may notice that ControlSrc is using a relative path by using the ~.

8. If you want, you can configure the feature to change the scope. The good thing about making SharePoint available in this way is that you can choose at which scope an administrator can activate or deactivate the library.

9. Press F5 to deploy the solution.

10. All the custom action does is just load the jQuery library; it is not using it in any way. You can check that it's loaded by pressing F12 in Internet Explorer and looking at which scripts have loaded. Go to the Script tab, and from the drop-down list you should be able to select jQuery-1.6.js.

Adding the Script to the Master Page

This method is unsupported if you are editing the default master page, so you will need to be working on a custom master page. It is worth remembering that you will need to update each master page you have if you want to include jQuery.

It's fairly straightforward to make this change. Open the master page, and in the head section add the script reference to the jQuery library:

```
<Head runat="server">
    . . .
<SharePoint:ScriptLink language="javascript" name="jQuery/jquery-1.6.js"  Defer="false"↵
 runat="server"/>
    . . .
</Head>
```

Or you can use this:

```
<script type="text/javascript" src="http://sharepoint/_layouts/jQuery/jquery-1.6.js"></script>
```

For more information on master pages and how to edit them, check out http://office.microsoft.com/en-us/sharepoint-designer-help/introduction-to-sharepoint-master-pages-HA102019628.aspx.

Using the ScriptLink method of loading jQuery, you have the choice to defer the loading until the page is ready, or you can get it to run asynchronously. In this example, because you want to make sure the library is loaded, you do not want to defer the loading. The path to jQuery is a relative path in the Layouts folder, which is why you can just use jQuery/jQuery-1.6.js. However, you can't refer to it in any other location, making it not an option for a sandboxed solution. Using the traditional script method of loading the file, you are free to choose its location, and it will load asynchronously. If the ScriptLink cannot find the JS file, it will display a SharePoint error, whereas the other method will just cause a JavaScript error in the browser.

Adding a Script Reference from Within an Application Page

Loading the library using an application page allows you to enable jQuery just for that one application and is an easy method to implement. It's very similar to the master page technique; however, you are using the existing content placeholders in the master page to allow you to insert the line to make the script load.

When you create an application page, you have the ability to add content into the content placeholders that the master page exposes. The placeholder you will want to use is PlaceHolderAdditionalPageHead. As the name suggests, it puts the contents in the head section of the page.

This is what the page looks like without any content in the placeholder:

```
<asp:Content ID="PageHead" ContentPlaceHolderID="PlaceHolderAdditionalPageHead"runat="server">

</asp:Content>
```

This is how it should look once you have added the `script` section:

```
<asp:Content ID="PageHead" ContentPlaceHolderID="PlaceHolderAdditionalPageHead"runat="server">

<SharePoint:ScriptLink language="javascript" name="jQuery/jquery-1.6.js"  Defer="false"↵
runat="server"/>

</asp:Content>
```

The script source location depends on whether you want to deploy this as a sandboxed solution. If you want it to be sandbox-compatible, make sure you're not going to load the file from the filesystem.

Creating a Visual Web Part in Visual Studio to Make jQuery Available on the Page

Using a Visual web part means that this solution will not be able to work in a sandboxed solution and means that jQuery will be available only in locations where the web part has been added. A Visual web part creates an ASCX control that is deployed to the `ControlTemplates` folder of the SharePoint root, and like the delegate control technique, you can just add the following to the control to enable jQuery to load:

```
<script type="text/javascript" src="http://sharepoint/_layouts/jQuery/jquery-↵
1.6.js"></script>
```

You can use this method for creating a web part, which just adds jQuery to the page, or the web part can include a full application, which uses jQuery to provide a fully functional web part.

Adding a Script Reference Dynamically Through Code

It's possible to dynamically inject the HTML required to load the jQuery library using a web part. This is very similar to the Visual web part method, but rather than declaratively telling the page to load the script, you are doing it programmatically.

To get things started, open Visual Studio 2010 and use the Empty SharePoint Project template to create a project named jQueryDynamicWebPart. Select "Deploy as a farm solution" and click Finish. Add a web part to the project by right-clicking the project and choosing Add ➤ New Item…. Name the web part jQueryDynamic, as shown in Figure 2-16.

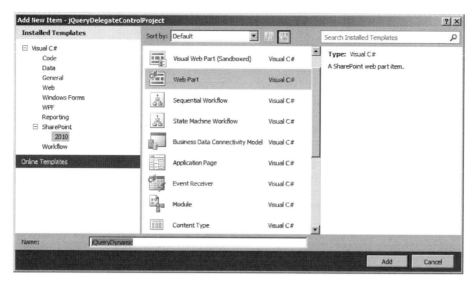

Figure 2-16. *Adding a web part to the project*

Open the jQueryDynamic.cs file that was just created if it's not already opened. Override the OnPreRender method and add the following:

```
protected override void OnPreRender(EventArgs e)
{
    // Register the jQuery script from "_layouts/jQuery/jquery-1.6.js"
    ScriptLink.Register(this.Page, "jQuery/jquery-1.6.js", false);
    base.OnPreRender(e);
}
```

Once you have added the line of code, you can deploy this web part and add it to a page. This will produce the following two lines of HTML on the page to load jQuery:

```
<script src="/_layouts/jquery/jquery.js?rev=1QT2rktNqE%2BC5kZ8LzXh3A%3D%3D" ↵
type="text/javascript"></script>
```

Summary

In this chapter, you saw the different ways you can deploy the jQuery library to your SharePoint environment. It's important to think carefully about the most suitable way for your organization to manage the deployment of jQuery. Once the jQuery has been deployed, you can consider the different options you have for making the library available for your solutions to consume. Again, you have to decide how much control you want and which approach is best for you. In the next chapter, you will begin to see how you can use this newly available library in your SharePoint environment.

CHAPTER 3

Common jQuery Features, Actions, and Methods

In this chapter, you will begin to see how you can use jQuery to work with HTML elements. You will start with what is arguably the most powerful of the features, and that is the jQuery selector. The selectors make working with elements in your application a cinch. You will also see the various ways you can create new elements and use the jQuery utilities. Finally, you will learn about the rich set of tools available to manipulate, transform, and handle events in your HTML.

Hello World

Creating an application page that has jQuery loaded will give you an excellent basis to begin learning what you can do using jQuery. In the first few examples, you will work with some of the main concepts, and the later examples will build upon the knowledge gained.

In the previous chapter, you explored the different ways you can make jQuery available to your environment and how to load jQuery to the SharePoint page. Apart from looking at the HTML of the page, there has been no real way to test that it has loaded correctly. Now that you have read about the basics of jQuery, it's time you wrote the obligatory "Hello World" example. You should already have deployed jQuery to your SharePoint environment and have it loading to a page using one of the methods discussed in the previous chapter.

To get started with the first "Hello World" example, open Visual Studio 2010 and use the Empty SharePoint Project template to create a project called MyjQueryApplicationPage, as shown in Figure 3-1.

Figure 3-1. Using the Empty SharePoint Project template to deploy the application page

In the SharePoint Customization Wizard, enter the URL you want to use to test the deployment of this application page, choose "Deploy as a farm solution," and click Finish. The application page gets deployed to the Layouts folder, which is why you need to choose a farm solution.

Next, add a new Application Page item called jQueryBasics.aspx, and open the file once it's created. You should be able to see the different content placeholders available to you from the default master page. Because I have opted to use the Site Actions method of adding jQuery to the page, I do not need to put anything in the head section. However, if you wanted to have only jQuery available to this page, you could have used the "Adding script" reference from within an application page, as described in Chapter 2.

Change the contents in the PageTitle content placeholder to jQuery Basics and the PageTitleInTitleArea to My jQuery Basics Page. I recommend deploying this page as it is just to make sure it loads correctly; there's nothing worse than wondering what's up with your jQuery code when it was just the page all along. If it's working fine, then you're good to add your first jQuery code. The solution has put the application page only on the file system (in the Layouts folder), so the only way you can get to it is to navigate to its URL directly:

```
http://sharepoint/_layouts/MyjQueryApplicationPage/jQueryBasics.aspx
```

You should see an empty page (how exciting), but it should have a title of My jQuery Basics Page, as shown in Figure 3-2.

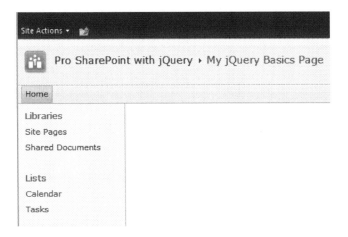

Figure 3-2. Testing an application page to make sure it works

Close the browser or click the Stop button in Visual Studio to stop debugging the application page. Now you're ready to add the first lines of jQuery.

Within the Main content placeholder, add the following code, which shows an alert when the page is ready. If you refer to the previous chapter, this piece of functionality was used to show that jQuery has loaded; its exact functionality will be explained later in the chapter.

```
$(document).ready(function() {
    alert('Hello World!');});
```

Deploy the solution again, and you should see the alert dialog once the page has loaded.

jQuery Basics

jQuery is most often used through its $ alias; in fact, you will see this symbol everywhere. The $ symbol is a shortcut for the jQuery() global function, and you will be writing it so much that you will be glad of the five characters it saves each time. But if you use the $ symbol in your own code or a third-party library, it could override the use of the symbol, causing your code not to work as expected. To make sure there are no conflicts when using the $, you can call jQuery.noConflict(), which will ensure that the jQuery function is the one being used.

The jQuery() Function

You can overload the jQuery() function (or $()) in four ways. It can be passed in a CSS selector; in a Document, Element, or Window object; in a string of HTML; or finally in a function. It also has a few utility functions that you will be learning about. Using CSS selectors is the most common, so you will be exploring them first.

jQuery(selector)

Using jQuery selectors makes working with elements on your page orders of magnitude easier than if you were just working with the JavaScript method of getObjectById(), as you will see in the later examples. jQuery allows you to select elements from the HTML document using the same selectors as available to you in CSS as well as a few more advanced selectors that will be covered later. By using just the selectors, all you're doing is returning those Document Object Model (DOM) elements, which does nothing on its own. In the next section, you'll add methods that will act on the group of elements you're returning from a query.

A few different selector types are available to help you select the elements that you want. It's worth noting at this point that in SharePoint there usually won't just be the HTML elements you have created on the page. The master page will be loading all of the standard SharePoint functionality. This is fantastic if you want to be able to select and work with the SharePoint elements, but if you're not selecting your own specific elements, then you may be interfering with SharePoint functionality. Selecting and editing the SharePoint UI may cause unforeseen issues and is not supported.

Basic Selectors

Table 3-1 lists the basic selectors.

Table 3-1. Basic Selectors

Name	Syntax	Example	Query
All selector	$('*')		All of the elements
ID selector	$('#id')	$('#myId')	Element with the matching id attribute
Class selector	$('.class')	$('.myClass')	Elements with the matching class name
Element selector	$('element')	$('p')	All elements with the matching tag

Let's try these selectors straightaway to see them in action; open the MyjQueryApplicationPage project in Visual Studio and edit the jQueryBasics.aspx file. Remove the existing contents of the PlaceHolderMain and PageHolderAdditionalPageHead content placeholders and replace the contents so they look like the following:

```
<asp:Content ID="PageHead" ContentPlaceHolderID="PlaceHolderAdditionalPageHead"
runat="server">
    <script type="text/javascript">
        $(document).ready(function () {
            // All Elements
            $('*').css('background-color', '#ADD8E6');
        });
    </script>
</asp:Content>
```

```
<asp:Content ID="Main" ContentPlaceHolderID="PlaceHolderMain" runat="server">
    <div id="myId">
        <p class="myClass">class is set to myClass</p>
        <p>Just a plain paragraph</p>
        <p class="myClass">class is also set to myClass</p>
    </div>
</asp:Content>
```

In this code, you are still using the document ready functionality. This time, however, when the DOM has loaded, it will execute the selector and set the CSS of the elements returned to a blue color. Once you have made the change to the code, recompile it and deploy to your SharePoint environment. You will notice that everything is blue; this is because the selector used in this first example is selecting all the elements on the page and setting their backgrounds to blue.

Now try the second example for Table 3.1, replacing $('*') with $('#myId'). This will change just the background of the <div id='myId'> to blue. Compile the code again and deploy the solution. This time, you will see that just the div has been selected by the jQuery query and the css() method has set its color, as shown in Figure 3-3.

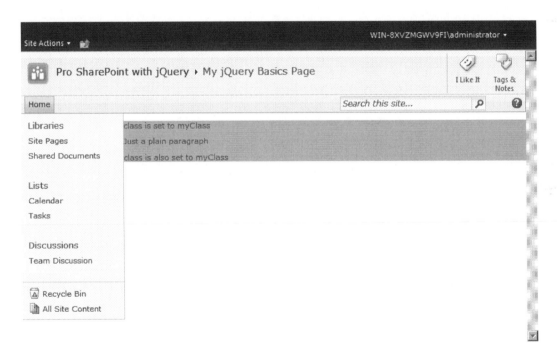

Figure 3-3. Setting the CSS of elements using the Id selector

Next, try to select just the elements with the myClass class by using $('.myClass'). You should see that just the elements with the class set are highlighted in the blue, as shown in Figure 3-4.

31

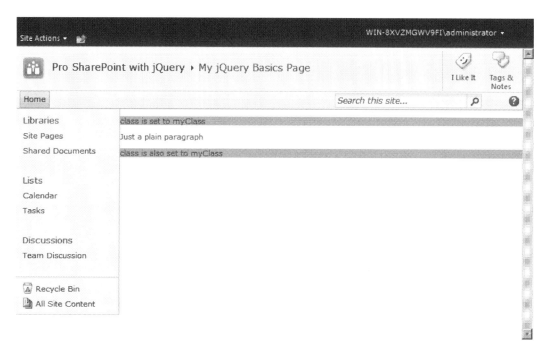

Figure 3-4. *Selecting and setting CSS using the* class *selector*

By now you should be beginning to see some of the potential of selectors. Once you begin to combine the selectors with the other functionality of jQuery such as manipulation, events, and visual effects, you will really see why jQuery is a tremendously powerful tool for developers.

The selectors that you have seen so far are the most basic available. You will use them the most throughout your applications, but sometimes you need to be able to create more powerful queries. The following sections will show you how you can further refine the queries to make sure you can easily and succinctly get the elements you need to work with.

Combining or Using Multiple Selectors

It is possible to combine selectors or use multiple selectors in order for you to have a more precise selection. For instance, if you wanted to select just the elements with the class of myClass within the myId div, then you can combine the id selector and the element selector as follows:

```
$('#myId .myClass')
```

This will ensure that only elements inside the myId element are selected. As mentioned, this precision can make sure that your jQuery code does not affect any elements on the page, which it should not.

Using multiple selectors allows you to combine the results of two queries into one result set. For example, if you want to select all paragraph elements with the class myClass and all the paragraph elements with the myOtherClass too, you can use the following syntax:

```
$('p.myClass, p .myOtherClass)
```

Hierarchy

HTML is mostly made up of nested elements, and the hierarchy selector allows for easy traversal of the DOM (see Table 3-2).

Table 3-2. Hierarchy Selectors

Name	Syntax	Example	Query
Child selector	`$('parent > child')`	`$('ul#people > li')`	All direct child elements of parent
Descendant selector	`$('ancestor descendant')`	`$('#myDiv1 p')`	All elements that are descendants of the ancestor
Next adjacent selector	`$('prev + next')`	`$('ul#people + p')`	All next elements matching next that are immediately preceded by a sibling prev
Next sibling selector	`$('prev ~ siblings')`	`$('ul#people ~ p')`	All elements on either side of the prev; must share the same parent

Using the same Visual Studio project as before, add the following div just below the one that already exists to enable you to see the hierarchy selectors in action.

```
<div id="myDiv1">
    <p>
        Paragraph before List</p>
    <ul id="people">
        <li>Phill</li>
        <li>Pip</li>
        <li>Les</li>
        <li>Denise</li>
        <li>Martin</li>
        <li>Helen</li>
        <li></li>
    </ul>
    <p>
        Paragraph after List</p>
    <div>
        <p>
            Paragraph inside another div</p>
    </div>
</div>
```

This time, change the jQuery method from the existing one to this one; you should know from Table 3-2 that this will select all li elements from the unordered list with the id attribute of people.

```
$(document).ready(function () {
    $('ul#people > li').css('background-color', '#ADD8E6');
});
```

The result of this query and CSS method call will produce the page shown in Figure 3-5.

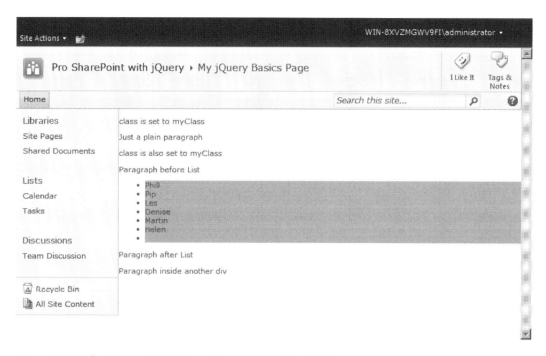

Figure 3-5. Selecting nested list items from an unordered list

Try working through the other examples from Tables 3.1 and 3.2 to see which elements get highlighted.

The next two sections introduce a way of filtering the elements that are queried by applying certain conditions on them.

Basic Filter

Filtering the selections allows for precise selection of the elements. Luckily, the jQuery filters are very comprehensive, and there are lots of different ways to make sure you can get only the elements needed as succinctly as possible. Another key benefit of using filters is that you can filter on their position in the DOM, state, or other variables without necessarily needing to know the element's type, ID, or class. Table 3-3 lists the filtering selectors.

Table 3-3. Filtering Selectors

Name	Syntax	Example	Query
Animated selector	:animated	$('div:animated')	All elements that are in the process of an animation at the time the selector is run
Last selector	:last	$('ul#people li:last')	Last-matched element
First selector	:first	$('#myId p:first')	First-matched element
Not selector	:not()	$('#myId p:not(.myClass)')	Elements not matching filter
Header selector	:header	$(':header')	All elements that are headers
Equals selector	:eq(index)	$('ul#people li:eq(2)')	Element at index
Greater than selector	:gt(index)	$('ul#people li:gt(2)')	Elements with index greater than index
Less than selector	:lt(index)	$('ul#people li:lt(2)')	All Elements with index less than index
Odd selector	:odd	$('ul#people li:odd')	All elements with an odd index number
Even selector	:even	$('ul#people li:even')	All elements with an even index number

Content Filter

As the name suggests, content filters allow you to select the elements based on their content, or lack thereof. The filter is not just restricted to the text in an element; it can also traverse to the parent element too. Table 3-4 lists the content filters.

Table 3-4. Filtering Selectors Based on Content

Name	Syntax	Example	Query
Contains selector	:contains()	$('ul#people li:contains(Pip)')	All elements that contain the specified text
Empty selector	:empty	$('ul#people li:empty')	All elements that have no children (including text nodes)
Has selector	:has()	$('div:has(ul)')	All elements that contain at least one element that matches the specified selector as a descendant
Parent selector	:parent	$('li:parent')	All elements that are the parent of another element, including text nodes

Child Filter

A key point to remember with child filters is that unlike most of the index-based selectors, it starts its indexing at one and not zero.

It you have the following unordered list on your page:

```
<ul id="people">
    <li>Phill</li>
    <li>Pip</li>
    <li>Les</li>
    <li>Denise</li>
    <li>Martin</li>
    <li>Helen</li>
    <li></li>
</ul>
```

and you have the following code being executed in your application:

```
$('ul#people li:eq(2)').css({ background: "yellow" });
```

```
$('ul#people li:nth-child(2)').css({ background: "orange" });
```

you will see that the zero-based :eq(index) has selected Les and nth-child(index) has selected Pip, as shown in Figure 3-6.

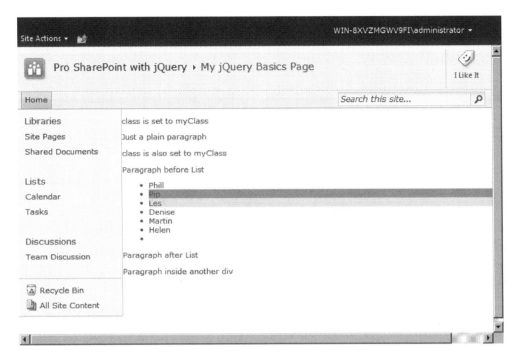

Figure 3-6. Showing how the difference in index base affects the selection

Table 3-5 lists the child selectors.

Table 3-5. Child Selectors

Name	Syntax	Example	Query
First child selector	`:first-child`	`$('div ul:first-child')`	Elements that are the first child of their parent
Last child selector	`:last-child`	`$('div span:last-child')`	Elements that are the last child of their parent
Nth child selector	`:nth-child(index/even/odd/equation)`	`$('ul li:nth-child(2)')`	Elements that are the nth-child of their parent
Only child selector	`:only-child`	`$('div button:only-child')`	Elements that are the only child of their parent

Visibility Filter

This pair of filters is very handy when you want only certain elements of your DOM to be seen or hidden depending on the state of the application (see Table 3-6).

Table 3-6. *Visibility Filters*

Name	Syntax	Example	Query
Hidden selector	:hidden	$('input:hidden')	All elements that are hidden
Visible selector	:visible	$('input:visible')	All elements that are visible

Attributes

Using attributes is a useful way to select elements. By being able to read any attribute, it makes it easy to select the elements that you want (see Table 3-7).

Table 3-7. *Attribute Filters*

Name	Syntax	Example	Query
Attribute contains prefix selector	[name|=value]	$('a[hreflang|="en"]')	Elements that have the specified attribute with a value either equal to a given string or starting with that string followed by a hyphen (-).
Attribute contains selector	[name*=value]	$('input[name*="dog"]')	Elements that have the specified attribute with a value containing a given substring.
Attribute contains word selector	[name~=value]	$('input[name~="dog"]')	Elements that have the specified attribute with a value containing a given word, delimited by spaces.
Attribute ends with selector	[name$=value]	$('input[name$="animal"]')	Elements that have the specified attribute with a value ending exactly with a given string. The comparison is case sensitive.
Attribute equals selector	[name=value]	$('input[value="Billy')	Elements that have the specified attribute with a value exactly equal to a certain value.

Name	Syntax	Example	Query
Attribute not equal selector	[name!=value]	$('input[name!="edit"]')	Elements that either don't have the specified attribute or do have the specified attribute but not with a certain value.
Attribute starts with selector	[name^=value]	$('input[name^="pet"]')	Elements that have the specified attribute with a value beginning exactly with a given string.
Has attribute selector	[name]	$('div[id]')	Elements that have the specified attribute, with any value.
Multiple attribute selector	[name=value] [name1=value2]	$('input[id][name$="dog"]')	Elements that match all of the specified attribute filters.

Form

More often than not, one of the requirements of an application is to capture data of some form or another, and having a specific set of filters to work with forms is brilliant. Let's add some more HTML to the existing application page to see how these filters behave and ideally gain an understanding of why they will be useful.

Add the following HTML after the last /div in the PlaceHolderMain content placeholder:

```
<form action="#">
<input type="button" value="Input Button" />
<input type="checkbox" />
<input type="file" />
<input type="hidden" />
<input type="image" />
<input type="password" />
<input type="radio" />
<input type="reset" />
<input type="submit" />
<input type="text" />
<select>
    <option>Option</option>
</select>
<textarea cols="10" rows="2">Text area</textarea>
<button>
    Button</button>
</form>
```

Table 3-8 lists the form selectors.

Table 3-8. Form Selectors

Name	Syntax	Example	Query
Button selector	:button	$('input:button')	All button elements and elements of type button
Checkbox selector	:checkbox	$('input:checkbox')	All elements of type checkbox
Checked selector	:checked	$('input:checked')	All elements that are checked
Disabled selector	:disabled	$('input:disabled')	All elements that are disabled
Enabled selector	:enabled	$('input:enabled')	All elements that are enabled
File selector	:file	$('input:file')	Elements of type file
Focused selector	:focus	$('input:focus')	Element if it is currently focused
Image selector	:image	$('input:image')	Elements of type image
Input selector	:input	$(':input')	All input, textarea, select, and button elements
Password selector	:password	$('input:password')	Elements of type password
Radio selector	:radio	$('input:radio')	Elements of type radio
Reset selector	:reset	$('input:reset')	Elements of type reset
Selected selector	:selected	$('select option:selected')	Elements that are selected
Submit selector	:submit	$('input:submit')	Elements of type submit
Text selector	:text	$('input:text')	Elements of type text

As with the other selectors you have seen, you are selecting only the elements. Try changing the existing jQuery code to set the border of these form elements using the examples in Table 3-8 (see Figure 3-7):

```
$(document).ready(function () {
    $('input:button').css({ border: "3px blue solid" });
});
```

Figure 3-7. Highlighting the button element using form selector

Setting the Selector Context

It is also possible to supply a context to the selector to limit its search scope to just elements within it, that is, jQuery(selector, [context]):

```
$('div.myClass').click(function() {
  $('p', this).Hide();
})
```

This code will hide all of the paragraphs, p, within the div with class myClass. If you did not supply the context, it would hide all of the p elements on the page.

Passing in a Document, Element, or Window to jQuery()

It is possible to pass in a Document, Element, or Window to the jQuery wrapper to enable it to use the jQuery methods you have at your disposal. Wrapping the document object and using the ready() method is a common way to put jQuery code into your script and wait until the DOM is available before executing the function. This technique is usually employed when wiring up your events to elements on the page because it needs to have the HTML elements to bind to.

The following code, which we will revisit later, gives an example of wrapping the document object and using the ready() method to add a click() event handler to a button.

```
$(document).ready(function() {
        $('#myButton').click(function())
            {
                // Do something;
            };
});
```

Passing in a String of HTML to jQuery(html)

The other methods that you have seen so far have been querying and selecting elements, which already exist in the DOM. By passing in HTML, you are able to create and insert new elements into the DOM on the fly. This method is particularly useful when you are working with data returned from a web service, because you can use the data to create new elements on the page easily.

```
var myData = GetMeData();
$.each(myData, function(index, value) {
    $('<li>' + value + '</li>').appendTo('#myDataList');
});
```

In this example, we are getting our data and using the $.each() utility. We are iterating through each item and creating a new list item, li, and appending it to our list with the id attribute of myDataList. You will notice that you need to include the full HTML tag with the angle brackets; this is to ensure that jQuery does not try to interpret it as a CSS selection.

41

Let's take a look at creating a little example to see how you can update the DOM on the fly. This code will use the HTML already written in this chapter.

```
$(document).ready(function () {

    // Create an array of the new people to add
    var newPeople = ["Sam", "Zoe", "Graeme", "Gemma"];

    // Use the each method to iterate through array
    $.each(newPeople, function (index, value) {

        // Create new List Item and append it to the people unordered list
        $('<li>' + value + '</li>').appendTo('ul#people');
    });

});
```

The list of people that contains Phill, Pip, Les, Denise, Martin, and Helen now has four more values: Sam, Zoe, Graeme, and Gemma, as shown in Figure 3-8.

- Phill
- Pip
- Les
- Denise
- Martin
- Helen
-
- Sam
- Zoe
- Graeme
- Gemma

Figure 3-8. *List item elements being dynamically added to a list*

This functionality of being able to write HTML is something that you will be doing in the full examples later in the book.

jQuery(callback)

You can use jQuery(function) or $(function) to call a function when the DOM is ready. This behaves in the same way that $(document).ready() does and can be used to call other $() functions on the page that require the DOM to have been loaded.

jQuery Utilities

jQuery also comes with a handy selection of utilities; you have seen one already, the each function. The utilities make working on the client side a lot easier for the developer. The following are some of the utilities you will likely be using:

- `$.each(function(index,Element))`: A generic iterator function that can be used to iterate over objects and arrays

- `$.support`: A collection of properties that represent the presence of different browser features or bugs

- `$.parseJSON`: Takes a well-formed JSON string and returns the resulting JavaScript object.

Common jQuery Actions and Methods

By now you should begin to understand what jQuery can do in terms of querying the DOM and see how this allows you to easily select the elements on the page. It's time to move on and see how jQuery can work with the elements on the page.

First you'll learn how to manipulate the elements on the page. jQuery has a large array of tools at your disposal that you can use to manipulate the DOM. When you are creating your applications or SharePoint customizations, it is important to be able to update the user interface either to show the user that they need to perform a certain action, to highlight a value in a table, or to manipulate another part of the page to change its look and feel. This is where the DOM manipulation comes into play. jQuery allows the developer to easily manipulate the properties and attributes of the elements on the page, whether that is to change a CSS class or update the text to a new value.

Let's start by taking a look at a simple HTML element that can work as our base for testing the jQuery manipulation:

```
<p id="ManipulationTest">My Test Text</p>
```

In the previous chapter, you learned that in order to highlight the elements that were being selected by the queries, you use a jQuery method called `css()`. Let's take another look at that code and break down what it is doing:

```
$('p#ManipulationTest').css("background-color", "yellow");
```

The element on the page was initially being rendered in the same way as it was written on the application page, as the jQuery method was loaded. However, the element's attributes were updated with the new changes applied from jQuery:

```
<p id="ManipulationTest" style="background-color: yellow;">My Test Text</p>
```

You should notice that the `style` attribute has been added with the `css` style as its value. It is the manipulation of these name-value pairs that allows the developer to manipulate the elements on the page.

Attributes

This section covers the different ways you can manipulate the attributes of an element using jQuery. Table 3-9 summarizes how to work with attributes.

Table 3-9. Working with Attributes

Name	Syntax	Example
Get attribute	`.attr(attributeName)`	`$('a#myLink').attr('src')`
Set attribute	`.attr(attributeName, value)`	`$('a#myLink').attr('href', 'http://SharePoint')`
Remove attribute	`.removeAttr(attributeName)`	`$('a#myLink').removeAttr('Target')`
Get property	`.prop(propertyName)`	`$('#myCheckbox').prop('checked')`
Set property	`.prop(propertyName, value)`	`$('#myCheckbox').prop('checked', true)`
Remove property	`.removeProp(propertyName, value)`	`$('#myCheckbox').removeProp('class')`

.attr()

The `attr()` method gives you the ability to get, set, or remove attributes on the element. If there is just the one argument passed to the method, then the value of the attribute will be returned. If the second argument is there, then the named attribute will be set to the value of the second parameter.

If you consider the following link, which you want to get the link for:

```
<a href="http://NotSharePoint" id="myLink">Link</a>
```

the following code within the document function will show you the link destination:

```
$(document).ready(function () {
    var linkLocation = $('a#myLink').attr('href');
    alert(linkLocation);
});
```

If you want to change the destination for the link, you can use the set attribute method to change its value. In this example, you will change the value and show what it used to be, keep the link on the page, but replace the script with the following:

```
<script type="text/javascript">
    $(document).ready(function () {
        ChangeLink();
    });

    function ChangeLink() {
        // Read the href attribute
        var originalLinkLocation = $('a#myLink').attr('href');

        // Set the href
        $('a#myLink').attr('href', "http://SharePoint");
```

```
            // Read the href attribute again
            var newLinkLocation = $('a#myLink').attr('href');

            alert('Link was to ' + originalLinkLocation + ' now it is ' + newLinkLocation);
        }
```

```
</script>
```

Figure 3-9 shows the result.

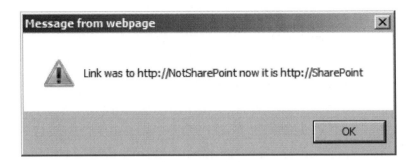

Figure 3-9. Alert showing the href attribute of the link

If you look at the HTML on the page, you can see that the link now points to the new location (see Figure 3-10).

```
⊟ <a id="myLink" href="http://SharePoint">
   ⌐ Text - Link
```

Figure 3-10. Viewing the updated source of the link

.prop()

The property method works in a similar way to the attr() method, but it will get, set, and remove properties from the element.

Class

The class methods allow for a simple way of working with the classes applied to an element (see Table 3-10).

Table 3-10. *Working with the class Attribute*

Name	Syntax	Example
Add class	`.addClass(class)`	`$('p').addClass('myClass')`
Has class	`.hasClass(class)`	`$('p').hasClass('myClass')`
Remove class	`.removeClass(class)`	`$('p').removeClass('myClass')`
Toggle class	`.toggleClass(class)`	`$('p').toggleClass('myClass')`

Being able to dynamically change the classes on elements makes it easy to highlight areas or controls on the page as required. For instance, if you want to change a normal paragraph, p, to reflect a warning, you can add the SharePoint CSS warning class (.ms-warning).

addClass()

Add the following paragraph to your application page with a real-world warning:

```
<p id="myWarning">Caution, I am a developer</p>
```

Next you need to update the ready function again to apply the styling to the element after the DOM is ready:

```
$(document).ready(function () {
    // Add the warning class to the myWarning paragraph
    $('p#myWarning').addClass('ms-warning');
});
```

The paragraph that contained no styling in the declarative HTML document now has the class applied (see Figure 3-11).

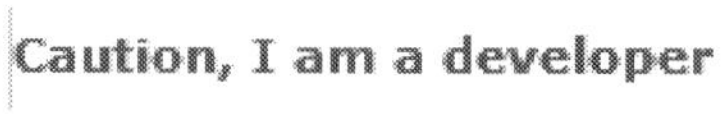

Caution, I am a developer

Figure 3-11. *A stark warning with the .ms-warning class applied*

If you take a look at the HTML, you can see it has a class of ms-warning, as shown in Figure 3-12.

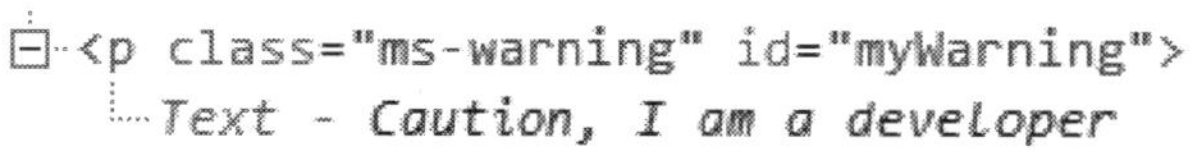

```
<p class="ms-warning" id="myWarning">
    Text - Caution, I am a developer
```

Figure 3-12. *You can see that the class is applied, which was not in the original HTML.*

hasClass()

The hasClass() method can be used to check whether a class exists on a selected element and then returns either true or false.

HTML and Text

These two sets of methods have been combined because their purpose is a similar one, but there is one key distinction that changes how they are used. Both methods allow you to either read the value or set the value. However, with the html() method, you are getting or setting the inner HTML of the element, and the text() method is working with the content (see Table 3-11).

Table 3-11. Working with Content of Elements

Name	Syntax	Example
Get HTML	.html()	$('div#myDiv').html()
Set HTML	.html(htmlString)	$('div#myDiv').html('<p>Hello World</p>')
Get text	.text()	$('p#myText').text()
Set text	.text(textString)	$('p#myText').text('Hello World')

To show how these methods work and the difference between them, add the following HTML to your application page. These two divs will have their content dynamically set when the page loads:

```
<div id="htmlDiv">
</div>
<div id="textDiv">
</div>
```

Within the script tags on your page, update the code to update the two divs, specifically, the first htmlDiv using the html(htmlString) method and the textDiv using the text(textString) method:

```
$(document).ready(function () {
    // Using the html method to set the innerHtml
    $("#htmlDiv").html('<a href="http://SharePoint">Link</a> - <b>HTML</b>');

    // Using the text method to set the element content
    $("#textDiv").text('<a href="http://SharePoint">Link</a> - <b>TEXT</b>');
});
```

If you take a look at the results (see Figure 3-13), you will see that there is something quite different going on between the two methods.

```
Link - HTML
<a href="http://SharePoint">Link</a> - <b>TEXT</b>
```

Figure 3-13. *Viewing the different output of HTML vs. text methods*

Basically, the HTML version (the top line) is treating the string as HTML and renders it appropriately, whereas the text version (the second line) escapes the HTML in order to render it as plain text. Both methods have their uses, but it's important to realize what will happen when you are choosing which one to use.

Value

The value method is used mostly with form elements as a way of getting values entered by the user; it also has a set method that could be used to prepopulate some data into the element (see Table 3-12).

Table 3-12. *Working with Element Values*

Name	Syntax	Example
Get value	.val()	$('#welcomeMessage').val()
Set value	.val(value)	$('#welcomeMessage').val('Good Day')

Using the following HTML, you can see how to work with the val methods:

```
<input type="text" id="textOne" />
<input type="text" id="textTwo" />
```

The following jQuery will get the value of the first text box and write it to the second text box as the user types in. Events have not yet been introduced in the book; all you need to know at this stage is that the code is getting the value from the first text box using $(this).val() and is setting the value in the second with $('input#textTwo').val(textOneValue). The this keyword is being used to get the object on which the event is running. In this example, it is the textOne input.

```
$(document).ready(function () {
    // Add event to run on Key Up of the textOne input text box
    $('input#textOne').keyup(function () {
        // Get value from the textOne input text box
        var textOneValue = $(this).val();
        // Set value of the second text box to that of the first
        $('input#textTwo').val(textOneValue);
    });
});
```

Deploy the solution and enter text into the first box; you will see it copied to the second box as the key is lifted up.

CSS

Table 3-13 lists the CSS functions.

Table 3-13. CSS Functions

Name	Syntax	Example
Get CSS style	.css(propertyName)	$('p#myParagraph').css()
Set CSS style	.css(propertyName, value)	$('p#myParagraph').css("background-color", "yellow");
Offset	.offset()	$("p#myParagraph").offset();
Offset using coordinates	.offset(coordinates)	$("p#myParagraph").offset(c.Left,c.Top);
Position	.position()	$('p#myParagraph').position();
Scroll left	.scrollLeft()	$('#myDiv').scrollLeft();
Scroll left by value	.scrollLeft(value)	$('#myDiv '). scrollLeft(300);
Scroll top	.scrollTop()	$('#myDiv '). scrollTop();
Scroll top by value	.scrollTop(value)	$('#myDiv '). scrollTop(100);
Get height	.height()	$('#myDiv '). height();
Set height	.height(value)	$('#myDiv '). height(150);
Get inner height	.innerHeight()	$('#myDiv '). innerHeight ();
Get inner width	.innerWidth()	$('#myDiv '). innerHeight (42);
Get outer height	.outerHeight([includeMargin])	$('#myDiv '). outerHeight (true);
Get outer width	.outerWidth([includeMargin])	$('#myDiv '). outerWidth(true);
Get width	.width()	$('#myDiv '). width ();
Set width	.width(value)	$('#myDiv '). width (600);

.css()

In the first examples on selectors, the code was using the CSS method to set the background color of the elements.

For instance, if you wanted to set the following paragraph to have a yellow background color, you can set it using the following method:

```
<p id="myParagraph">I am stylish</p>
```

```
$('p#myParagraph').css("background-color", '"yellow");
```

It is also possible to set multiple CSS values at the same time using property-value pairs. If you look at the same paragraph but want to set the font weight at the same time, you can do it like this:

```
$(document).ready(function () {
    $('p#myParagraph').css({ 'background-color': 'yellow', 'font-weight': 'bold' });
});
```

The result will show that the plain paragraph now has a yellow background and its font weight is bold (see Figure 3-14).

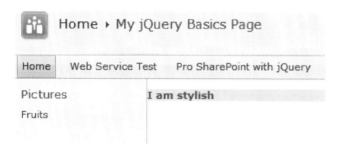

Figure 3-14. *Styled element using the CSS functions*

Using css('parameterName), you can also retrieve individual CSS values; a difference worth noting is that it will bring back the units as well. For example, if you want to get the width of an element and use css(parameterName), you will get a result such as 300px. If you use just the width() method, then it excludes the unit. Using just the width() method is the jQuery recommendation if you are using the width value to perform a calculation.

Width and Height

You can use jQuery in different ways to get the dimension of your element, and the results vary because of what exactly they're measuring. Figure 3-15 shows the three different ways that the height can be obtained: height, innerHeight, and outerHeight.

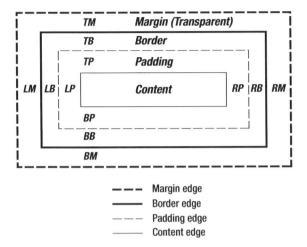

Figure 3-15. *Showing the different properties of an element. Copyright © 2011 W3C® (MIT, ERCIM, Keio), All Rights Reserved. http://www.w3.org/Consortium/Legal/2002/copyright-documents-20021231*

- height(): Returns computed height of the content.

- innerHeight(): Returns computed height including the padding but not the border.

- outerHeight(true/false): Returns computed including padding and border. If you set the optional parameter to true, then you can include the margin in the result too.

The same applies to the width methods.

Offset

The offset() method can be used to find the coordinates of the element relative to the document as well as setting the value. The get method will return an object with left and top properties to allow you to retrieve the coordinates.

Place any element on the HTML page, and using the ID selector, get the element and use the offset() method on it. Here's an example:

HTML

```
<p id="myParagraph">Where am I?</p>
```

jQuery Code

```
$(document).ready(function () {
    var myOffset = $('p#myParagraph').offset();
    alert("Left offset: " + myOffset.left + " Top offset: " + myOffset.top);
});
```

Running this code will show an alert with the coordinates of the element, as shown in Figure 3-16.

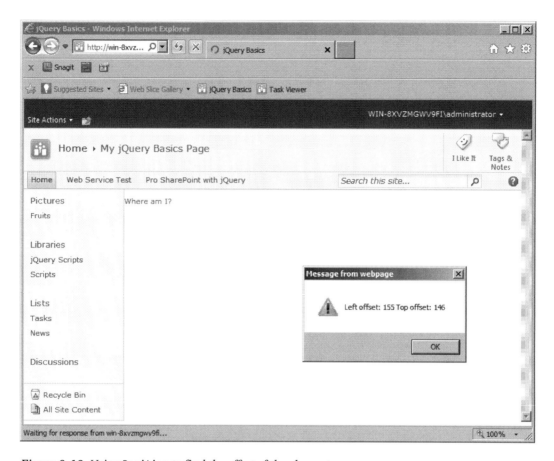

Figure 3-16. *Using* Position *to find the offset of the element*

Traversing

Traversing in jQuery gives the developer a way to walk the DOM by finding how elements are related to each other. Being able to select an element using jQuery is very easy to achieve, and the traversing methods takes the pain out of then refining the selection or simply exploring the HTML structure.

Filtering

Table 3-14 lists the filtering selection.

Table 3-14. Filtering Selection

Name	Syntax	Example
Equals	`.eq(index)` `.eq(-index)`	`$('li').eq(2)`
Filter	`.filter(selector)`	`$('li').filter(':even')`
First	`.first()`	`$('li').first()`
Has	`.has(selector)`	`$('#myDiv').has('p')`
Is	`.is(selector)`	`$('#myDiv').is('div')`
Last	`.last()`	`$('li').last()`
Not	`.not(selector)`	`$('#myDiv').not('li')`
Slice	`.slice(start,[end])`	`$('li').slice(2)`

Tree Traversal

The tree traversal selectors make it easy to walk up or down the Document Object Model (DOM) tree to discover neighboring, parent, or child elements (see Table 3-15).

Table 3-15. Tree Traversal Selectors

Name	Syntax	Example
Children	`.children([selector])`	`$('#myList').children()`
Closest	`.closest(selector)`	`$('p').closest('div')`
Find	`.find(selector)`	`$('p').find('span')`
Next	`.next([selector])`	`$('li').next()`
Parent	`.parent([selector])`	`$('p').parent()`
Parents	`.parents([selector])`	`$('li').parents('.detail')`
Previous	`.prev(selector)`	`$('li').prev()`
Siblings	`.siblings([selector])`	`$('li').siblings()`

Miscellaneous

Table 3-16 lists the rest of the selectors.

Table 3-16. Miscellaneous

Name	Syntax	Example
Add	.add(selector)	$('#myListItem').add('#myParagraph')
And self	.andSelf()	$('#liTwo').children().andSelf()
Contents	.contents()	$('#myIframe').contents()

The add method is really useful for adding extra elements to the collection, and the andself method allows you to add elements and make sure that the result from the first query is included too.

Events

For browser-based applications to have any kind of interaction, you need to be able to handle events that occur; these could be browser events or user events, such as a mouse click, browser ready, or page close.

If you're creating an application that is requiring the users to enter lots of details, the last thing you want them to do halfway through is accidentally click a link or the back button and lose five minutes of data entry. By handling events effectively, you can give the user a rich experience and ensure that the code executes appropriately when it is required.

Document Loading

There are three main types of document-loading event:

- Load
- Ready
- Unload

Load: load(handler(eventObject))

The load() method binds an event handler to the load() JavaScript event, allowing code to be executed when the page has been loaded

.load(handler(eventObject)) takes a function handler(eventObject) to execute when the event is triggered. The load method can be called using .load([eventData], handler(eventObject)) to allow the developer to pass in a map of data to in turn be passed onto the event handler.

Ready: .ready(handler)

The `ready()` method is used to bind an event handler to execute as soon as the DOM has been loaded. This is important if you want to use the elements on the page, because they are not available until the DOM is ready. The ready function is commonly used to house the entire jQuery script:

```
$(document).ready(function(){
    // jQuery code here
});
```

I prefer to use the ready function to wire up all events to the required elements and put other JavaScript functions outside of this block.

To ensure that the jQuery alias works as it should, it is possible to pass in a parameter to the ready method to use as the alias for the jQuery() function. You can pass in the normal $ to ensure the alias will work, or you could even pass in your own alias, and it will still do as you would expect:

```
jQuery(document).ready(function (CleverStuff) {
    CleverStuff("#myParagraph").text("I work when called CleverStuff!");
});
```

Unload: unload(handler(eventObject))

The `unload()` method adds an event handler to handle events as the `unload` JavaScript event is called. The `unload` event is called when the user navigates away from the page. There are many different scenarios that can cause this event to fire:

- Link has been clicked
- New address has been typed into the address bar
- Forward/back button has been clicked
- Browser has been closed
- Page has been refreshed

Because there are differences of how browsers handle the `unload` event, it is worth thoroughly testing on all supported browsers to check the exact behavior.

Handling Event Attachment

With a keyboard and mouse at hand or even a touchscreen, there are lots of ways that a user can raise an event within the browser. Whether it's selecting a choice from a drop-down menu, typing in their username, or double-clicking an icon, jQuery has really simplified handling these events, and in this section you will learn how to attach events and handle the interactions of your beloved users.

The first step to look at is binding and unbinding events. What is needed to handle an event successfully is to wire up the element with the event to fire upon. It's also possible for an element to have multiple events attached to it, such as a text box you can raise an event for when it gets the focus as well as when it is clicked, for example.

Bind()

Binding allows you to attach event handlers to elements to handle their events; this is a key tool for building interactive user interfaces.

```
.bind( eventType, [eventData], handler(eventObject) )
```

Take a look at the following example, which is using the bind method to attach the click event to all paragraphs (don't do this in your live SharePoint environment and blame me!). It will then call the function (see Figure 3-17).

```
$(document).ready(function () {
    $('p').bind('click', function() {
        var pValue = $(this).text();
        alert(pValue);
    });
});
```

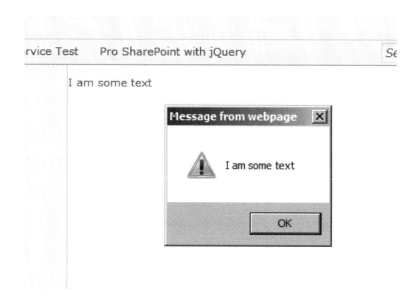

Figure 3-17. Clicking the text will cause the alert the show.

Sometimes when an event is fired, you need to pass in additional information to the handling function to enable it to perform further functionality. There is an optional parameter on the bind method, which allows you to pass in a JSON-formatted object to the handling function. The data object is available within the handling function in the event.data object. It is worth mentioning that the jQuery documentation (http://api.jquery.com/bind/) says, "The event object is often unnecessary and the parameter omitted, as sufficient context is usually available when the handler is bound to know exactly what needs to be done when the handler is triggered." However, I thought I would include it just to make you aware of its existence.

```
$(document).ready(function () {

    var importantData = "My Event Data";

    $('p').bind('click', { i: importantData }, function (event) {
        alert(event.data.i);
    });
});
```

As mentioned, the first parameter can take one or more events or custom events to allow multiple events to be handled. For example, click mouseover would perform the same function on both a click event and a mouseover event. If you want to perform different functions on different events but for the same element, you can do so using the following syntax:

```
$(document).ready(function () {
    $('p').bind({
        'click': function () {
            alert('Click Event');
        },
        'mouseover': function () {
            alert('Mouse Over Event');
        }
    });
});
```

In the previous example, we are passing in a map of type and value pairs into the method to allow it to bind to multiple events.

As well as using the bind method to add event handlers, you can also use a shortcut version to bind the handler to the element. The following two lines behave in the same way; both will perform the myClickFunction when clicked.

```
$('p').bind('click',  myClickFunction);
$('p').click(myClickFunction);
```

The shortcut events are displayed in the following tables.

Mouse Events

Table 3-17 lists mouse events.

Table 3-17. Mouse Events

Name	Syntax
Click	.click(handler(eventObject)
Double-click	.dblclick(handler(eventObject)
Focus in	.focusin(handler(eventObject)
Focus out	.focusout(handler(eventObject)
Hover	.hover(handlerIn(eventObject),handlerOut(eventObject)
Mouse down	.mousedown(handler(eventObject)
Mouse up	.mouseup(handler(eventObject)
Mouse enter	.mouseenter(handler(eventObject)
Mouse leave	.mouseleave(handler(eventObject)
Mouse move	.mousemove(handler(eventObject)
Mouse out	.mouseout(handler(eventObject)
Mouse over	.mouseover(handler(eventObject)
Mouse up	.mouseup(handler(eventObject)

As you can see, with most of the mouse events, it's a simple case of calling the method with the function to handle the event, just like the previous click example. The only exception is the hover event, which has an In handler and an Out handler, which are used, for instance, if you want to put a border around an image when the mouse hovers over it. When the mouse leaves, it will call the Out function to remove the border.

Mouse events can apply to any HTML element, making them very useful for providing mouse-based interactions with your user interface.

Form Events

Next up are the form events; these events, as the name suggests, are for handling form-based events (see Table 3-18).

Table 3-18. Form Events

Name	Syntax
Blur	`.blur(handler(eventObject)`
Change	`.change(handler(eventObject)`
Focus	`.focus(handler(eventObject)`
Select	`.select(handler(eventObject)`
Submit	`.submit(handler(eventObject)`

Most of the events are fairly self-explanatory and do as the name suggests. The one worth explaining a bit further is the blur event. The blur event is essentially the opposite of the focus event; it's when the element loses focus that the event is fired.

Keyboard Events

Table 3-19 lists the keyboard events.

Table 3-19. Keyboard Events

Name	Syntax
Key down	`.keydown(handler(eventObject)`
Key press	`.keypress(handler(eventObject)`
Key up	`.keyup(handler(eventObject)`

Even though the keyboard events can be bound to any element, they will apply only to the element with focus. More often than not, the keyboard events are used with form elements.

With the event binding so far, we have been using a jQuery selector to get the elements to apply the binding to and then adding the required binding method. With this method of wiring up the element to events, you need to really know all the elements are there at the beginning because any new elements added to the DOM will not have the event handler attached to them. Let's take a look at another example and see this behavior in action.

The HTML is just a simple div with two paragraphs that have the myParagraph class:

```
<div id="myDiv">
    <p class="myParagraph">
        Click me!</p>
    <p class="myParagraph">
        Click me!</p>
</div>
```

The jQuery uses the class selector to select the two paragraphs and attaches the click handler. The code also creates a new identical paragraph element and appends it to the parent div.

```
$(document).ready(function () {
    // Bind click handler to the paragraph elements with the myParagraph class
    $('p.myParagraph').bind("click", function () { alert("You clicked me"); });
    // Create new paragraph with the class and appends it to the 'myDiv' DIV element
    $('<p class="myParagraph">Click me too!</p>').appendTo('#myDiv');
});
```

Running this code will allow you to click the paragraph elements, and an alert will show. However, you will notice that when you click the paragraph "Click me too!" that the alert does not show even though it has the correct class. This makes sense because it wasn't part of the query selection where you added the event. If you swapped the two methods around, then it would work, but there is another way that allows you to say "Bind these elements and all future elements that match this selector." This method is called the live() method; its opposite is the die() method.

Live(eventType,eventData,handler): Deprecated as of Version 1.7; See On()

To add an event to an element and to all future elements that match, you can create the query using the live() method. Working from the previous example, it is only a small change to allow you to handle all new elements you add.

```
$(document).ready(function () {
    // Bind click handler to the paragraph elements with the myParagraph class using
Live
    $('p.myParagraph').live("click", function () { alert("You clicked me"); });
    // Create new paragraph with the class and appends it to the 'myDiv' DIV element
    $('<p class="myParagraph">Click me too!</p>').appendTo('#myDiv');
});
```

The difference is slight, but it makes a big impact. Now if you deploy the solution again, you will be able to click the new item, and the event will fire.

Die(): Deprecated as of Version 1.7; See Off()

Similar to the unbind method, the die() method allows you to unhook events attached using the live() method. As with the unbind(), you can remove all bindings with the parameterless constructor, you can remove an event type by passing in its name, and you can remove a specific event by event type and function.

```
$('p').die()
$('p').die('click')
$('p').die('click', myClickFunction)
```

For .die() to function correctly, the selector used with it must match *exactly* the selector initially used with .live().

On(): jQuery 1.7+ Only

The on method works in a similar fashion to the live() method where the element is selected and the action can be bound for all existing and all future elements matching the selector. The event can be unbound using the off() method.

```
$('.myClass').on('click', function(event){
        alert("Element with myClass has been clicked");
});
```

Off(): jQuery 1.7+ Only

Die will detach the event from the elements; the selector must match the one used for on(). In this example, it is removing the event that was enabled from the earlier on() example:

```
$("#myDiv").off('click', '.myClass');
```

Why Is This Useful?

The live() and on() methods are especially useful if you want to work with elements that are outside of your control or if you are dynamically generating the HTML. If, for example, you wanted to keep a log of all links clicked within a page, you could use live() to bind to the links and all others that may come afterward. When using a web service, as long as you make sure the new elements you are creating will meet the query conditions, you can ensure they have the same event handling behaviors as existing elements.

Unbind()

If a binding is no longer required, then it is possible to unbind it from the element. There are three ways to remove the bindings from an element: delete all bindings, delete bindings by type, or delete a specific binding by type and function.

To remove all bindings, the unbind method is called without any parameters:

```
$('p').unbind();
```

Removing the event is simply done by passing in the type; this will remove all bindings of that type:

```
$('p').unbind('click');
```

Or, if a specific function was bound to an element, it could be unbound like so:

```
$(document).ready(function () {

    var clickFunctionOne = function() {
        alert('Click Function One');
    };

    var clickFunctionTwo = function() {
        alert('Click Function Two');
    };
```

```
$('p').bind('click', clickFunctionOne); // Bind clickFunctionOne to click event
$('p').bind('click', clickFunctionTwo); // Bind clickFunctionTwo to click event
$('p').trigger('click'); // Fire click event - Will show the two alerts
$('p').unbind('click', clickFunctionTwo); // Remove clickFunctionTwo from click
event

        // Click on a p now and only the first function will fire
});
```

In this code, we are creating two variables, clickFunctionOne and clickFunctionTwo, for the functions to be called on the click event. The two functions will behave the same way as if we had passed in the function like in the first binding example. By using variables, we can pass the variable we want to remove (clickFunctionTwo) to the unbind method to remove only that method.

Trigger

The last few sections have covered how to bind events to the HTML elements on the page. What happens if you want to trigger one of the events without the user? Well, luckily most of the methods also support a parameterless call that will trigger the event:

```
$('#myElement').dblclick();
```

The previous code will fire the double-click event for the element.

You should now have an idea of how to attach event handling to the HTML elements on your page. It's also important to know how to detach the event handling; this is where the unbind method comes into play.

Manipulation

In this section, you will learn how to manipulate the DOM. You have seen some of the methods that do some manipulation already such as attr() to modify attributes and css() to alter the CSS.

There are three main types of DOM insertion that jQuery offers: inside, outside, and around. Inside is used to insert content inside an existing element. Outside lets you insert content outside an element, such as before or after it. Finally, there is around, which allows you to wrap or unwrap existing elements, such as adding a div around a collection of paragraphs.

DOM Insertion Inside

Table 3-20 lists the functions for inserting elements inside an element.

Table 3-20. Inserting Elements Inside an Existing Element

Name	Syntax
Append	`.append()`
Append to	`.appendTo()`
Prepend	`.prepend()`
Prepend to	`.prependTo()`

The append() and prepend() methods behave in a similar way; the only difference is that the prepend will insert the element at the beginning, and append will insert it at the end. Both methods can take HTML content as their parameter; in this example, I have found the class of the list in the navigation page and will add two extra items:

```
$(document).ready(function () {
    $('.s4-specialNavLinkList').append('<li>I have been appended</li>');
    $('.s4-specialNavLinkList').prepend('<li>I have been prepended</li>');
});
```

The results, although not the prettiest, show how you can add elements to existing SharePoint elements, or even elements that you have created yourself, as shown in Figure 3-18.

Figure 3-18. Elements inserted into the SharePoint 2010 navigation menu

With the two methods so far, the syntax is the elements you want to append or prepend the new elements to. With PrependTo() and AppendTo(), it works the other way around; you specify the content and then say where you want it to go.

This example of AppendTo() is moving the Site Actions element and appending to the same menu as before:

```
$(document).ready(function () {
    $('#zz9_SiteActionsMenu_t').appendTo('.s4-specialNavLinkList');
});
```

'#zz9_SiteActionsMenu_t is the site action element ID, and we are appending this element to the nav list. As before, because we used append(), it's at the end of the list, as shown in Figure 3-19.

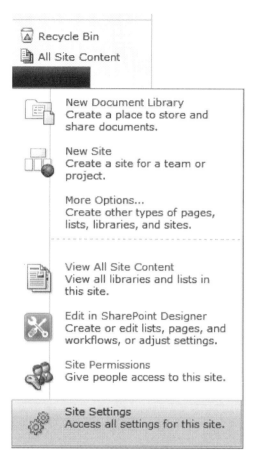

Figure 3-19. Adding an existing element to another location

DOM Insertion Outside

Table 3-21 lists the functions for inserting an element outside an existing element.

Table 3-21. Inserting Elements Outside an Existing Element

Name	Syntax
After	`.after()`
Before	`.before()`
Insert after	`.insertAfter()`
Insert before	`.insertBefore()`

Rather than just the locations of the beginning and end like append() and prepend() give you, the outside methods give you greater control on where to place the elements you are manipulating.

Look at the following HTML:

```
<div id="myDiv">
    <p class="myParagraph" id="firstParagraph">I am the first paragraph</p>
    <p class="myParagraph" id="secondParagraph">I am the second paragraph</p>
</div>
```

What you want to do is add a new paragraph in the middle of these two; luckily, they have an ID each so you can choose to insert after the first paragraph:

```
$(document).ready(function () {
    // Using a variable to hold the new element
    var newParagraphVariable = $('<p>I am a new paragraph</p>');
    $('#firstParagraph').after(newParagraphVariable);
});
```

The result of this after method is shown in Figure 3-20.

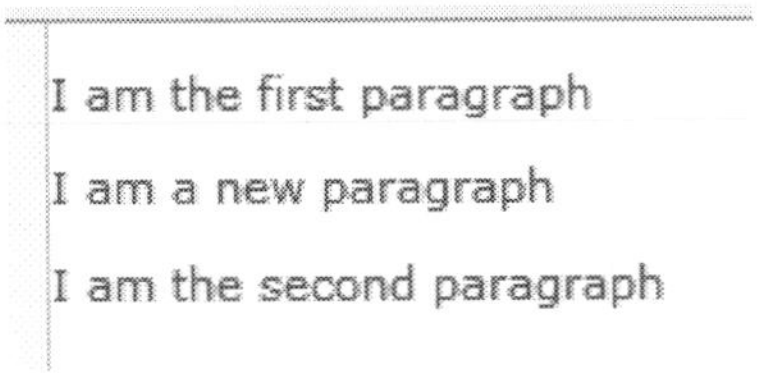

I am the first paragraph

I am a new paragraph

I am the second paragraph

Figure 3-20. New element added after the first paragraph

As you would expect, the before method will insert the element before the specified element. The InsertBefore() and InsertAfter() methods perform the same function as the before and after methods; it's just that the syntax is different. As with appendTo() and prependTo(), the element to insert comes before the destination.

The following two lines do exactly the same thing, the first using InsertAfter:

```
$('<p>I am a new paragraph</p>').insertBefore('#secondParagraph');
$('#secondParagraph').before('<p>I am a new paragraph</p>');
```

DOM Insertion Around

Table 3-22 lists the functions for inserting elements around an existing element.

Table 3-22. Inserting Elements Around an Existing Element

Name	Syntax
Unwrap	.unwrap()
Wrap	.wrap()
Wrap all	.wrapAll()
Wrap inner	.wrapInner()

As mentioned previously, the around set of methods is used to wrap existing elements with new elements, essentially putting them into a container.

In the following example, you will be using the toggle() method to wrap and unwrap a set of images. The example is using the following style that has been placed in the head ContentPlaceHolder of the page:

```
<style type="text/css">
    .myInnerDiv
    {
        margin: 10px;
        border: 2px solid black;
        display: inline-block;
    }
</style>
```

The HTML containing the images is as follows:

```
<div id="myOuterDiv">
    <button id="myButton">
        Unwrap\Wrap</button>
    <img alt="Apple" src="apple.png" class="myFruit" />
    <img alt="Lemon" src="lemon.png" class="myFruit" />
</div>
```

The images I am using have been placed in the same folder in the Layouts directory as the ASPX page, as shown in Figure 3-21.

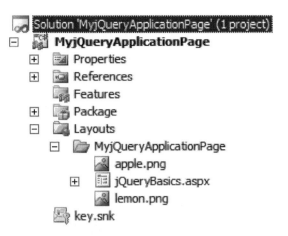

Figure 3-21. Images have been added to the project, so they will be deployed.

Finally, here is the jQuery code:

```
$(document).ready(function () {
    $("#myButton").toggle(function () {
        $(".myFruit").wrap("<div class='myInnerDiv'></div>");
    }, function () {
        $(".myFruit").unwrap();
    });
});
```

The toggle() method alternates between the two functions provided, so on the first click, it will wrap the elements with the myFruit class using the myInnerDiv div, and when the button is clicked for a second time, it will unwrap the same elements.

Unwrapped Page and the Underlying HTML

Figure 3-22 shows the original img elements without wrapping.

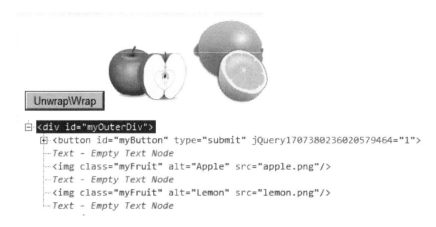

Figure 3-22. Original img elements without wrapping

Now once the button is clicked, it will wrap the elements. To help visualize this, the div, which is being wrapped, has been styled with a trendy border, as shown in Figure 3-23.

Figure 3-23. Images now show the border coming from the wrapping div

If you refresh the view in the Internet Explorer Developer Tools, you will notice that the two fruit elements are now wrapped in the innerDiv div, as shown in Figure 3-24.

```
<div id="myOuterDiv">
   <button id="myButton" type="submit" jQuery1707380236020579464="1">
   Text - Empty Text Node
   <div class="myInnerDiv">
      <img class="myFruit" alt="Apple" src="apple.png"/>
   Text - Empty Text Node
   <div class="myInnerDiv">
      <img class="myFruit" alt="Lemon" src="lemon.png"/>
   Text - Empty Text Node
```

Figure 3-24. The HTML shows how the img tags are now wrapped by the div.

You have seen in the previous example that when the elements have been wrapped, they were wrapped individually. The class selector that was used brought back the two fruits, and each of them was wrapped with the div. If you want to wrap the elements returned from the selection as a group, you can use the `.wrapAll()` method.

Changing the jQuery code to the following will wrap both elements into the same div; this code will do it on page load rather than requiring the button click:

```
$(document).ready(function () {
    $(".myFruit").wrapAll("<div class='myInnerDiv'></div>");
});
```

The result is shown in Figure 3-25.

Figure 3-25. Both images are now wrapped in a single div.

The final method to look at is the `wrapInner()` method, which allows you to wrap the inner elements of the selector with the provided element. For instance, say you have the following HTML where instead of having images of fruit, you just have the names in paragraphs:

```
<div id="myFruits">
    <p class="myFruit">Apple</p>
    <p class="myFruit">Lemon</p>
</div>
```

If you want to wrap the contents, that is, Apple and Lemon inside a b tag to make it bold, then you can use the following jQuery:

```
$(document).ready(function () {
    $(".myFruit").wrapInner("<b></b>");
});
```

The result will be that each element matching the query will have its inner content wrapped with the tag, as shown in Figure 3-26.

```
<div id="myFruits">
   <p class="myFruit">
      <b>
         Text - Apple
   <p class="myFruit">
      <b>
         Text - Lemon
```

Figure 3-26. p tags are now wrapped in the b tag.

DOM Replacing

Table 3-23 lists the DOM replacing methods.

Table 3-23. Replacing Elements

Name	Syntax
Replace with	`.replaceWith()`
Replace all	`.replaceAll()`

As well as being able to insert new elements, you can also replace existing elements. In this example, you will look at replacing the page logo.

Using the developer toolbar, you can find out that the image to replace is nested underneath the anchor element with an ID of `ctl00_onetidProjectPropertyTitleGraphic`, so using the direct descendent selector, you can get the image to replace:

```
$(document).ready(function () {
      $("#ctl00_onetidProjectPropertyTitleGraphic>img").replaceWith("<img
src='apple.png' border='0' alt='Fruit' />");
      });
```

Running this code returns the logo shown in Figure 3-27,

Figure 3-27. Standard Team Site logo that will be replaced

which becomes the logo shown in Figure 3-28.

Figure 3-28. Replacing an element is easy with the replaceWith method.

Although this example is a good one to show what you can achieve with jQuery, always be aware that just because you can do something with jQuery doesn't mean it's the best way. If you wanted to change this icon, you should do it through the Site Settings ➤ Title, Description, and Icon page.

replaceAll() is the same as replaceWith(), but the source and target are reversed.

DOM Removing

Table 3-24 shows DOM removing elements.

Table 3-24. Removing Elements

Name	Syntax
Detach	.detach()
Empty	.empty()
Remove	.remove()

You've inserted and replaced, and now you will see how to remove. There are some clever features of the remove methods, which will allow you to detach something from the DOM but keep it to be attached or inserted elsewhere.

Working through a couple of demonstrations will help here. Using these two lists with some sample content, you will see how the remove operations behave:

```
<h2>List One</h2>
<ol id="myListOne">
        <li>Item One</li>
        <li>Item Two</li>
        <li>Item Three</li>
    </ol>
<h2>List Two</h2>
    <ol id="myListTwo">
        <li>Other Item One</li>
        <li>Other Item Two</li>
        <li>Other Item Three</li>
    </ol>
```

Deploying just this so far would display two lists, each containing three list items (see Figure 3-29).

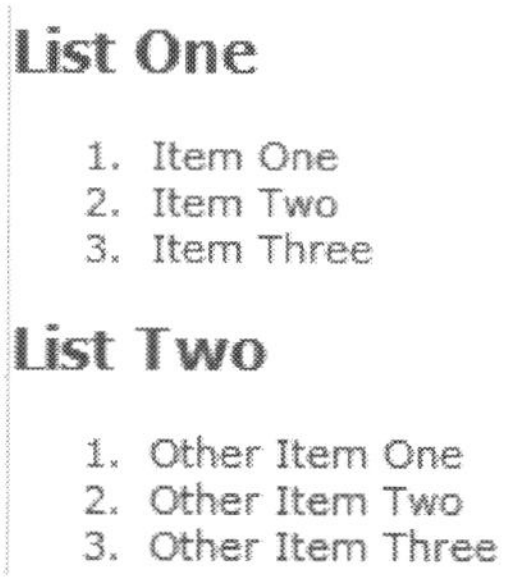

List One

1. Item One
2. Item Two
3. Item Three

List Two

1. Other Item One
2. Other Item Two
3. Other Item Three

Figure 3-29. Orginal elements with two unordered lists with three list items

If you use the following jQuery script, you will see that it is using each of the removal methods. The first removes all items from the second list. The detach method is removing the Item Two element from the first list and storing it into a variable. The next method is removing Item Three, and finally the element being stored in the variable is being appended to the second list.

```
$(document).ready(function () {
    // Remove all items from List Two
    $('#myListTwo').empty();

    // Detach the second item from List one (Item Two)
    var itemTwo = $('#myListOne>li:nth-child(2)').detach();

    // Remove new second item (Item Three as Item Two has been detached)
    $('#myListOne>li:nth-child(2)').remove();

    // Append the detached item to the second list
    $('#myListTwo').append(itemTwo);
});
```

The result is shown in Figure 3-30.

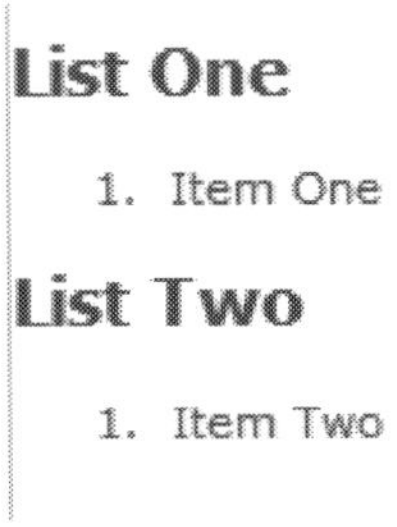

List One

1. Item One

List Two

1. Item Two

Figure 3-30. The child elements have been detached and reattached to a different parent element.

Summary

In this chapter, you saw a great deal of the arsenal that jQuery offers. When you are building your jQuery applications in SharePoint, you will find that selectors are an invaluable tool, and knowing the different ways you can select the elements you want will make this task that much easier. You should also understand the different events available, from the $(document).ready() function, which is used in pretty much every jQuery application I have written, to the events that you will seldom use but that are worth knowing about. Being able to create HTML code on the fly is such a useful function to have, and you will see later in the book how this can be applied when retrieving data from various sources to populate elements on a page.

Because of the interactive nature of jQuery and the speed in which you can knock out a small test application, I strongly advise you to create a few more test pages with various elements and different IDs, class names, and attributes to learn more about how you can interact with them. When it comes to writing your solutions, being able to draw on this experience will help you in the long run.

CHAPTER 4

Debugging jQuery

This chapter will introduce the necessary tools and knowledge you need in order to debug issues that you will come across when writing code. Most SharePoint developers are used to writing managed code where it's fairly straightforward to put in a breakpoint and step through the code. Luckily, this can still be done with JavaScript files in Visual Studio 2010 (as long as the debugger is attached to the right process). Sometimes it is easier to debug in the browser, because one of the benefits of working on the client side is that most modern browsers have tools that allow you to debug "on the fly."

To explore the debugging options, it's easiest to start with just a Content Editor web part with the jQuery code entered in HTML mode. The examples will assume you have the jQuery library deployed. You will also learn what will happen if the jQuery library is not available and how to handle it.

To make it simple to work with the JavaScript file in the examples, you will be working with a JavaScript file that will sit in a document library.

Creating the JavaScript File to Debug

Follow these steps to create the JavaScript file:

1. In your SharePoint environment, create a new document library called Scripts. You will not need to use a document template or versioning.

2. Create a file locally on your machine called DebuggingjQuery.js. This will be the file to which you will be adding your jQuery code. Add the following code and then save the file:

   ```
   $(document).ready(function () {
       });
   ```

3. Upload the JavaScript file to your Scripts document library.

4. To be able to reference this JavaScript file in the Content Editor web part, you will need its URL. The easiest way of finding this is to just right-click its name in the All Documents view and click "Copy shortcut."

5. Go to a SharePoint web part page and add a Content Editor web part from the Media and Content category, as shown in Figure 4-1.

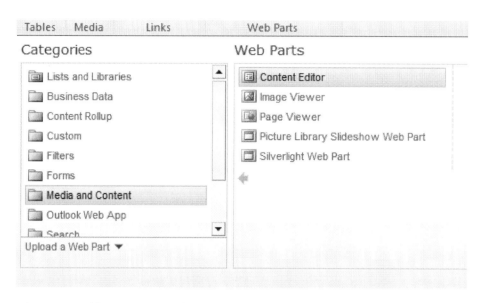

Figure 4-1. Adding a Content Editor web part

6. Once the web part has been added, click the "Click here to add new content" hyperlink.

7. In the Ribbon's Editing Tools ➤ Format Text tab, find the HTML drop-down box in the Markup section and click Edit HTML Source, as shown in Figure 4-2.

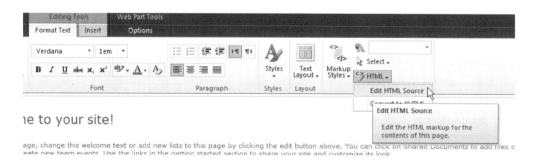

Figure 4-2. Editing the HTML mode to add the script *tag*

8. In the HTML Source dialog, you will be adding a script reference to the JavaScript file in the document library. Add a script reference using the URL you copied earlier in the example. Once done, click OK and then click OK again in the Tool pane. Here is how it looks for my URL; make sure you put the correct path for your own environment:

```
<script type="text/javascript" src="http://win-8xvzmgwv9fi/Scripts/↵
DebuggingjQuery.js"></script>
```

9. The jQuery script should now be loading on the page! A quick way to check is to press F12 in Internet Explorer, navigate to the Script page, and in the drop-down look to see whether the JavaScript file is being referenced, as shown in Figure 4-3.

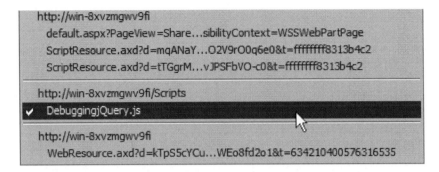

Figure 4-3. Checking that the DebuggingjQuery file has loaded using IE Developer Tools

Now that you have a JavaScript file, after any changes you make, you can just update the file and re-upload, making sure you overwrite the file. This will make it easier for you to work through the difference exercises and debug the code.

Alert: It's Not a Debugger but It Can Help!

You know that the JavaScript is being referenced because you saw that the file was appearing in the list of scripts for the page. Now, wouldn't it be nice if there were a little something that could pop up just to let us know it's there? The simplest way of making sure that something has happened in JavaScript is to add a simple alert. Let's use something like this:

```
alert('Something has happened');
```

This is what you saw earlier in the book to show that an event has occurred. The easiest way to make sure that jQuery has loaded is to use the following jQuery code:

```
$(document).ready(function()
{
  alert('Hello jQuery');
});
```

Update the DebuggingjQuery.js file with the previous code using Notepad and re-upload it to the document library. This time when the page loads, you will be shown the beauty of the JavaScript alert, as shown in Figure 4-4.

Figure 4-4. *Alert showing that the JavaScript is working*

There are places where an alert might be appropriate, but it's not the most suitable way to do all of your debugging.

- It's a blocking process; in other words, everything else will wait until you click OK before proceeding.

- Alerts *will* drive you completely crazy if you accidently leave 15 of them in your code and every other second one pops up for you to swat down.

- Some modern browsers will suppress multiple alerts so they can get "taken care of" before you get to see them.

Console

The console provides a less intrusive way of recording events that have occurred in your code; console output doesn't block the process as alerts do. Most modern browsers come with a developer dashboard that can show you the output from a console call. The following jQuery code is calling a function that in turn is logging the event in the console, see Figure 4-5; the syntax is nice and easy to remember:

```
$(document).ready(function () {
    DoSomething();
});

function DoSomething() {
    console.log('DoSomething was called');
}
```

Figure 4-5. Viewing console log information in IE Developer Tools' Console tab

The console will be an invalid object unless IE Developer Tools or any other tool that creates the console object is enabled. If a debugger is attached, such as Visual Studio, you will get the error message shown in Figure 4-6:

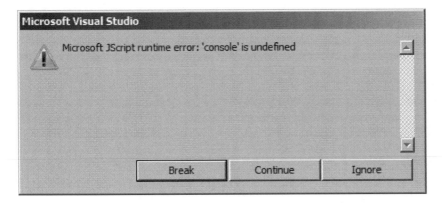

Figure 4-6. Error if IE Developer Tools is not running

Clicking Continue and then F12 in the browser will allow you to use the console logging method. There is a really cool wrapper for `console.log` available that will help get around the issue; see `http://benalman.com/projects/javascript-debug-console-log/`.

Stepping Through Your Code

You can use two main methods to step through your code: using an IDE like Visual Studio or using a browser tool. Like in managed code, it is possible to put a breakpoint into your code so the browser will break its execution and allow you to inspect objects as well as step through the process.

Stepping Through Code Using Visual Studio

If you deploy a solution using Visual Studio 2010, pressing the F5 key launches the browser with the debugger attached to Internet Explorer. In your code, any breakpoints you have entered will stop execution. Take a look at the example in Figure 4-7; you will see that one of the lines has been highlighted. This is where the breakpoint has been set by clicking in the left margin.

```javascript
$(document).ready(function () {
        CountQuickLaunchElements();
    });

    function CountQuickLaunchElements() {
        alert('Try to count quick launch children using incorrect ID selector');
        var childCount;
        childCount = $('#ms-quickLaunch').children().count;
        alert("Children: " + childCount);

        alert('Try to count quick launch children using correct CLASS selector');
        childCount = $('.ms-quickLaunch').children().Count;
        alert("Children: " + childCount);
    }
```

Figure 4-7. Stepping into code using the Visual Studio debugger and a breakpoint

The code is meant to show how many child elements there are of the Quick Launch menu, but at the moment it is showing this in the alert (Figure 4-8) for both selector queries. This is because the property that is being retrieved does not exist.

Figure 4-8. Alert showing that something is wrong in the code

Deploying this solution will allow you to inspect your objects and see what's going on. Once you go to the page with this code and it reaches this point in execution, it will break to Visual Studio, and you can debug your solution. If you want to test a jQuery method or inspect any objects, you can use the Immediate window too, just as you would for writing C# or VB code. If you do this on the children methods for one of the selectors, you will be able to see that there is no count method. Instead, the code should be using length. Update the code to the following to see whether it works:

```
$(document).ready(function () {
    CountQuickLaunchElements();
});

function CountQuickLaunchElements() {
    alert('Try to count quick launch children using incorrect ID selector');
    var childCount;
    childCount = $('#ms-quickLaunch').children().length;
    alert("Children: " + childCount);

    alert('Try to count quick launch children using correct CLASS selector');
    childCount = $('.ms-quickLaunch').children().length;
    alert("Children: " + childCount);
}
```

This time, you will see that the first alert shows it found zero children, and the second time it will show how many it found.

Alternatively, if there is a method call in the code that does not exist, such as the following (which uses a selector but a method that is not defined)

```
$('.ms-quickLaunch').Spin();
```

you will get the following message, telling you that you need to check to make sure you're using a valid method:

```
Microsoft JScript runtime error: Object doesn't support property or method 'Spin'
```

Stepping Through Code Using the Browser

Using the same code from the Visual Studio example, it is as simple to debug your JavaScript. Edit the .js file from the earlier debugging examples with the following erroneous code:

```
$(document).ready(function () {
    DoSums();
});

function DoSums() {
    var firstNumber = 10;
    var secondNumber = "Four";
    var thirdNumber = numberStoredInVariable;
    var result = firstNumber + secondNumber + numberStoredInVariable;
    console.log(result);
}
```

Once the code has been saved, upload it to the Scripts document library, overwriting the original. Next navigate back to the SharePoint page where the Content Editor web part page is. You'll notice that nothing happens (that you can see). Press F12 to bring up IE Developer Tools, navigate to the Scripts tab, and from the drop-down box choose your script. This time click the "Start debugging" button. The script will have already executed on the page load, so in order to debug it, you will need to refresh the page by pressing F5. The debugger should catch one of the errors in the script: that the `numberStoredInVariable` variable does not exist, as shown in Figure 4-9.

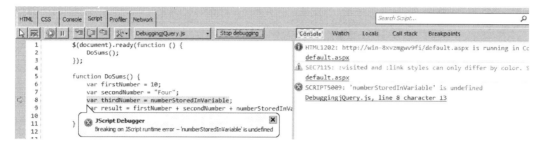

Figure 4-9. *Finding out what's going on using the IE Developer Tools script debugger*

To remedy this issue, edit the `DoSums` method in the JavaScript file to the following and reupload the file:

```
function DoSums() {
    var firstNumber = 10;
    var secondNumber = "Four";
    var numberStoredInVariable = 6;
    var thirdNumber = numberStoredInVariable;
    var result = firstNumber + secondNumber + numberStoredInVariable;
    console.log(result);
}
```

This time, the script will run without any errors, but if you look into the Console tab, you will see the result that is logged:

```
LOG: 10Four6
```

This is obviously not what you want. Edit the code again, and this time change the following:

```
var secondNumber = "Four";
```

to this:

```
var secondNumber = 4;
```

Finally, you will see in the console that the correct answer is recorded:

```
LOG: 20
```

Inspecting Objects

In the next example, you will see how you can inspect objects to see their properties. Edit the JavaScript file with the following new code that gets a menagerie of animals and outputs their name to the console:

```
$(document).ready(function () {
    GetAnimals();
});

function GetAnimals() {
    var animals = ['Cat', 'Dog', 'Goat', 'Narwhal', 'Platypus'];

    $(animals).each(function (index, element) {
        console.log("Animal number " + index + ": is a " + element);
    });
}
```

Deploy the code and put a breakpoint on the first line in the GetAnimals method. Attach the debugger once again by clicking "Start debugging" and refresh the page. Once the page hits the breakpoint, change to the Locals view in the right pane. You should see that there is an entry for animals, but as yet it is undefined. Press F10 to step to the next code section. After you have done this, you should see that the animals variable is now instantiated, and the array is populated with values. Click the + to expand the section to see the elements in the array, as shown in Figure 4-10.

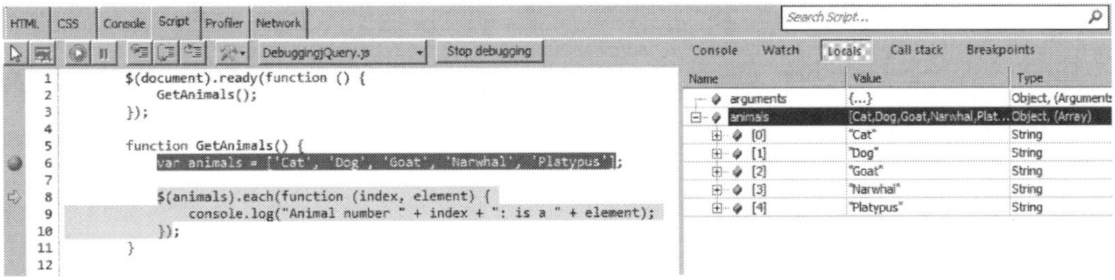

Figure 4-10. The Locals window makes it easy to inspect your objects.

This is useful when you want to see the properties of an object or want to see what has come back from a web service call, for example. Press F5 to continue all execution, and if you change back to the Console tab, you will see the output of the code.

It's also worth mentioning that you can write on-the-fly jQuery into the Console tab; this can be a very quick way of testing a new idea or concept before you write your script.

Checking Whether jQuery Has Loaded

If you want to make sure that jQuery has loaded, you can use the following code at the start of your JavaScript file:

```
if (!(window.jQuery)) {
    alert("jQuery has not been loaded");
    // Use pure JavaScript to make sure users experience isn't hindered
} else if (!(window.jQuery.fn.jquery == '1.0')) {
    var jQueryVersion = window.jQuery.fn.jquery;
    alert("This version you wanted: 1.0 was not loaded it was " + jQueryVersion);
```

```
    } else {
        alert("jQuery has loaded fine!");
    }
```

In this simple example, the first check is seeing whether jQuery has loaded by using `window.jQuery`. By negating the `if` statement, you are able to show a message or take the necessary action to ensure that the site operators or the end users are aware that the page will not be able to provide the jQuery functionality. It's also possible to check for a specific version of jQuery by looking at the `window.jQuery.fn.jquery` property.

Using a Logging Framework

Many logging frameworks are available to allow a more robust and flexible framework. A list of such frameworks is available at `http://ajaxpatterns.org/Javascript_Logging_Frameworks`.

Moving to Production

Don't forget to remove those alerts if you don't want your end users to see them. That will also help reduce the file size of the final JavaScript file.

Make sure that you also respect the JavaScript code as you would any other that you write and include `try/catch` statements in your code to make sure you are not going to cause the JavaScript execution to fail unexpectedly and break all the JavaScript functionality on the page.

```
try
  {
     // Run your code
  }
catch(err)
  {
      //Handle error
  }
```

Summary

In this chapter, you saw how it's possible to display alerts and log issues to the console as well as how to inspect objects. Whether you want to debug using the power of Visual Studio or whether you prefer to do your debugging in the browser, both provide an excellent way to get to the root of any issues and allow a, ideally quick, resolution to the problem!

Lots of tools are available for the Firefox browser, namely, Firebug (`http://getfirebug.com/`), which is similar to IE Developer Tools, and Firefinder (`http://robertnyman.com/firefinder/`), which is a simple way to test selection queries. Finally, I recommend using Fiddler for helping find out what data is being exchanged with web services (`www.fiddler2.com`); it can be a real lifesaver when trying to make sure you are getting the right data out of a JSON object.

CHAPTER 5

Viewing SharePoint Data Using jQuery

This chapter will introduce the different ways you can use jQuery to work with SharePoint data. As mentioned in Chapter 1, some of the great features that SharePoint offers developers are the document libraries and lists. As in the previous chapter, this chapter will include lots of hands-on examples to help you understand what's going on and how to take it to the next level.

SharePoint already offers an easy to use user interface for working with SharePoint data. The lists and libraries generate forms for you, and you can customize the forms using InfoPath.

Most of the data is presented in a grid fashion as in Figure 5-1, there are other styles to use but they are more on the functional side of things rather than the pretty.

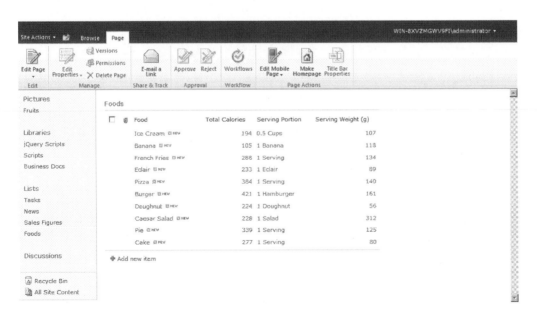

Figure 5-1. A SharePoint custom list displaying food items

Consider a list of products that you want to sell: seeing them all in a grid is certainly functional, but it won't deliver a particularly high "wow" factor for your audience. Maybe a carousel would be a better option to allow a user to spin through the options.

You can access SharePoint data using jQuery in three ways. The first is using the Server Object Model to load data and using jQuery just to work with the data. The second method is using the SharePoint web services, and the third is using the SharePoint 2010 Client Object Model.

Creating a jQuery Web Part to View Images from a Picture Library

In this series of examples, you will learn some of the ways you can access images stored in a picture library. You will be learning useful concepts as the examples progress, building upon what you have learned already.

In the first example, you will access the images by manually telling jQuery the location of the files to use, making this a static example. This example will be displaying images of five fruits that have been put into a document library called Fruits, as shown in Figure 5-2. Each of the fruits has a small version (e.g., apple_small.png) and a large version (e.g., apple_large.png).

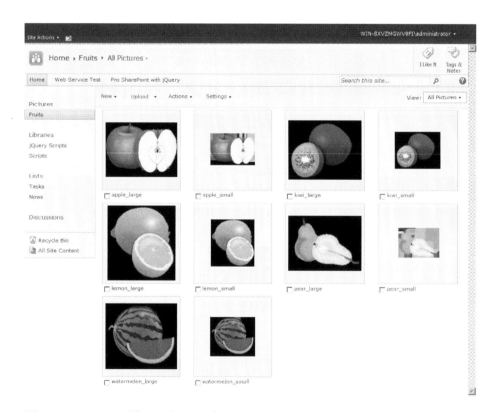

Figure 5-2. Picture library showing fruit images

The images, although they have a transparent background, appear to have a black background when viewed in the picture library. Don't worry about that, though, because they will display correctly when using them later.

It's time to create the Visual Studio project. Open Visual Studio and use the new Empty SharePoint Project template that sits under SharePoint ➤ 2010. Name the project jQueryFruitsExample, and click OK. The Visual web part you will be adding needs to be deployed as a farm solution, so select that option and click Finish. You will notice that there is indeed a Visual web part project that exists already; however, using this makes renaming the web part to something other than the default VisualWebPart1 a little tricky.

Now you have an empty SharePoint solution. Let's add a Visual web part, right-click the project, and choose Add ➤ New Item. Select a Visual web part from the SharePoint 2010 category, call it jQueryFruitWebPart, and click Add. Once the project has opened, then you should be presented with the ASCX code, as shown in Figure 5-3.

***Figure 5-3.** An empty ASCX control has been added to the project.*

The first thing you should do is add some text to the web part and deploy it at this stage (see Figure 5-4).

***Figure 5-4.** Adding some text will allow you to test that the web part is working.*

Why are you deploying it right now? It's for a very simple reason—one that was drummed into me by my colleague (Thanks, Nick!). You want to make sure the very minimum works; if you're having problems here, then it's easier to debug now than after filling a web part with all its moving parts.

Now let's make one change: double-click the `Elements.xml` file that resides underneath the jQueryFruitWebPart folder in Solution Explorer. This file tells SharePoint what to do with the web part and where it can be found for the user. Change the only property element in the file with the name `Group,` so that the value is `SharePoint and jQuery Examples` instead of the default `custom` value (see Figure 5-5).

```xml
<?xml version="1.0" encoding="utf-8"?>
<Elements xmlns="http://schemas.microsoft.com/sharepoint/" >
  <Module Name="jQueryFruitWebPart" List="113" Url="_catalogs/wp">
    <File Path="jQueryFruitWebPart\jQueryFruitWebPart.webpart" Url="jQueryFruitWebPart.webpart" Type="GhostableInLibrary" >
      <Property Name="Group" Value="SharePoint and jQuery Examples" />
    </File>
  </Module>
</Elements>
```

Figure 5-5. *Adding a group to the web part will make it easier to find.*

Press F5, and once the browser has opened add the web part to the page, go to Site Actions ➤ Edit Page, and click the "Add a web part" link on the web part zone where you want to put the web part. In the Categories list, you will see SharePoint and jQuery Examples (all the of the web parts you create in this book will be put here to make them easy to find). When you click the category, you should see the jQueryFruitWebPart (see Figure 5-6), which you have just deployed. Select it and click the Add button.

Figure 5-6. *The web part is appearing in the correct group.*

Click Stop Editing from the Ribbon, and prepare to be astounded by the web part (see Figure 5-7).

jQueryFruitWebPart

Hello World

Figure 5-7. *The web part successfully shows the "Hello World" text, meaning you're good to carry on.*

Yes, my readers, you are on the way to a great web part! Close the browser, which will actually retract the web part and detach the debugger. If someone went to the page now, they would get an error such as the following:

```
Web Part Error: A Web Part or Web Form Control on this Page cannot be displayed or imported.
The type jQueryFruitsExample.jQueryFruitWebPart.jQueryFruitWebPart, jQueryFruitsExample,
Version=1.0.0.0, Culture=neutral, PublicKeyToken=34595caa37df5ff3 could not be found or it
is not registered as safe.
```

This error makes sense because we retracted everything the solution; however, the web part does still exist in the web part gallery. If you try to select it from the gallery, you will be presented with a warning telling you "The operation could not be completed because the item was removed from the gallery."

The next stage is to add a JavaScript (*.js) file to contain the JavaScript. This could all be inline in the ASCX file, a bit like what was happening with the application page from the previous chapter, but this is not a best practice. You should get used to separating the elements; just as you would expect to put CSS into its own file, you should be doing the same with your jQuery code.

Back in Visual Studio, add a JavaScript file (from the Web category) to the jQueryFruitWebPart folder and name the file jQueryFruit.js (see Figure 5-8).

Figure 5-8. *The JavaScript file for the jQuery code is added to the project.*

When the file is added, its deployment type is set as NoDeployment, which isn't much use for us. To deploy this to a location where it can be used, change the deployment type to ClassResource. By changing this to ClassResource, the Deployment location becomes {ClassResourcePath}\jQueryFruitsExample\jQueryFruitWebPart\. This is a special location for supplying resources for our web part. On my file system, the file will be deployed to C:\Program Files\Common Files\Microsoft Shared\Web Server Extensions\wpresources\jQueryFruitsExample\1.0.0.0__34595caa37df5ff3\jQueryFruitsExample\jQueryFruitWebPart. To make this path a bit more manageable, change the deployment location to Scripts (see Figure 5-9).

Figure 5-9. Deploying the JavaScript as a class resource to the Scripts folder

So, now when the solution is deployed, the JavaScript file will be deployed to this location on the file system. Right-click the project in Visual Studio and choose Deploy. Once it has deployed, then you will be able to navigate to the folder location and see the file. It is also necessary to do this so you can get the full URL and GUID required to use this file from the web part, as follows:

1. Navigate to `C:\Program Files\Common Files\Microsoft Shared\Web Server Extensions\wpresources\`.

2. Locate the `jQueryFruitsExample` folder and navigate down until you get to the `jQueryFruit.js` file.

3. From the address bar in Explorer, copy the location from `wpresources` onward to the clipboard. For example, I have `wpresources\jQueryFruitsExample\ 1.0.0.0__34595caa37df5ff3\Scripts\jQueryFruit.js`.

You may wonder why you're using this method of deploying the file rather than just putting it in the `Layouts` folder. The main advantage of deploying the file as a `ClassResource` is the caching. The script will be loaded from the server only the first time it is referenced, and all references thereafter will be loaded from the browser's cache. As the scripts grow in size and complexity, any benefits like this become increasingly important. You can find more information on this method of JavaScript deployment here: `http://blogs.msdn.com/b/sharepointdev/archive/2011/02/15/creating-a-web-part-with-client-side-script.aspx`.

Open the ASCX file again, and add the following `<script>` reference to tell the web part where to find the JavaScript file. Here you can paste what's on the clipboard, making sure you put a / at the start and replace all backslashes with forward slashes:

```
<script type="text/javascript" src="/_wpresources/jQueryFruitsExample/↵
1.0.0.0__34595caa37df5ff3/Scripts/jQueryFruit.js" />
```

The ASCX file should look like Figure 5-10.

```
<%@ Assembly Name="$SharePoint.Project.AssemblyFullName$" %>
<%@ Assembly Name="Microsoft.Web.CommandUI, Version=14.0.0.0, Culture=neutral, PublicKeyToken=71e9bce111e9429c" %>
<%@ Control Language="C#" AutoEventWireup="true" CodeBehind="jQueryFruitWebPartUserControl.ascx.cs" Inherits="jQueryFruitsExample.jQueryFruitWebPart.jQueryFruitWebPartUserControl" %>
<script type="text/javascript" src="_wpresources/jQueryFruitsExample/1.0.0.0__34595caa37df5ff3/Scripts/jQueryFruit.js"></script>

Hello World
```

Figure 5-10. *The script link has been added to load from the resources location.*

At the moment, nothing would happen because the JavaScript file is empty. So, add the following jQuery script to let you know that the JavaScript file has been loaded and that jQuery is also working too:

```
$(document).ready(function () {
    alert("I loaded");
});
```

As a tip, I always find it easier to write the empty function with all the brackets and braces before adding the body to make sure they all match up:

```
$(document).ready(function() { });
```

Then I expand it with the body between the two braces. So long as you make sure the brackets and braces are added in pairs, then it should help you make sure you don't have any strays.

Once you have added the alert, you are OK to deploy again and test to make sure you get that alert. Great, now you have your basic web part set up and raring to go. The first thing to look at is just to make sure you can display one of the images on the page. Navigate to the picture library where your images are stored, and click one of the images you want to use from the list. In the pop-up dialog, copy the file location by right-clicking either the name or the preview and then choose Copy Shortcut.

In the ASCX file, add a new image tag and use the URL on your clipboard as the source URL. Make sure you supply an ID because you will be using this in the JQuery code to manipulate this element:

```
<img alt="Fruit" id="myFruitImage" src="Fruits/apple_small.png" />
```

You can make the path relative if you want as I have done here. Fruits is the picture library, and apple_small.png is my image. Make sure you take into account that if you're using a managed path, you will need to set the source appropriately. If I deploy, then I get a beautiful picture of an apple (see Figure 5-11).

jQueryFruitWebPart

Figure 5-11. *Image successfully loading from the image library*

There's nothing jQuery-like here yet, but let's attach a `toggle` event to the image element so that when it is clicked, it will swap between two images. Open the `jQueryFruit.js` file and enter the following code:

```
$(document).ready(function () {
    // Bind toggle event to the img element with name #myFruitImage
    // Each click will alternative between the two methods SetAppleImage and SetLemonImage
    $('#myFruitImage').toggle(SetAppleImage, SetLemonImage);
});

function SetAppleImage() {
    // Call the Set Image method passing in Apple image name
    SetImage("apple_small.png");
}

function SetLemonImage() {
    // Call the Set Image method passing in Lemon image name
    SetImage("lemon_small.png");
}

function SetImage(imageName) {
    // Call the Set Image method passing in Apple image name
    $('#myFruitImage').attr("src", "Fruits/" + imageName);
}
```

In this jQuery code, the document ready event is being used to bind the `toggle` event to the element that the user should click to toggle between the two images. The code is also being a good citizen and has just one function to update the image's source attribute (`SetImage`) and has separate functions to pass in the desired fruit names. The `SetImage` method has a parameter to take in the image name, and this variable is being used when building up the `src` value.

Once you deploy this solution, you may find that the functionality isn't doing what you expected; it might still be showing you the alert that was set in the first deployment that has now been removed. This is because of the clever caching mechanisms, meaning that the old version is cached in the user's browser and is being used. To force the browser to get the latest version of the JavaScript file from the server, do a full-page refresh using Ctrl+F5. Remember this tip when you have made a change and can't see the changes.

A good test to make sure you're working with the correct version of the JavaScript file is to use the Internet Explorer Developer Tools. Go to the Script tab, and from the drop-down list find the script you are working with. Compare the contents to the version that you believe should be running; if there is a difference, do a full refresh.

Clicking the image will alternate between calling the two methods; this shows us the first picture and then the second.

If you wanted to loop through all of the images in the picture library, you could hard-code all of the values and loop through them in an array, but that would require updating the JavaScript every time you wanted to update the pictures. In the next example, you will be using the Server Object Model in the web part to write a JavaScript array of the images to load from the picture library.

Replace the JavaScript with the following. What this will do is cycle through the images every three seconds. The `setInterval` is a JavaScript method that will call the supplied function in the first parameter at a duration set by the second parameter in milliseconds. In this case, it will call the function to change the image to the next in the sequence.

```
// Global variable to track current fruit index
var currentFruit = 0;

$(document).ready(function () {

    // Check to make sure Fruits array has been created
    if (typeof Fruits != "undefined") {

        // Get the first fruit
        GetFruit();

        // Get timer to call the GetFruit method every 3 seconds
        setInterval('GetFruit()', 3000);
    } else {
        // Set imgage to the error image from the Layouts folder
        $('#myFruitImage').attr("src", "_LAYOUTS/1033/IMAGES/ERROR.GIF");
        alert("Fruits array is undefined");
    }


});

function GetFruit() {

    // If at the end of the Array then start again from 0
    if (currentFruit == Fruits.length - 1) {
        currentFruit = 0;
    }

    // Update the src attribute with the path to the fruit image
    $('#myFruitImage').attr("src", "Fruits/" + Fruits[currentFruit]);

    // Increment current fruit so next time it gets the next item
    currentFruit++;
}
```

This code is using an array called Fruits, which will contain the file names of the files in the picture library. The eagle-eyed reader will note that the code does not define the Fruits array anywhere. Deploy the solution now, and you will see this error-handling line:

```
if (typeof Fruits != "undefined") {
```

This will capture if the array does not exist, and it will show the alert and change the picture to the SharePoint Error image.

The task of creating this array will fall to the web part code. In the web part, you are able to use the Server Object Model, and you also have the ability to use the Pages Client Script Manager. Take a look at the following code, which uses an SPQuery to obtain the name of all images in the picture library where the name contains _small.

First, add a using statement for System.Web.Collection.Generic.

Next, update the class to the following:

```
public class jQueryFruitWebPart : WebPart
{
    // Visual Studio might automatically update this path when you change the Visual↵
Web Part project item.
    private const string _ascxPath = @"~/_CONTROLTEMPLATES/jQueryFruitsExample/↵
jQueryFruitWebPart/jQueryFruitWebPartUserControl.ascx";

    protected override void CreateChildControls()
    {
        Control control = Page.LoadControl(_ascxPath);
        Controls.Add(control);
    }

    protected override void OnLoad(EventArgs e)
    {
        base.OnPreRender(e);
        LoadFruitArray();
    }

    private void LoadFruitArray()
    {
        // Get the Page Client Script Manager
        var cs = Page.ClientScript;

        // Try and get the Fruit List from the current Web
        var fruitList = SPContext.Current.Web.Lists.TryGetList("Fruits");

        // If list not found then return
        if (fruitList == null) return;

        var fruits = new List<string>();

        // Query to select just the image names from the list with _small in the name
        var query = new SPQuery
        {
            Query = "<Where>" +
            "<Contains>" +
            "<FieldRef Name='NameOrTitle' />" +
            "<Value Type='Text'>_small</Value>" +
            "</Contains>" +
            "</Where>",
            ViewFields = "<FieldRef Name='NameOrTitle' />",
            ViewFieldsOnly = true
        };

        var fruitListItems = fruitList.GetItems(query);
```

```
        // Iterate through each list item
        foreach (SPListItem item in fruitListItems)
        {
            // Add the Item Name i.e. 'apple_small.jpg'
            fruits.Add(string.Format("'{0}'", item.Name));
        }

        // Combine all array elements as comma delimited
        var fruitItems = string.Join(",", fruits.ToArray());

        // Register Fruit array to the page Client Script Manager
        cs.RegisterArrayDeclaration("Fruits", fruitItems);
    }
}
```

The code will add the following JavaScript to the page:

```
<script type="text/javascript">
//<![CDATA[
var Fruits =  new Array('apple_small.png','kiwi_small.png','lemon_small.png', ↵
'pear_small.png','watermelon_small.png');
//]]>
</script>
```

The power here comes from the fact that you are able to inject JavaScript into the page by making use of the Client Script Manager, accessible in the web part from the `Page.ClientScript` property. In this example, an array is being inserted, but you also have the ability to insert script blocks, references to other scripts, and more besides.

Deploy the solution, and you should see that the web part loops through the images every three seconds, and because of the query supplied, it will show only the small images.

With this example, it's important to break the solution down to see exactly how the web part is working. The web part code-behind is using the Server Object Model to obtain the list of images to use. This could easily be pulling down announcements from an announcement list, and once it has the items, it could use the Client Script Manager to create an array on the page that the jQuery code can iterate through.

SharePoint Sandboxed Solutions

One of the restrictions of working within a sandboxed solution is that you are constrained to data within the current site collection. This means calls to web services and databases are not permitted on the server side. There is, however, a very neat way in which you can talk to external systems, and that is by using Business Connectivity Services (BCS).

BCS gives SharePoint a standardized way to communicate with external systems. Once a BCS model (which contains details of how to connect), the methods used to perform CRUD functionality, and the structure of the data returned have all been defined, the model can be used throughout SharePoint. A BCS model contains one or more external content types (ECTs), and these ECTs can be used with an external list. An external list behaves in an almost identical way to a standard SharePoint list for your end users and developers; the key point is that the data is not being stored in the SharePoint database. Instead, the data store is the external system defined in the model. Once the ECT has been created, it doesn't matter what the external system is. It could be a web service, a Microsoft SQL Server database, an Oracle database, or even custom objects from a .Net Assembly. You can use the SharePoint API to retrieve the data in a standardized fashion. The key here is that if you want to work with external data in a sandboxed solution, you can configure an external list and use the Client Object Model or web services to talk to the list (because it's within the site collection), but the data it will return will be from the external system.

Office 365 also allows you to talk to external systems via an external list configured for a BCS model. This means you can have access to data that lives in the cloud or, if you make use of the Azure Service Bus (`www.microsoft.com/windowsazure/features/servicebus/`), on-premise data in a sandbox-only environment such as Office 365.

SharePoint Web Services

Using web services is a fantastic way of producing application pages and web parts that can retrieve data dynamically using Ajax. Modern web sites rarely require postbacks when dealing with data on a page, and you will learn in this section how jQuery and the SharePoint web services can work in harmony.

jQuery has a number of ways it can talk to web services (see Table 5-1); here you will explore the different Ajax methods you can use.

Table 5-1. Retrieving Data Using jQuery

Name	Syntax
Ajax	`$.ajax()`
Get	`$.get()`
GetJSON	`$.getJSON()`
Load	`$.load()`
Post	`$.post()`

In this scenario, you will be creating a News web part, which will display the latest three news articles from an announcements list called News. The news articles will have only a small amount of information, but when the user clicks a story, the full story will be retrieved and displayed alongside the title.

To start, add three items to an announcements list. It doesn't matter what they are; just make sure you add a title and some sort of body too. If you're feeling adventurous, you could stick in an image or table. If you're struggling to think of some good text for the body, just head to `www.lipsum.com` and generate some *Lorem Ipsum* text.

Create a new Empty SharePoint Project item called myjQueryNews as a farm solution and add a Visual web part called MyNewsWebPart. Once it's created, open the `Elements.xml` file and change the `Group` property to `SharePoint and jQuery Examples`. Do a "Hello World" deployment test by adding some text to the ASCX control and deploying it. If I t comes back OK, add and test a JavaScript file, as done previously in jQueryFruitsExample. Don't forget to deploy the JavaScript as a class resource and include the `<script>` tag to point to the file in the `_wpresources` location. In this example, you will also be deploying a CSS file. Add a CSS file to the project in the same location as the JS file and choose to deploy it as a class resource, but this time, instead of putting it in a `Scripts` folder, choose to put it in a `Styles` folder (see Figure 5-12).

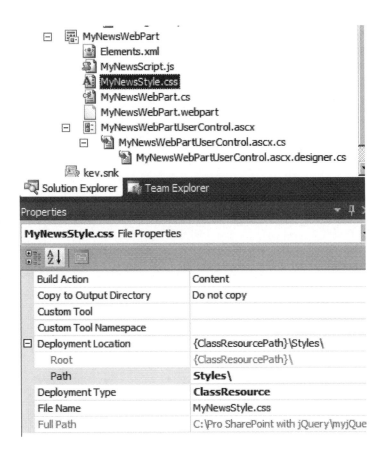

Figure 5-12. Deploying a CSS style sheet and JavaScript file as a class resource

You are now ready to start piecing together this News web part. Right-click the project name and choose Deploy. This will put the JS and CSS files into the web part resources folder so that you can make a note of their locations. Navigate to C:\Program Files\Common Files\Microsoft Shared\Web Server Extensions\wpresources\myNewsWebPart. There you will find the identifier for your web part. Navigate down a layer, and you will see two folders, one for the scripts and one for the styles. In the ASXC file, you will need to add a reference to the script and also a link to the style sheet. The ASCX should look like the following but with your own resources path:

```
<%@ Assembly Name="$SharePoint.Project.AssemblyFullName$" %>
<%@ Assembly Name="Microsoft.Web.CommandUI, Version=14.0.0.0, Culture=neutral,↵
 PublicKeyToken=71e9bce111e9429c" %>
<%@ Control Language="C#" AutoEventWireup="true" CodeBehind="MyNewsWebPartUserControl↵
.ascx.cs" Inherits="myjQueryNews.MyNewsWebPart.MyNewsWebPartUserControl" %>
<script type="text/javascript" src="_wpresources/myNewsWebPart/↵
1.0.0.0__d423462d89d62895/scripts/MyNewsScript.js"></script>
<link href="_wpresources/myNewsWebPart/1.0.0.0__d423462d89d62895/↵
styles/MyNewsStyle.css" rel="stylesheet" type="text/css" />
```

I have removed some of the assembly references that were not needed for this example. The next stage is to add the HTML that will be used for displaying the news articles:

```
<!-- Id to hold the articles loaded by the Web Service-->
<div id="News" />

<!-- News Story Template -->
<div id="NewsStory-Template" class="NewsStory" style="display: none">
    <h2></h2>
    <div class="NewsArticle" style="display: none" />
</div>
```

This HTML is very succinct. The `<div>` with the `id` of `News` is where the articles will be placed once loaded from the web service. `NewsStory-Template` is a template for each news item. There are number of benefits of creating an HTML template. The first is that the way the news items are displayed is completely separate from the code. As long as the class names remain the same, the code will work. It also means that a designer can embellish the ASCX control using a WYSIWYG editor, and it won't interfere with the JavaScript code. The other main benefit is that if the code weren't using a template, the elements would need to be built up dynamically in the JavaScript code, which can get very messy for complex elements.

The styling in the CSS is very simple, but it does what it needs to do:

```
.NewsStory
{
    border: thin solid #000000;
    padding: 10px;
}

.NewsArticle
{
    padding: 10px;
}
```

The JavaScript file will need to contain the following:

```
$(document).ready(function () {

    // Load News Articles
    LoadAllNewsArticles();

    // Bind the click event of the News Header to load the article
    $('.NewsStory>.NewsStoryHeader').live('click', function () {
        var article = $(this).find('.NewsArticle');

        // If News Story is visible then hide it
        if (article.is(':visible')) {
            article.hide();
        } else {
```

```
            // If the News Article has not been loaded then load it
            if (article.is(':empty')) {
                // Load the article, pass in the article element
                LoadArticle(article);
            }

            // Hide all of the other articles
            $('.NewsArticle').hide();

            // Show the News Article
            article.show();
        }

    });
});

function LoadAllNewsArticles() {
    // URL of the List Data Web Service being passed in the list name News
    var taskUrl = "/_vti_bin/ListData.svc/News/";

    // Use Ajax method to call Web Service
    $.ajax({
        type: "GET",
        url: taskUrl,
        dataType: 'json',
        success: function (data) {

            //Iterate through each News Item returned
            $.each(data.d.results, function (i, result) {

                // Clone the hidden Template News Story
                var newsClone = $('#NewsStory-Template').clone();

                // Remove ID as not needed and don't want duplicats
                newsClone.removeAttr('id');

                // Set the text of the H2 element to the Title of the news story
                newsClone.find('.NewsStoryHeader').text(result.Title);

                // Stored the News Item id into the jQuery Data object of the element
                newsClone.data("articleId", result.Id);

                // Show the Element as the template is hidden by default
                newsClone.show();

                // Append the News Story to the News Div
                $('#News').append(newsClone);
            });
        },
```

```
            error: function () {
                alert("Error");
            }
        });
    }

    function LoadArticle(articleElement) {
        // Retrieve the Article ID from the parent element Data object
        var id = articleElement.parent().data("articleId");

        // Build the URL to retrieve the Body of the news story
        var taskUrl = "/_vti_bin/ListData.svc/News(" + id + ")/Body";

        // Use the GetJson Method to obtain the Body form the RestFul Web Service
        $.getJSON(taskUrl, function (data) {
            // Apend the Article body to the Article Element which was passed in as a parameter
            articleElement.append($(data.d.Body));
        });
    }
```

When you deploy the solution, the web part will load the titles (see Figure 5-13).

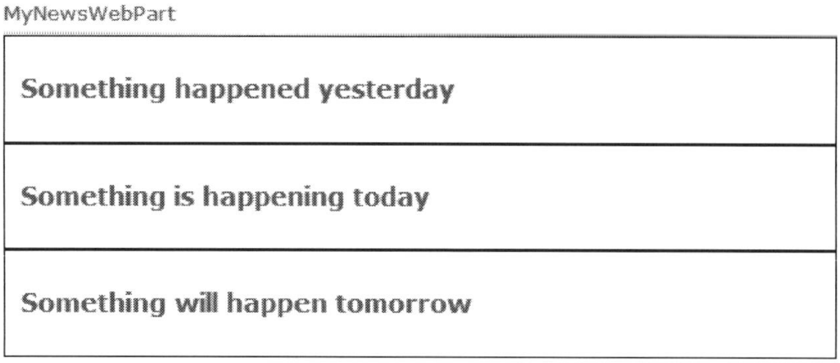

MyNewsWebPart

Something happened yesterday
Something is happening today
Something will happen tomorrow

Figure 5-13. News items being returned from the web service

Click one of the news items, and it will asynchronously load the article details (see Figure 5-14).

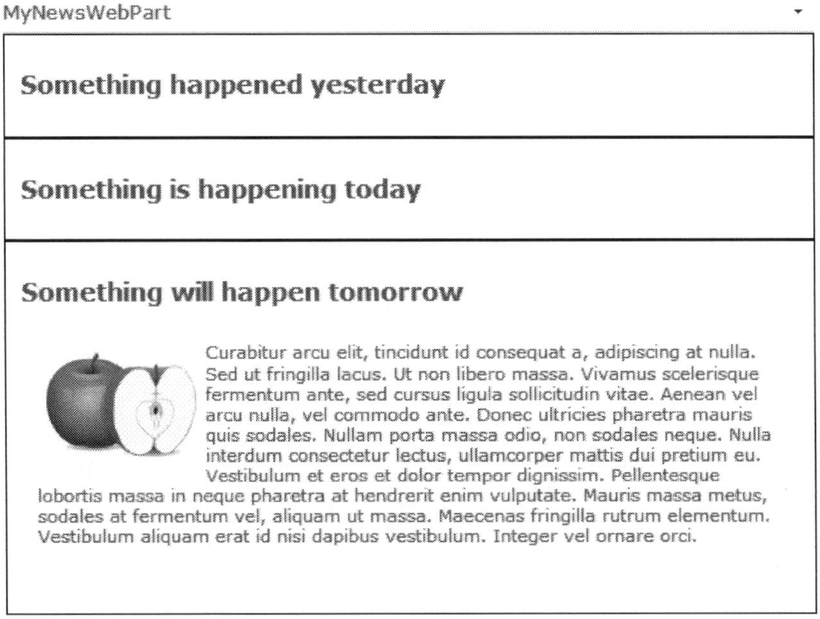

MyNewsWebPart

Something happened yesterday

Something is happening today

Something will happen tomorrow

 Curabitur arcu elit, tincidunt id consequat a, adipiscing at nulla. Sed ut fringilla lacus. Ut non libero massa. Vivamus scelerisque fermentum ante, sed cursus ligula sollicitudin vitae. Aenean vel arcu nulla, vel commodo ante. Donec ultricies pharetra mauris quis sodales. Nullam porta massa odio, non sodales neque. Nulla interdum consectetur lectus, ullamcorper mattis dui pretium eu. Vestibulum et eros et dolor tempor dignissim. Pellentesque lobortis massa in neque pharetra at hendrerit enim vulputate. Mauris massa metus, sodales at fermentum vel, aliquam ut massa. Maecenas fringilla rutrum elementum. Vestibulum aliquam erat id nisi dapibus vestibulum. Integer vel ornare orci.

Figure 5-14. The body of the news article has been dynamically loaded.

That's pretty neat. This code is using two different types of web service call; let's take a look at each in turn.

For retrieving the news articles, the Ajax method is used. The Ajax method is used to perform asynchronous HTTP (Ajax) requests; in this example, you will see that it is using a GET request. You can also use a POST. The default is GET, so if this option is omitted, then GET will be used. The URL is simple path of the web service to call. The SharePoint RESTful web services will return JSON, so you need to set the option so it knows how to handle the data coming back. The two remaining options are the functions to call on success and errors. Lots more configuration options are available for this method; you can find them at http://api.jquery.com/jQuery.ajax/.

```
// Use Ajax method to call Web Service
$.ajax({
    type: "GET",
    url: taskUrl,
    dataType: 'json',
    success: function (data) {

// Code to run
        });
    },
    error: function () {
        alert("Error");
    }
});
```

To retrieve the body for a specific news article, the $.getJson method is used instead:

```
// Use the GetJson Method to obtain the Body form the RestFul Web Service
$.getJSON(taskUrl, function (data) {
    // Code to run
});
```

This is much more succinct way of getting the JSON data from the web service.

In both of the methods, the news article data from the web service is being put into the data object. The Ajax call returns a collection of news items, and the code reads in just the Title field. The GetJSON method returns just one result. The question is, how do you know which properties are available on the data object? One way to find out is to just put a breakpoint in the JavaScript code and inspect the data object to see what properties are available. Another useful way is by using Fiddler (www.fiddler2.com). Fiddler is a free web debugging tool that, when running, will show calls to the web services from your JavaScript code and will even show you the JSON being returned (Figure 5-15).

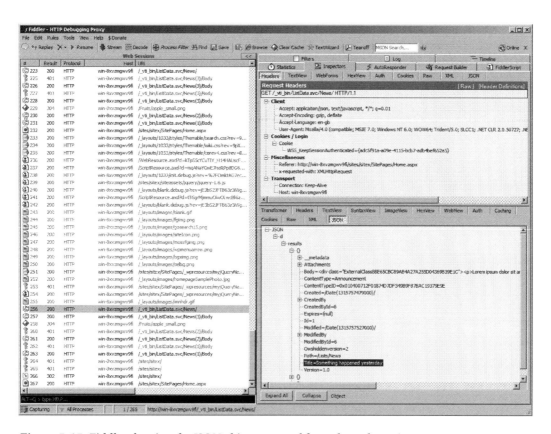

Figure 5-15. *Fiddler showing the JSON object returned from the web service*

Looking at the bottom-right pane, you can see the JSON that is being returned; the object is accessible in the jQuery code; for example, data.d.ContentType would return Announcement.

The $.get and $.post methods are essentially just a shortcut version of the full $.ajax method and can be used to easily perform either function. It's worth explaining the difference between GET and POST here: GET calls should be idempotent. In other words, you're not changing anything; you should be able to call the method an unlimited number of times and get exactly the same results. POST is used when you want to send something to the server and have some sort of action performed.

$.load is the final method to look at here; it allows the jQuery code to load data from the server and place the returned HTML into the matched element.

SharePoint 2010 Managed Client Object Model

The Client Object Model was introduced in SharePoint 2010 as an easier way of working with SharePoint data from a client computer, whether it is a .NET application, a Silverlight application, or an application that uses JavaScript in the browser. The Client Object Model is designed to allow you to write code similar to code you would write for the Server Object Model. It doesn't contain all of the methods of the full Server Object Model, but it does give you a convenient way of accessing site, web, and list information that you will be using later in the book. The part of the Client Object Model that you will be using for working with jQuery is the ECMAScript programming interface, which gives access to the API using JavaScript or Jscript.

The first thing to look at is how the Client Object Model actually works (see Figure 5-16).

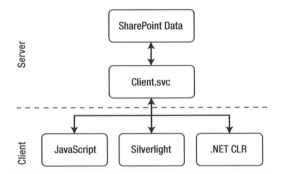

Figure 5-16. The Client Object Model

The JavaScript proxy that you will be using calls the Client.svc web service. The useful thing about using the Client Object Model is that the queries to the service are batched to ensure that the calls are as efficient as possible across the network.

SP.js

SP.js is the JavaScript file used for the ECMA Client Object Model. Because loading this JavaScript file is crucial to being able to use the SharePoint Client Object Model, you will need a way of telling your own script to wait until this file has been loaded before progressing. There is a very useful method available that allows you to do just that: ExecuteOrDelayUntilScriptLoaded. The ExecuteOrDelayUntilScriptLoaded method takes a function to call as well as the script that it should wait for. Once the script has loaded, then the function will execute:

```
$(document).ready(function () {
    ExecuteOrDelayUntilScriptLoaded(getWebUserData, "sp.js");
});
```

To see this in action, take a look at this example, which shows the title and login name for the currently logged on SharePoint user once the page has loaded:

```
$(document).ready(function () {
    // Wait until SP.JS has loaded before calling getWebUserData
    ExecuteOrDelayUntilScriptLoaded(getWebUserData, "sp.js");
});

var context = null;
var web = null;
var currentUser = null;

function getWebUserData() {
    // Get the current user
    context = new SP.ClientContext.get_current();

    // Get the current web
    web = context.get_web();

    // Get the current user
    currentUser = web.get_currentUser();

    // Load the current user
    context.load(currentUser);

    // Execute the query
    context.executeQueryAsync(onSuccessMethod, onFailureMethod);
}

function onSuccessMethod() {
    alert('User name:' + currentUser.get_title() + '\n Login Name:' +↵
 currentUser.get_loginName());
}

function onFailureMethod(sender, args) {
    alert('request failed ' + args.get_message() + '\n' + args.get_stackTrace());
}
```

With the Client Object Model, you build up the objects you want to retrieve from SharePoint by using the various get and load functions, and it's not until the query is executed that the data is requested from SharePoint. This reduces the number of round-trips to the server. It can take some time to get used to that you need to build and then place your order and wait for the service to return the objects before you can work with the properties.

The first thing you need to do when working with the Client Object Model is to get the current context. In the previous example, the next step is to get the current web; and from the web you are getting the current user. You use the `context.load(currentUser)` method to let the query know the object you want back from the server. It doesn't get the object immediately; it's only until the `executeQueryAsync` is called that `currentUser` will available for the code to request its properties. Once the query has executed successfully, then you are able to get the title and login name from the current user object and display it in the alert message.

Summary

This chapter showed you some of the different ways you can work with SharePoint data. You are able to use a web part to inject JavaScript values to the HTML page, you can load data from the web services, and finally you can use the SharePoint 2010 Client Object Model. It's important to think about the method that will be most suitable for your application and choose appropriately. In the following chapters, you will see in more detail how you can leverage these different methods of accessing SharePoint data to create awesome web parts and application pages.

CHAPTER 6

Building a Task List Viewer Application Page

So far in this book, you have learned how to deploy and use the jQuery library, as well as how to use jQuery to work with data residing in SharePoint. Now that you're familiar with the basic concepts, it is time to move on to your first project, which will incorporate what you've learned and also introduce some new ideas to explore.

Planning the Task List Viewer

In this chapter, you'll create an application that allows users to see tasks in a task list and to easily move them between the different statuses.

Consider how users interact with the SharePoint task list normally. There are two main ways of working with this task list,

One way is to navigate to the list itself. Here, you can see the list of tasks available. If you wish to update the status of a task, you must click the task and choose Edit Item, as shown in Figure 6-1, or choose Edit Item from the edit control block.

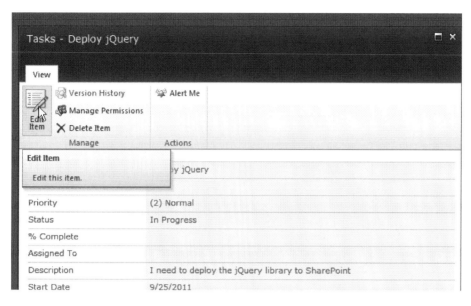

Figure 6-1. Editing a task using the SharePoint user interface

The second option is to use the task list as a web part. You access the property that you want to update either by clicking the item name and choosing Edit Item or by using the edit control block.

So, updating the status of a task list item currently takes four steps:

- Click the task name or the edit control block

- Click Edit Item

- Change the Status value

- Click Save

The application you'll create in this chapter is designed to streamline this process.

Task List Viewer Requirements

The scenario is that management has asked for an easy way to go to an application page, see all of the tasks from a specific task list and their current status, and change the status as necessary.

The following are the requirements for the application:

- It should be easy to see the status of the task.

- No postbacks should occur when the status changes, Use SharePoint web services and jQuery.

- It should take only one click to move between states.

- It should be easy to view the details of the task.

- The application will be concerned with only Not Started, In Progress, and Completed tasks.

- A task can move up or down only one status at a time. For example, it can't go from Not Started to Completed without going through In Progress.

I am sure you'll agree that this is a relatively simple set of requirements. In the next chapter, you will expand on this project to include editing functionality and more.

Task List Viewer Prerequisites

This example assumes that you have already deployed jQuery to your SharePoint environment and that you have a task list created to use as a source of your tasks.

For my example, I used a Team Site template that has a task list created automatically as part of the template. I added three very relevant tasks to this task list, which is named Tasks, as shown in Figure 6-2.

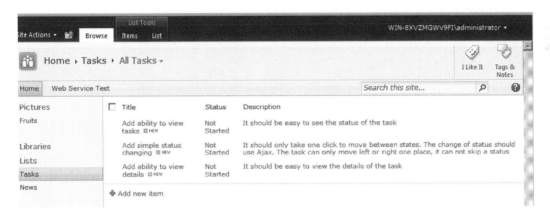

Figure 6-2. Task list with tasks to use with the project

With everything prepared, you are ready to begin to create the project.

Creating the Task List Viewer Application Page

The Task List Viewer application will be an application page that allows end users to view and update tasks. You could create a version that uses a web part, but for this example, you will use an application page to provide as much screen real estate as possible.

Adding an Application Page

The first step is to create and test a simple application page to make sure that everything is working correctly.

1. Create a new Empty SharePoint project in Visual Studio 2010 called jQueryTaskViewerApplication, choose to deploy it as a Farm Solution, and click OK.

2. Add a new application page to the project and name it jQueryTaskViewer.aspx.

3. In the new application page, change the PageTitle content placeholder value to Task Viewer and the PageTitleInTitleArea to My jQuery Task View.

4. Add some text to the Main content placeholder so that you can tell it has deployed properly. Your page should look something like this:

```
<asp:Content ID="Main" ContentPlaceHolderID="PlaceHolderMain" runat="server">
Task viewer ahoy!
</asp:Content>

<asp:Content ID="PageTitle" ContentPlaceHolderID="PlaceHolderPageTitle"
runat="server">
Task Viewer
</asp:Content>

<asp:Content ID="PageTitleInTitleArea" ContentPlaceHolderID=↵
"PlaceHolderPageTitleInTitleArea" runat="server">
My jQuery Task Viewer
</asp:Content>
```

5. Deploy the application page by pressing F5 in Visual Studio.

6. Navigate to the application page by entering its path:

http://SharePoint/**_layouts/jQueryTaskViewerApplication/jQueryTaskViewer.aspx**

Providing that everything has worked as you hope, you should see the application page displaying your message of choice, as shown in Figure 6-3.

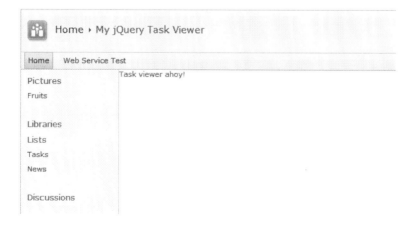

Figure 6-3. Deployed application page

7.   After checking that the application page shows the correct information, close
     the browser.

Adding the HTML to Display Tasks

The next step is to add the HTML to display the tasks. Open the jQueryTaskViewer.aspx file in Visual
Studio and add the following to the Main placeholder. You can remove the sample text you added for the
previous deployment test.

```
<!-- Task Content -->
<div id="taskContent">
    <!-- Not Started Tasks -->
    <div id="notStartedTasksColumn" class="taskColumn">
        <h3>
            Not Started</h3>
        <div class="taskDiv" id="notStartedTasksDiv">
            <ul />
        </div>
    </div>
    <!-- In Progress Tasks -->
    <div id="inProgressTasksColumn" class="taskColumn">
        <h3>
            In Progress</h3>
        <div class="taskDiv" id="inProgressTasksDiv">
            <ul />
        </div>
    </div>
    <!-- Completed Tasks -->
    <div id="completedTasksColumn" class="taskColumn">
        <h3>
            Completed</h3>
        <div class="taskDiv" id="completedTasksDiv">
            <ul />
        </div>
    </div>
</div>

    <!--
    Template for Task List Items
Wrapped in UL to make it easier to design,
Style added to make it not show on page
    -->
    <ul class='hiddenTemplate'>
        <li id="TemplateListItem" class="task">
```

```
        <div class="taskDetailDiv">
            <p class='taskTitle'>
                Title</p>
            <p class='taskDescription'>
                Description</p>
        </div>
    </li>
</ul>
```

This HTML sets up three columns: one for each status of the tasks. Each status has a header and an unordered list of the tasks. There is also a template for the list items, even though the list item is currently wrapped in the ul tag. This is just so that it's easier to design the element in whichever integrated development environment (IDE) you choose. The template will be hidden by using a CSS class that just sets display: none. When using this template, you will just be cloning the inner list item element, rather than the whole list.

Styling the Task List

Now it's time to add some CSS to give this application a proper look and feel. Add a CSS file to the jQueryTaskViewerApplication folder called style.css, as shown in Figure 6-4.

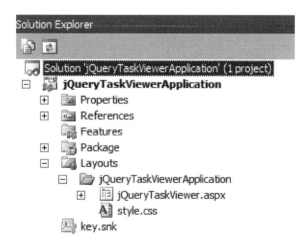

Figure 6-4. CSS file in application folder of the Layouts folder

Add the following CSS to the newly added file:

```
.taskColumn
{
    float: left;
    width: 30%;
}
```

```
.taskTitle
{
    font-weight: bold;
}

.taskDiv ul
{
    list-style: none;
    margin: 0px;
    padding: 4px;
    min-height: 100px;
}

.taskDiv li
{
    font-size: 90%;
    display: block;
    padding: 0.4em 0 0.4em 0.5em;
    text-decoration: none;
}

#notStartedTasksDiv li
{
    border-left: 12px solid #71af0e;
    border-right: 3px solid #71af0e;
    background-color: #e9f9d0;
    border-bottom: 1px solid #71af0e;
}

#notStartedTasksDiv li:hover
{
    background-color: #71af0e;
    color: white;
}

#inProgressTasksDiv li
{
    border-left: 12px solid #efb600;
    border-right: 3px solid #efb600;
    background-color: #f1efae;
    border-bottom: 1px solid #efb600;
}

#inProgressTasksDiv li:hover
{
    background-color: #efb600;
    color: white;
}
```

```
#completedTasksDiv li
{
    border-left: 12px solid #ef0b00;
    border-right: 3px solid #ef0b00;
    background-color: #f3c8c6;
    border-bottom: 1px solid #ef0b00;
}

#completedTasksDiv li:hover
{
    background-color: #ef0b00;
    color: white;
}

.hiddenTemplate
{
    display: none;
}
```

This CSS code styles the tasks so that users can easily identify the three different statuses:

- Green means Not Started

- Orange means In Progress

- Red means Completed

Visual Studio 2010 makes it easy to add the reference to the CSS class. Open the .aspx file again, and drag the CSS file from the Solution Explorer to the PageHead content placeholder. It will create the necessary link tag for you:

```
<asp:Content ID="PageHead" ContentPlaceHolderID="PlaceHolderAdditionalPageHead"↵
 runat="server">
    <link href="style.css" rel="stylesheet" type="text/css" />
</asp:Content>
```

Note that the href is a relative path to the style.css file, which is in the same directory as the .aspx file on the server.

You *could* deploy the application now, but you would see nothing spectacular. That's because all of the magic will come from the jQuery code you will be adding next.

Creating the jQuery JavaScript

With the new application page in place, it is time to look at the code that will drive this application. There are a few steps to take before wiring up the web service calls, the events, and the elements.

To begin, add the JavaScript file, check that the jQuery library is accessible, and show a message.

1. Add a .js file to the same folder as the .css and .aspx files. Name the JavaScript file jQueryTaskViewerScript.js, as shown in Figure 6-5. This technique is a simple way of adding a JavaScript library that relates to this application page only. It will be deployed to the same location as the page itself in the Layouts folder, and can be referenced using a relative path in the script and link tags.

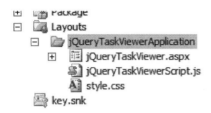

Figure 6-5. CSS and JavaScript files

2. In the .js file, add the following to test it can use jQuery:

```
$(document).ready(function () {
    alert("jQuery loaded!");
});
```

3. As with the CSS file, drag the JavaScript file from the Solution Explorer to the PageHead, which should now look like the following:

```
<asp:Content ID="PageHead" ContentPlaceHolderID="PlaceHolderAdditionalPageHead"↩
 runat="server">
    <link href="style.css" rel="stylesheet" type="text/css" />
    <script src="jQueryTaskViewerScript.js" type="text/javascript"></script>
</asp:Content>
```

4. Deploy the solution. You should see that you that you're on track, as shown in Figure 6-6.

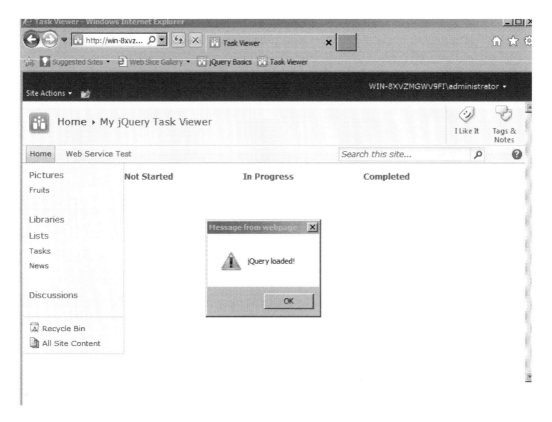

Figure 6-6. *jQuery is working.*

Viewing Tasks

Now you know that jQuery is working correctly, go ahead and add the following JavaScript:

```
$(document).ready(function () {
    // Wait until SP.JS has loaded before calling GetTasks
    ExecuteOrDelayUntilScriptLoaded(GetTasks, "sp.js");

});

var tasks;
var taskListName = "Tasks";

function GetTasks() {

    // Get the current context
    var context = new SP.ClientContext.get_current();
```

```
    // Load the web object
    var web = context.get_web();

    //Get the list
    var list = web.get_lists().getByTitle(taskListName);

    // Get all the items in the list
    tasks = list.getItems('');

    // Load the web in the context and retrieve only selected columns to improve performance
    context.load(tasks, 'Include(ID,Title,Body,Status)');

    //Make a query call to execute the above statements
    context.executeQueryAsync(OnGetTasksSucceeded, OnGetTasksFailed);

}

function OnGetTasksSucceeded() {
    // Get the collection
    var taskCollection = tasks.getEnumerator();

    // Iterate through tasks
    while (taskCollection.moveNext()) {

        // Load the current task in iteration
        var task = taskCollection.get_current();

        // Get the list to add the task details to
        var taskList = GetTaskListElementByTaskStatus(task.get_item('Status'));

        // If there is a suitable task list, then add task element
        if (taskList != null) {
            addTaskToList(taskList, task.get_item('ID'), task.get_item('Title'),↵
 task.get_item('Body'));
        }
    }
}

// Error handler
function OnGetTasksFailed(sender, args) {
    alert('Request failed. ' + args.get_message() + '\n' + args.get_stackTrace());
}

function GetTaskListElementByTaskStatus(status) {

    var taskList;

    // Switch on the status value to make sure it gets added to
    // the correct list
    switch (status) {
        case "Not Started": taskList = $('#notStartedTasksDiv>ul');
            break;
```

```
            case "In Progress": taskList = $('#inProgressTasksDiv>ul');
                break;
            case "Completed": taskList = $('#completedTasksDiv>ul');
                break;
            default:
                // Code only supports Not Started, In Progress
                // and Completed tasks
                taskList = null;
        }

        return taskList;

}

function addTaskToList(list, id, title, description) {
        // Create a copy of the <li> template
        var itemTemplate = $('#TemplateListItem').clone();

        // Remove the unnecessary id attribute
        itemTemplate.attr('id', null);

        // Set the title to the task title
        itemTemplate.find('.taskTitle').text(title);

        // Add Task Element created from template
        list.append(itemTemplate);
}
```

When writing jQuery code, be sure to remember that you should still treat the code as you would any other managed code. You should avoid repeating lines of code, add comments, and create functions to separate logic. When deploying such a JavaScript file to production, it makes sense to minimize the code to remove comments and shorten variable lengths in order to keep the file size to a minimum, which is a consideration if thousands of users will be downloading this file in order to use your application.

In the ready event of the document library, the code is making a call to the GetTasks method. The GetTasks method is using the Client Object Model to retrieve the tasks from the task list. In the context.load method call, a second parameter is passed in, which tells the Client Object Model to return only the required fields:

```
context.load(tasks, 'Include(ID,Title,Body,Status)');
```

If you take a look at the difference this makes in retrieving the data from the server, you will see how useful it is to be able to specify just the data that is returned. Fiddler is a great way to inspect the data being retrieved. Without the second parameter, you can see all of the information coming back for just one of the task items in the list, as shown in Figure 6-7.

```
_Child_Items_
  {}
      _CopySource=(null)
      HasCopyDestinations=(null)
      IsCurrentVersion=True
      Level=1
      ModerationComments=(null)
      ModerationStatus=0
      _ObjectIdentity_=740c6a0b-85e2-48a0-a494-e0f1759d4aa7:web:34ba0a3d-dc18-43e8-84e3-66778df07163:list:471df59d-90c2-4647-998f-af93d19cb5f2:item:8,0
      _ObjectType_=SP.ListItem
      _ObjectVersion_=3
      _UIVersion=512
      _UIVersionString=1.0
      AssignedTo=(null)
      Attachments=False
      Author
          _ObjectType_=SP.FieldUserValue
          LookupId=6
          LookupValue=WIN-8XVZMGWV9FI\administrator
      Body=It should be easy to see the status of the task <div></div>
      ContentTypeId
          _ObjectType_=SP.ContentTypeId
          StringValue=0x010800E30B16BDB5299A4C9B910646004CE43B
      Created=/Date(2011,8,27,22,9,25,0)/
      Created_x0020_Date=2011-09-27 22:09:25
      DueDate=(null)
      Editor
          _ObjectType_=SP.FieldUserValue
          LookupId=6
          LookupValue=WIN-8XVZMGWV9FI\administrator
      File_x0020_Type=(null)
      FileDirRef=/Lists/Tasks
      FileLeafRef=8_.000
      FileRef=/Lists/Tasks/8_.000
      FileSystemObjectType=0
      FolderChildCount=0
      FSObjType=0
      GUID=/Guid(0f859b6d-aa9d-4b59-a320-04a0064cbd5e)/
      Id=8
      ID=8
      InstanceID=(null)
      ItemChildCount=0
      Last_x0020_Modified=2011-09-27 22:09:25
      MetaInfo=
      Modified=/Date(2011,9,15,12,37,39,0)/
      Order=800
```

Figure 6-7. Viewing the JSON returned from the Client Object Model web service call using Fiddler

The size for the three list items is 2.5KB. You see all the superfluous information that isn't needed for the application, so it makes no sense to bring everything back. Adding the second parameter to the context.load method call changes things considerably, as shown in Figure 6-8.

```
⊟·{}
   ⊟·_Child_Items_
      ⊟·{}
         _ObjectIdentity_=740c6a0b-85e2-48a0-a494-e0f1759d4aa7:web:34ba0a3d-dc18-43e8-84e3-66778df07163:list:471df59d-90c2-4647-998f-af93d19cb5f2:item:8,0
         _ObjectType_=SP.ListItem
         _ObjectVersion_=3
         Body=It should be easy to see the status of the task <div></div>
         ID=8
         Status=In Progress
         Title=Add ability to view tasks
      ⊟·{}
         _ObjectIdentity_=740c6a0b-85e2-48a0-a494-e0f1759d4aa7:web:34ba0a3d-dc18-43e8-84e3-66778df07163:list:471df59d-90c2-4647-998f-af93d19cb5f2:item:10,0
         _ObjectType_=SP.ListItem
         _ObjectVersion_=4
         Body=<div>It should only take one click to move between states. The change of status should use Ajax. The task can only move left or right one place, it can not skip a status</div>
         ID=10
         Status=Not Started
         Title=Add simple status changing
      ⊟·{}
         _ObjectIdentity_=740c6a0b-85e2-48a0-a494-e0f1759d4aa7:web:34ba0a3d-dc18-43e8-84e3-66778df07163:list:471df59d-90c2-4647-998f-af93d19cb5f2:item:11,0
         _ObjectType_=SP.ListItem
         _ObjectVersion_=1
         Body=<div>It should be easy to view the details of the task<div></div>
         ID=11
         Status=Not Started
         Title=Add ability to view details
   ObjectType_=SP.ListItemCollection
```

Figure 6-8. Only the relevant information is now in the JSON.

This version uses 1.2KB for the three list items, and now all the information from those tasks fits into one screenshot!

■ **Note**   One of the considerations when working on client-side logic is to send and retrieve only the minimum amount of data with the server. By just being careful in this example, the size of request has shrunk by 50 percent.

Determining which columns to use for the Include parameter of context.load can be a little confusing, as the column names do not always match the display names. An example of this is the Description field of the sample task list. Looking at the list settings reveals the columns shown in Figure 6-9.

Columns

A column stores information about each item in the list. Because this list allows multiple content ty

Column (click to edit)	Type
% Complete	Number
Assigned To	Person or Group
Description	Multiple lines of text
Due Date	Date and Time
Predecessors	Lookup
Priority	Choice
Start Date	Date and Time
Status	Choice
Task Group	Person or Group
Title	Single line of text
Created By	Person or Group
Modified By	Person or Group

Figure 6-9. *Viewing the columns of the task list*

If you wanted to use the ID, Title, Description, and Status columns, you would expect to enter the following:

```
context.load(tasks, 'Include(ID,Title,Description,Status)');
```

However, if this code is executed, the error handler will catch an error, as shown in Figure 6-10.

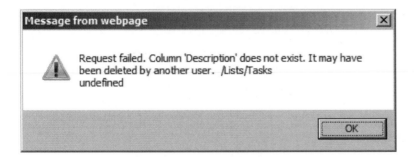

Figure 6-10. *An error occurs when you use the incorrect column name.*

The problem is that you need to use the internal field name. To discover the internal name, click the column name in the list settings and check out the URL. The field name is appended at the end of the URL. For the Description column, the internal field name is Body, as shown in Figure 6-11.

121

Figure 6-11. Viewing the actual field name

Changing the parameter to Body allows the code to work as expected:

```
context.load(tasks, 'Include(ID,Title,Body,Status)');
```

If you want to use a column that has a space in its name, the space will be converted to a value. For example, My Field becomes My_x0020_Field, and you should include the _x0020_ when trying to access the field.

Setting up a template in the HTML and using it in the jQuery makes this code as clean as possible. By cloning the hidden element on the page, all you need to do is set the nested element's values and then use a switch statement to append it to the correct location.

Once all the code is in the JavaScript file and you have taken the time to see what's going on, you can go ahead and deploy the application page. As shown in Figure 6-12, you will see that all three tasks are set to Not Started. You can begin to appreciate how this new view of the data makes the status of the tasks remarkably clear.

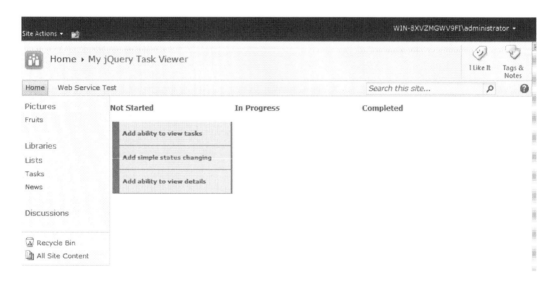

Figure 6-12. Viewing task information for the first time

To further test the application, open the task list and set the "Add ability to view tasks" item to Completed. Also, move the "Add ability to view details" item to In Progress (that's the next task!). Return to the application page, which should now display the tasks in the correct column, as shown in Figure 6-13.

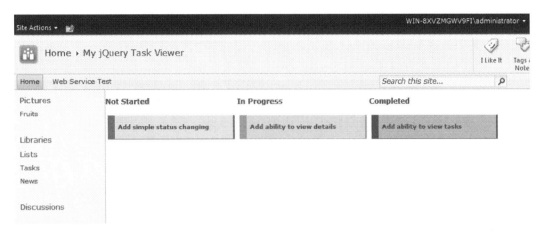

Figure 6-13. Making sure the tasks are in the correct columns

At this stage, the first of the tasks has been completed, but as you can see in Figure 6-13, there is more work to be done. Close the browser, and let's continue with our In Progress task of adding the functionality to view the details of the tasks in the list.

Viewing Task Details

Open the JavaScript file. The eagle-eyed will have noticed that the code is already returning the task's description, but it is not being used anywhere. It's time to set the description field and display that alongside the task title. Amend the addTaskToList function to add the description as follows:

```
function addTaskToList(list, id, title, description) {
    // Create a copy of the <li> template
    var itemTemplate = $('#TemplateListItem').clone();

    // Remove the unnecessary id attribute
    itemTemplate.attr('id', null);

    // Set the title to the task title
    itemTemplate.find('.taskTitle').text(title);

    // Set the description to the task description
    itemTemplate.find('.taskDescription').html(description);

    // Add Task Element created from template
    list.append(itemTemplate);
}
```

When setting the value of the task description, using the html function ensures it is rendered correctly, as the field information is stored as HTML. If you use the text method, the result will display all of the tags, which is not the desired effect.

123

After making these changes to the code, deploy the solution again. Now you will see the details of each task, as shown in Figure 6-14. (If you do not see the changes, press Ctrl+F5 for a refresh, to make sure you're using the latest version of the JavaScript file.)

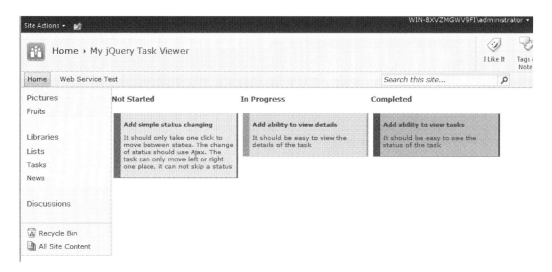

Figure 6-14. *Checking that the description appears with the task*

Success—it is now possible to view the details of the tasks! So, there is just one more task required to meet the application specifications set out earlier in the chapter.

Changing the Task Status

Now things get very interesting, as the previous functionality could have been achieved using any number of methods, such as creating a web part to display the data. This next step makes use of the client-side interaction to allow end users to easily manipulate tasks in the list.

A consideration here is deciding whether you want the users' interactions to update the server immediately or you want to allow the users to make all of their client-side changes before committing to the server. There are pros and cons for each approach. If other people trying to access the data should see the most up-to-date version, then the instant option is preferable. On the other hand, if users may be making a lot of changes in their browser, and may or may not wish to commit their changes, then it is best to allow them to update their changes only via a save button. For this example, each time a task is changed, its status is automatically updated in the list.

Updating the CSS and HTML

A few changes are required in order to provide a neat user interface for the user to be able to move the tasks between statuses. The easiest way in this example is to add two arrow images to the page: a right arrow and a left arrow. If the user clicks the right arrow, the task will move up a stage. If the user clicks the left arrow, the task will go back a stage. Figure 6-15 shows an example of what you will be creating.

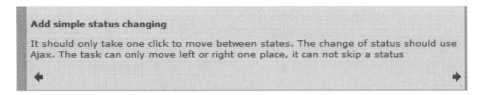

Figure 6-15. *A sneak peek at the arrows that will allow the user to move a task between states*

HTML and CSS

Only slight changes to the HTML are required. Because the code is making use of the List Item template, you just need to update the TemplateListItem element, as follows (in bold):

```
    <ul class='hiddenTemplate'>
        <li id="TemplateListItem" class="task">
            <div class="taskDetailDiv">
                <p class='taskTitle'>
                    Title</p>
                <p class='taskDescription'>
                    Description</p>
            </div>
<div class="moveButtonsDiv">
                <img class="moveLeftButton moveButton" src="/_layouts/images/ARRLEFTA.GIF" ↵
  alt="Move Left" />
                <img class="moveRightButton moveButton" src="/_layouts/images/ARRRIGHTA.GIF" ↵
  alt="Move Right" />
            </div>
        </li>
    </ul>
```

This example uses two handy buttons that sit in the Layouts folder. If you wish to use your own buttons, you can do so.

The CSS changes just help put the buttons in the correct location at either side of the task:

```
.moveButtonsDiv
{
    display: inline-block;
    width: 100%;
}

.moveButton
{
    cursor: pointer;
}

.moveLeftButton
{
    float: left;
}
```

```
.moveRightButton
{
    float: right;
}
```

Updating the JavaScript

With the buttons added to the HTML and the styling done, it's time to wire up the clicking events. You will need two events: one to move the task backward, which will be on the left button click, and one to move the task forward, which will be on the right button click. You can use the live event handler here, because as the tasks are retrieved, the jQuery code will be adding new task elements, which also need to have the buttons wired up. As discussed in Chapter 3, the live event handler will attach the event to all existing and all future elements that match the query—very handy in our circumstances! Add the events as follows:

```
// Create object to make it easy to
// choose direction
var direction = {
    Left: "Left",
    Right: "Right"
};

$(document).ready(function () {
    // Wait until SP.JS has loaded before calling GetTasks
    ExecuteOrDelayUntilScriptLoaded(GetTasks, "sp.js");

    $('.moveLeftButton').live("click", (function () {
        // Change status to the left
        ChangeStatus(this, direction.Left);
    }));

    $('.moveRightButton').live("click", (function () {
        // Change status to the right
        ChangeStatus(this, direction.Right);
    }));
});
```

The direction variable allows you to use direction as you would use an enum in C#. For example, it later makes it easier when doing comparisons such as the following:

```
if (moveDirection == direction.Right)
{
// Do something
}
```

In the preceding code, the direction is being passed into another new function, which will update the task.

The first parameter in the ChangeStatus method, this, is the object that was clicked. In this case, it is the task element list item. The ability to use this makes it easy to work with the element where the event is being handled.

Before adding the main functionality of the status changing, you need to update a couple places in the code to store variables so they can be used throughout the code. The first of these changes is to update the OnGetTasksSucceeded method to pass the Status to the addTaskToList method, as follows:

```
function OnGetTasksSucceeded() {

    // Remove all current tasks
    $('.taskDiv>ul').empty();

    // Get the collection
    var taskCollection = tasks.getEnumerator();

    // Iterate through tasks
    while (taskCollection.moveNext()) {

        // Load the current task in iteration
        var task = taskCollection.get_current();

        // Get the list which to add the tasks details
        var taskList = GetTaskListElementByTaskStatus(task.get_item('Status'));

        // If there is a suitable task list, then add task element
        if (taskList != null) {
            addTaskToList(taskList, task.get_item('ID'), task.get_item('Title'),↵
  task.get_item('Body'), task.get_item('Status'));
        }
    }
}
```

The status and the task ID will be stored using the data method against the element. Navigate to the addTaskToListMethod and add the following lines:

```
function addTaskToList(list, id, title, description, status) {
    // Create a copy of the <li> template
    var itemTemplate = $('#TemplateListItem').clone();

    // Remove the unnecessary id attribute
    itemTemplate.attr('id', null);

    // Set the title to the task title
    itemTemplate.find('.taskTitle').text(title);

    // Set the description to the task description
    itemTemplate.find('.taskDescription').html(description);

    itemTemplate.data('status', status);
    itemTemplate.data('taskId', id);
```

```
    // Only show possible direction of movement
    switch (status) {
        case "Not Started": itemTemplate.find('.moveLeftButton').hide();
            break;
        case "Completed": itemTemplate.find('.moveRightButton').hide();
            break;
    }

    // Add Task Element created from template
    list.append(itemTemplate);
}
```

The new switch statement ensures that users can move left or right on the task only when they're supposed to. They should not be able to move backward from Not Started or forward from Completed. This small piece of code handles this requirement nicely. Basically, it checks if it is either at the start or end of the chain to see if it can go any further in either direction.

Next, at the top of the OnGetTasksSucceeded method, add the following method call to clear out all tasks from the lists, so that this method can be reused once a task has been updated:

```
    // Remove all current tasks
    $('.taskDiv>ul').empty();
```

At the bottom of the .js file, add the following new function, which takes the task element:

```
function ChangeStatus(taskElement, moveDirection) {
    // Get the parent list item of the task
    var taskListItemElement = $(taskElement).parents("li:first");

    // Get the new status based on the existing status
    // and the direction it is moving
    var updatedStatus = GetNewStatus(taskListItemElement, moveDirection);

    // Return if invalid new status
    if (updatedStatus == null) {
        return;
    }

    // Update the SharePoint Task List item with the new status
    updateTaskStatus(taskListItemElement.data('taskId'), updatedStatus);


    // Get the tasks again from the server
    GetTasks();
}
```

As mentioned previously, the first parameter of the ChangeStatus function is the element that was clicked in the event handler. The object it gives you is not a jQuery object, so to be able to perform functions such as finding the parent li element, you need to wrap it using $().

The GetNewStatus method is used to inspect the current status of the task by retrieving the value from the data object for the element. Then, using a switch statement, it returns the next status based on the direction.

```javascript
function GetNewStatus(element, moveDirection) {

    // Retrieve the Status from the element's data object
    var currentStatus = element.data("status");

    var newStatus = null;

    // Get the new Status depending on the direction request
    // i.e., moving left or right
    if (moveDirection == direction.Left) {
        newStatus = GetLeftStatus(currentStatus);
    }
    else if (moveDirection == direction.Right) {
        newStatus = GetRightStatus(currentStatus);
    };

    return newStatus;
}

function GetLeftStatus(currentStatus) {
    var newStatus = null;
    switch (currentStatus) {
        case "In Progress": newStatus = "Not Started";
            break;
        case "Completed": newStatus = "In Progress";
            break;
    }
    return newStatus;
}

function GetRightStatus(currentStatus) {
    var newStatus = null;
    switch (currentStatus) {
        case "Not Started": newStatus = "In Progress";
            break;
        case "In Progress": newStatus = "Completed";
            break;
    }
    return newStatus;
}
```

Now that you have the next status available, you can update the task. In the ChangeStatus method, you see that the ID of the task list item was stored in the data store for the task list item element, and can be easily retrieved and passed through to the update method.

```javascript
function ChangeStatus(taskElement, moveDirection) {
    // Get the parent list item of the task
    var taskListItemElement = $(taskElement).parents("li:first");
```

```
    // Get the new status based on the existing status
    // and the direction it is moving
    var updatedStatus = GetNewStatus(taskListItemElement, moveDirection);

    // Return if invalid new status
    if (updatedStatus == null) {
        return;
    }

    // Update the SharePoint Task List item with the new status
    updateTaskStatus(taskListItemElement.data('taskId'), updatedStatus);

    // Get the tasks again from the server
    GetTasks();
}
```

The updateTaskStatus method is almost identical to the GetTasks method, but with a couple of key differences. The first is that instead of retrieving all of the items from the list, you can use the getItemById method, which will allow you to pass in the ID of the list item you wish to retrieve. The second difference is that instead of just getting data from the list, you are setting data via the set_item method. Keep in mind that all the Client Object Model code does is build the query in the background. The query will not be executed until you call load or update, as in this example.

```
function updateTaskStatus(id, status) {

    // Get the current context
    var context = new SP.ClientContext.get_current();

    // Load the web object
    var web = context.get_web();

    //Get the list
    var list = web.get_lists().getByTitle(taskListName);

    //Get the list item to update
    var listItem = list.getItemById(id);

    //Set the new property value
    listItem.set_item('Status', status);

    // Call the update method to commit the change
    listItem.update();
}
```

Now that all the changes have been made, it's time to take the application for a spin. Deploy the solution and check out the new ability to be able to move items between the different statuses, as shown in Figure 6-16.

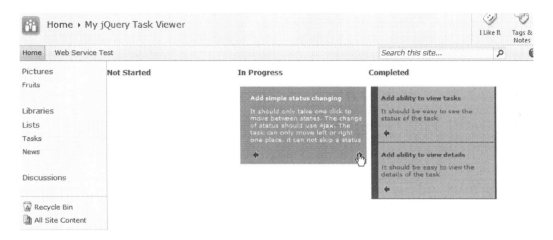

Figure 6-16. The tasks can finally be moved between states using the arrows.

So, all of the project requirements have been fulfilled, and it did not take too much code to build the application. One of my favorite things about using jQuery is the speed with which solutions can be created. I suppose the last thing to do is to move all of the tasks to the completed stage and give yourself a well-deserved pat on the back.

Summary

In this chapter, you have used the Client Object Model to return the tasks from a task list. You have seen how easy it is to parse the information returned from the Client Object Model to create new elements on the page and position them where required. In SharePoint, you may frequently need to create a solution that is getting information from somewhere, such as the Client Object Model or a web service, and you will want to display the data in a variety of different ways. Using a template to build up an element, and then using the selectors to add the new element to any number of places, makes creating the solution a breeze.

CHAPTER 7

Adding Controls to Create, Edit, and Delete Tasks

In this chapter, you will learn how you can improve upon the Task View List application to allow the end user to create, edit, and delete tasks without ever leaving the application page. This is one of the great advantages of using client-side code because you can read, write, and update data dynamically without needing to do a page postback to refresh the data.

This chapter will show how easy it is to further develop an application with SharePoint and jQuery. To start, you will see how to add the ability to delete a task (which is the easiest functionality to implement), to add a new task, and finally to edit an item in-place. SharePoint makes these kinds of actions on a list item fairly painless through its use of the Edit Control Block (ECB) and the dialogs in SharePoint 2010; what you will learn here is how to streamline these actions using jQuery.

Deleting a Task

Deleting a task will be an easy introduction to this chapter because all that is required on the HTML side is to add a new element that, when clicked, will remove the item from the task list and then refresh the tasks on the page. But wait, you may think, people have clumsy fingers, and we don't want people accidentally deleting items left, right, and center, so we'll also give users a chance to change their minds.

To get started, open the jQueryTaskViewerApplication project from the previous chapter; you'll be using this throughout the rest of the chapter.

Adding the HTML

To add the HTML, follow these steps:

1.   Open the jQueryTaskView.aspx file; this is the one that holds the HTML you are going to be updating first. As usual, the following couple of steps are ones that you could easily pass off to a designer to configure as long as the designer gives you the necessary IDs and classes; however, seeing as though you're on your own here and doing it all yourself, we'll walk through the tasks.

2. Locate the template that is being used to render each task. It makes sense if
    you want to be able to remove a task that it should be done in a location as
    close to the task element as possible. There is no point in putting a delete
    section at the top of the page if the user has to find the task they want to
    remove and then look it up in a list to then delete it. The section you are
    interested in is this one:

```
<ul class='hiddenTemplate'>
    <li id="TemplateListItem" class="task">
        <p class='taskTitle'>
            Title</p>
        <p class='taskDescription'>
            Description</p>
        <div class="moveButtonsDiv">
            <img class="moveLeftButton moveButton" src="/_layouts/images/↵
ARRLEFTA.GIF" alt="Move Left" />
            <img class="moveRightButton moveButton" src="/_layouts/images/↵
ARRRIGHTA.GIF" alt="Move Right" />
        </div>
    </li>
</ul>
```

3. The previous HTML is currently producing a task that looks like Figure 7-1; it's
    time to add some elements to allow the end user to delete a task.

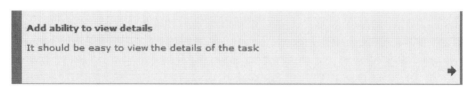

Figure 7-1. Task element

4. The button that the user will click to initiate the deletion of a task will just be a
    simple *X*. To make sure the user is certain that this is indeed the task they want
    to remove, a couple more elements are required. Add the following bold HTML
    just inside the TemplateListItem list item element:

```
<li id="TemplateListItem" class="task">
        <div class="deleteDiv">
                <span class="deleteButton delete">x</span>
                <span class="confirmDelete" style="display: none">Are you sure?↵
<span class="yesDeleteButton delete">Yes</span><span class="noDeleteButton
delete">No</span></span>
        </div>
```

The HTML now has an *X* for the user to click. You'll want to ask the end user "Are you sure?" as well as offer Yes and No options. The `confirmDelete` span is hidden initially using `display: none` because you need to wait until the user tries to delete the task before asking them if they're sure. Using some smart jQuery code, you can ensure that the user will see the right elements at the right time to ensure the user experience is as intuitive as possible. There are also a few classes and IDs used to help identify them in the jQuery code as well as to make it look nice!

Adding the CSS

Add the following CSS to the `Style.css` file, which will give the user some visual feedback:

```
.deleteDiv
{
    float: right;
}

.delete
{
    background: red;
    color: white;
    font-weight: bolder;
    padding: 3px;
    margin: 5px 5px 0px 5px;
    border: white solid thin;
    border-top: 0px;
    cursor: pointer;
}

.deleteButton:hover
{
    font-size: 1.3em;
}

.yesDeleteButton
{
    background: darkgreen;
}

.yesDeleteButton:hover
{
    background: greenyellow;
}

.noDeleteButton
{
    background: darkred;
}
```

```
.noDeleteButton:hover
{
    background: palevioletred;
}
```

Figure 7-2 shows what the UI will look like if you deploy the project.

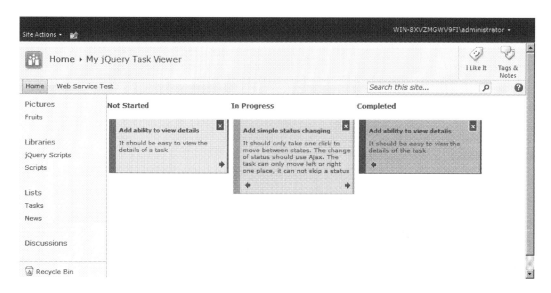

Figure 7-2. *Tasks with delete button*

Adding the jQuery Code

With the styling done, it's time to move on to the jQuery. If you take a minute to think about what you have so far, it's easy to imagine what the code will be doing:

- The code should allow the user to click the delete button, and when the button is clicked, the code should show the hidden confirmation buttons and question and hide the delete button.

- If the user clicks No, the code should hide the confirmation and show the delete button again.

- If the user clicks Yes, the code should delete the task and refresh the tasks on the page.

Adding the Event Handlers into $(document).ready()

Now follow these steps:

1. In the jQueryTaskViewerScript.js file, locate the document.ready function:

```
$(document).ready(function () {
...
});
```

At the bottom of this function, before the closing braces, });, you will want to add three functions that handle the three buttons you have just added: the delete, Yes, and No buttons. It's worth mentioning that the code is using a span as a button. By using the click handler, it's possible to use almost any element as a button and handle its event when clicked.

2. The first button to look at is the delete button. As mentioned earlier, rather than allowing the user to go in for the kill and just delete the task straightaway, you will present the user with the option to back out. The elements already exist, and the following code shows the confirmDelete span tag, which contains the question as well as being the parent element for both the Yes and No spans. Clicking the button will also hide itself to save on real estate on the task.

```
$('.deleteButton').on("click", function () {
    $(this).siblings('.confirmDelete').show();
    $(this).hide();
});
```

You will notice that the event handler is using the On method of binding; this is because the elements are created dynamically. If the code were using $('.deleteButton').click() instead, it would not be applied to anything because the elements would not exist in the document.ready function. The On method is great because it will apply the event handler to all existing and future elements that match its selector.

Because the delete button shares the same parent as the confirmation text, it's possible to use the Siblings method to select and show the span. Using $(this).hide() will hide the element that was handled, and this will hide the delete button for you.

3. Now that the delete button is configured, add the No button. This again is a simple one because all it is doing is the reverse of the delete button. The buttons toggle between the two states. This time, however, because the button is nested, it's necessary to use the parent method to get to the correct level to be able to show and hide the correct elements.

```
$('.noDeleteButton').onOn("click", function () {
    $(this).parent('.confirmDelete').hide();
    $(this).parent().siblings('.deleteButton').show();
});
```

    4.   The Yes button is going to be the call to the function that does the actual deletion. This makes the event "wiring up" a simple affair. The deleteTask is being called, which takes the Yes button element as the parameter. This is so you can get a reference to the task element and task that should be deleted.

```
$('.yesDeleteButton').onOn("click", function () {
    deleteTask(this);
});
```

The code in the document.ready function should appear like the following, now with the previous changes made:

```
$(document).ready(function () {
    // Wait until SP.JS has loaded before calling GetTasks
    ExecuteOrDelayUntilScriptLoaded(GetTasks, "sp.js");

    $('.moveLeftButton').on("click", (function () {
        // Change status to the left
        ChangeStatus(this, direction.Left);
    }));

    $('.moveRightButton').on("click", (function () {
        // Change status to the right
        ChangeStatus(this, direction.Right);
    }));

    $('.deleteButton').on("click", function () {
        $(this).siblings('.confirmDelete').show();
        $(this).hide();
    });

    $('.noDeleteButton').on("click", function () {
        $(this).parent('.confirmDelete').hide();
        $(this).parent().siblings('.deleteButton').show();
    });

    $('.yesDeleteButton').on("click", function () {
        deleteTask(this);
    });
});
```

I still find it impressive how little code is required here. Granted, the hard work is later in the JavaScript file, but the key here is keeping the separation of the UI from the main functions as loose as possible so that it is easy to adapt if something changes in either the user interface or the code.

Adding the Function to Delete the Task

Now follow these steps:

1. To delete the task list item from the task list, you will need to get a reference to the current task that the function is working on. Luckily, because of some up-front planning, you know that the parent list item element contains the ID of the task inside its data container. Add this code after the closing braces of the document.ready function:

```
function deleteTask(taskElement) {

    // Get the parent list item of the task
    var taskListItemElement = $(taskElement).parents("li:first");

    // Get the current context
    var context = new SP.ClientContext.get_current();

    // Load the web object
    var web = context.get_web();

    //Get the list
    var list = web.get_lists().getByTitle(taskListName);

    var taskId = taskListItemElement.data('taskID');

    // Get Item to delete by If from the list
    var itemToDelete = list.getItemById(taskId);

    // Add Delete method to the query
    itemToDelete.deleteObject();

    // Execute the query to perform the deletion
    context.executeQueryAsync(DeleteTaskSuccess, DeleteTaskFail);
}
```

    The previous code shows that once the parent element has been retrieved using the passed-in Yes button element parameter, it's just a case of traversing up the tree to its parent list item element. The rest of the code in the function should be familiar because it has been used a fair amount in this Task Viewer application. The difference here is that once the element has been plucked from the list, it is promptly deleted.

2. The final two methods can be put together; they're the two methods that occur if things go either right or wrong. The "right" is very simple; all the code does is make a call to the same GetTasks method that is called when the page loads. It removes all existing task elements from the page and reloads them. It is also possible to just delete the element from the page and not require the extra trip to retrieve all of the tasks from the task list. The second method shows us what went wrong in an alert.

```
function DeleteTaskSuccess() {
    GetTasks();
}

function DeleteTaskFail(sender, args) {
    alert('Request failed. ' + args.get_message() + '\n' + args.get_stackTrace());
}
```

3. With all of the code now written, build and deploy the solution to see it in action. You will see the newly added red *X* (Figure 7-3), which when clicked will ask you if you are sure you want to delete the item. Try clicking No first, and then next time click Yes to remove the item.

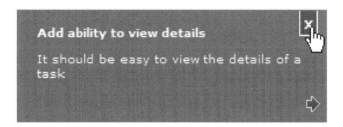

Figure 7-3. *Task element with delete button*

Once you have clicked the button, the delete options are available, as shown in Figure 7-4.

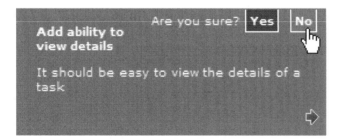

Figure 7-4. *Element showing confirmation once the delete button has been clicked*

Deleting an item from a list is a very simple task when using jQuery; here the method of deleting the item was using the client object model, but it is possible to use another method of your choosing too, such as using the web services. The beauty is that it makes no difference to your code or the user interface how you do it!

Adding a New Task

This section will deal with adding tasks. Again, this is something you will want to make as easy as possible. If the user needs to click in four different places to be able to add a task, then there is a high chance that when adding their fifth task, they're going to be feeling a little bit frustrated. The following example simplifies the task creation by creating the task with just a name, as you can see in Figure 7-5. There are a lot of fields that you can fill in for a task. In this example, you will be creating a task that has only a title name because it's the only required field for a task, but the concepts will allow you to extend this if you want. You will also allow users to add multiple tasks without lifting their fingers off the keyboard!

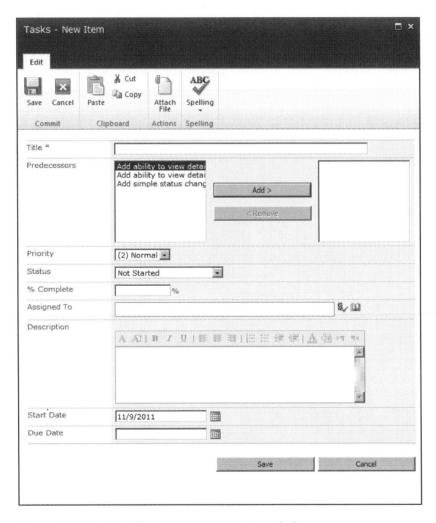

Figure 7-5. Standard SharePoint 2010 New Item dialog

Adding the HTML

To add the HTML, follow these steps:

1. The first step will be to add the user interface; it's going to be simple because there is only one piece of information that the user will be submitting, and that is the task name. To submit the task name, the user will be using a text input tag. A label will tell the user what it is they are entering, and a button will allow the user to add the item. The button will not be the only way to add a task, as you'll discover. Open the jQueryTaskViewer.aspx file.

2. Find the PlaceHolderMain content placeholder and just inside add the following HTML. It's simply a div for positioning, a text input to take the new task title (limited to 50 characters), and a button. A newTask class has been added for styling, and some IDs have been added to help in the jQuery:

```html
<div id="newTaskDiv">
    <input id="newTaskTitle" class="newTask" type="text" maxlength="50" />
    <input type="button" class="newTask" id="addTaskButton" value="Add New Task" />
</div>
```

Adding the CSS

Add the following CSS to make this new task addition feature look fabulous! Add it to the bottom of the CSS file:

```css
#newTaskDiv
{
    padding: 5px;
}

#newTaskTitle
{
    width: 350px;
}

.newTask
{
    border: 3px solid #cccccc;
    padding: 5px;
    background-color: white;
}

#addTaskButton:hover
{
    border: 3px solid #ff1943;
    cursor: pointer;
}
```

Adding the jQuery

Now that you've created the design, it is time to crack open the jQueryTaskViewerScript.js file and start doing some coding. You will be binding two main events in the document.ready function. The first is to handle the click event of the button to add the task, and the second is to handle it when the user presses Enter after they have finished entering their task name. This piece of code will allow the user to rapidly add items without having to switch between the keyboard and mouse.

Adding the Event Handlers into $(document).ready()

Follow these steps:

1. Add the button click handler first. This method is retrieving the text entered by the user. If the title is empty, then it will show an alert; otherwise, it will pass the new tasks title to the AddNewTask method:

```
$('#addTaskButton').click(function () {
    // Get the Users title
    var title = $('#newTaskTitle').val();

    // If no value is set then show alert and set focus
    if (title == '') {
        alert('Please enter a value');
        $('#newTaskTitle').focus();

    } else {
        AddNewTask(title);
    }

});
```

2. The second event handler is bound to the keyup event of the text box where the end user will be entering the title. The keycode of the key that was pressed is available from the event object. Enter is 13, and Esc is 27. The Esc button is used to clear the box if the user changes their mind, and the Enter button is clever because instead of needing to maintain two locations of what to do when someone tries to add a task, it just calls the click event of the button. This means that any changes need to be added only to the click event handler.

```
$("#newTaskTitle").keyup(function (event) {
    switch (event.keyCode) {
        // Handle the Enter button to call button click
        case 13: $('#addTaskButton').click();
            break;
        // Handle the ESC key press to clear value
        case 27: $(this).val('');
            break;
    }
});
```

Adding the Function to Create and Add the Task

The next step is to add the task to the task list. This is done in the AddNewTask method, which will do all of the grunt work.

1. The AddNewTask method has a parameter for the task name. There is the usual code to connect to the SharePoint list; however, now the code is using the addItem and set_item methods to create the item and to then set the title field with the name that the user has supplied to the task. Once the query has executed, the tasks are refreshed to the page, and the new task name text box is cleared and gets the focus again to allow the user to seamlessly add their next task.

```
function AddNewTask(taskName) {
    // Get the current context
    var context = new SP.ClientContext.get_current();

    // Load the web object
    var web = context.get_web();

    //Get the list
    var list = web.get_lists().getByTitle(taskListName);

    // create the ListItemInformational object
    var listItemInfo = new SP.ListItemCreationInformation();

    // add the item to the list
    var listItem = list.addItem(listItemInfo);

    // Assign Values for fields
    listItem.set_item('Title', taskName);

    // Apply changes to Item
    listItem.update();

    //Make a query call to execute the above statements
    context.executeQueryAsync(AddTaskSuccess, AddTaskFail);
}

function AddTaskSuccess() {
    // Task has been added so refresh
    GetTasks();

    // Reset the input box
    $('#newTaskTitle').val('');

    // Add focus to carry on adding
    $('#newTaskTitle').focus();
}
```

```
function AddTaskFail(sender, args) {
    alert('Request failed. ' + args.get_message() + '\n' + args.get_stackTrace());
}
```

2. Deploy the solution (Figure 7-6) and check out the neat new functionality you
    have added. Add five items and see how long it takes—not very long at all. You
    can test what happens if you enter no information and press Enter, what
    happens if you enter some text and press Esc, or the two different ways you
    can submit your new task. Once you have exhausted yourself with adding
    tasks, it is nice and easy to delete them thanks to the functionality you added
    in the previous coding example!

Figure 7-6. *Add New Task functionality now available*

With the delete and add tasks completed, ideally you are seeing how it is possible to extend a jQuery application within SharePoint to add more functionality. There is one task left to achieve in this chapter, and that is to be able to edit a task inline.

Editing an Existing Task

This section will show you how, with some clever hiding and showing of elements, it is possible to give the end user an inline editing experience. Instead of having to hunt for the way to edit a task, the user can simply double-click the task, and it will transform into an editable region where they can edit both the task title and the description. In this example, the description can be edited as simple text rather than using a rich text editor, although there is no reason why you couldn't implement a richer text box if you wanted. Like the other examples in this chapter, the aim here is to provide a pleasant user interface that does not require the page to post back as changes are made.

Adding the HTML

To add the HTML, follow these steps:

1. Open jQueryTaskView.aspx. Adding the ability to edit a task will be similar to how we added the ability to delete a task, because we will be adding the new HTML elements to the task template. You can probably appreciate about now how much easier it is when you can work with just one template.

2. You will want to add a new div tag that will contain the editing elements. The layout of the elements is designed to mirror how the task details are displayed. The following bold section indicates the new code to add:

```
<ul class='hiddenTemplate'>
    <li id="TemplateListItem" class="task">
        <div class="deleteDiv">
            <span class="deleteButton delete">x</span> <span class=↵
"confirmDelete" style="display: none">
                Are you sure?<span class="yesDeleteButton delete">↵
Yes</span><span class="noDeleteButton delete">No</span></span>
        </div>
        <div class="taskDetailDiv">
            <p class='taskTitle'>
                Title</p>
            <p class='taskDescription'>
                Description</p>
        </div>
        <div class="editDiv" style="display: none">
            <p>
                <input class="editTaskTitle edit" type="text" maxlength="50" />
            </p>
            <p>
                <textarea class="editTaskDescription edit" rows="4"↵
cols="30"></textarea></p>
            <span class="editTaskSaveButton editButton">Save</span>↵
<span class="editTaskCancelButton editButton">
                Cancel</span>
        </div>
        <div class="moveButtonsDiv">
            <img class="moveLeftButton moveButton" src="/_layouts/images/↵
ARRLEFTA.GIF" alt="Move Left" />
```

```
                        <img class="moveRightButton moveButton" src="/_layouts/images/↵
        ARRRIGHTA.GIF" alt="Move Right" />
                    </div>
              </
```

The edit `div` is hidden by default. This is because it should be visible only when a task is actually being edited. An alternative to having this `div` and its child elements for each task always being created is to dynamically add them when entering edit mode using jQuery. You would want to do this to save creating all of the elements for editing each task, because in reality you may edit only one or two of them. Creating them dynamically will save you from increasing the HTML size and potentially decreasing performance. The HTML contains an input box for the title; it has the `maxlength` of 50 just like the new task text box, and there is also a text area that will allow the user to enter the body of their task. The final two elements are buttons to allow the user to either save and submit their changes or cancel the editing.

Adding the CSS

Add the CSS required to style these new elements to `style.css`:

```css
.edit
{
    width: 90%;
    padding: 5px;
    background-color: white;
    font: inherit;
    border: 0;
}

.editTaskDescription
{
    height: 120px;
    overflow: hidden;
}

.editButton
{
    font-weight: bolder;
    padding: 5px;
    border: white solid thin;
    cursor: pointer;
    color: white;
}

.editTaskSaveButton
{
    background: darkgreen;
}
```

```
.editTaskSaveButton:hover
{
    background: greenyellow;
}

.editTaskCancelButton
{
    background: darkred;
}

.editTaskCancelButton:hover
{
    background: palevioletred;
}
```

Adding the jQuery

If you deployed this now, it wouldn't look any different because the edit div is hidden and there is no jQuery to show the elements needed to enter edit mode. It's time to open the jQueryTaskViewerScript.js file and start plugging in some of that jQuery that we like creating.

Adding the Event Handlers into $(document).ready()

Follow these steps:

1. As with the previous event handler "wiring up," the following code will go into the document.ready function at the end but before the closing braces. Double-clicking the task element will hide the current details, copy the contents of the title and description into the editable elements, and then show the edit elements. It goes a little something like this:

```
$('.task').on("dblclick", function () {

        // Makes it easier to see what
        // the code is dealing with
        var taskElement = $(this);

        // Hide the task details
        taskElement.children('div.taskDetailDiv').hide();

        // Show the edit elements
        taskElement.children('div.editDiv').show();

        // Get the title from the Task Title Paragraph
        var title = taskElement.find('p.taskTitle').text();

        // Get the description from the Task Title Paragraph
        var description = taskElement.find('p.taskDescription').text();

        // Set the text of the editable Text input to the title
```

```
        taskElement.find('input.editTaskTitle').val(title);

        // Set the text of the editable Text Area input to the description
        taskElement.find('textarea.editTaskDescription').text(description);
    });
```

2. Test the code; it will yield something like Figure 7-7.

Figure 7-7. Task on the page in normal mode

But then, with a swift double-click of your mouse, it will become like
Figure 7-8.

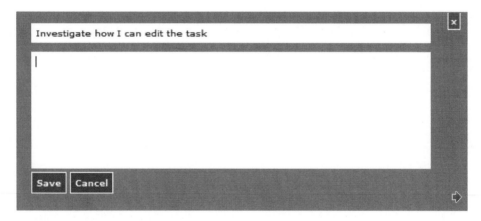

Figure 7-8. Double-clicking a task turns it into edit mode.

3. The next step is to wire up the two buttons; it's important to give the user the
    ability to "back out" of a decision such as editing by including a cancel option
    of sorts. If you were to just leave the user with only a save button, then to be
    able to stop editing they would need to refresh the page, which we don't like.

4. The cancel event again goes into the document.ready section at the end; it
    needs to use an on event binder because the elements aren't on the page when
    the document does become ready. The code uses the $(this) function to get
    the button element that was clicked, and by walking up the tree using the
    parents method, it can find the containing li that hides and shows its child
    elements.

```
$('.editTaskCancelButton').on("click", function () {
    // Get the task by traversing the tree to the li element
    var taskListItemElement = $(this).parents("li:first");

    // Hide the edit div
    taskListItemElement.children('div.editDiv').hide();

    // Show the default details div
    taskListItemElement.children('div.taskDetailDiv').show();
});
```

5. The final method to put into the document.ready function is the handler for the
    save button, arguably the most important one of all. This will simply call a
    function elsewhere in the JavaScript file.

```
$('.editTaskSaveButton').on("click", function () {
    // Update task
    UpdateTask(this);
});
```

Adding the Function to Update the Task

We've created the user interface side of things, so it's time to pass the new information for the task that
you got from the user into a method to make the changes to the SharePoint task list. When making
changes to a SharePoint list item, remember that you will need to provide your own validation that
matches that required by the list. If you tried to update a list item and left a required field empty, you
would get an exception, so it is worth making sure your data entry is validated before submission.

Go to the bottom of the JavaScript file and add the following chunk of code:

```
function UpdateTask(taskElement) {
    // Get the parent list item of the task
    var taskListItemElement = $(taskElement).parents("li:first");

    // Get the updated text
    var taskTitleElement = taskListItemElement.find('input.editTaskTitle');
    var updatedTitle = taskTitleElement.val();

    // If no title is set then show alert and set focus
    if (updatedTitle == '') {
        alert('Please enter a value for the task title');
        taskTitleElement.focus();
        return;
    }

    // Read the description form the text area
    var updatedDescription = taskListItemElement.find('textarea.editTaskDescription').text();

    // Get the current context
    var context = new SP.ClientContext.get_current();
```

```
    // Load the web object
    var web = context.get_web();

    //Get the list
    var list = web.get_lists().getByTitle(taskListName);

    var taskId = taskListItemElement.data('taskID');

    // Get Item to update by Id from the list
    var listItem = list.getItemById(taskId);

    //Set the new property value
    listItem.set_item('Title', updatedTitle);
    listItem.set_item('Body', updatedDescription);

    // Call the update method to commit the change
    listItem.update();

    GetTasks();
}
```

The code is getting the text from the input elements that have been filled out by the user. It is checking to make sure that the required Title field has a value, and then it is using the set_item method of the task list item to update the value. It's all very simple—and hopefully useful!

Summary

In this chapter, you saw how to delete a task, but only after a user has confirmed their choice with options to continue or cancel. You also learned that you can efficiently add items by using the keypress handler to call your jQuery functions. Finally, you saw that by thinking about how you can hide and show elements, it is possible to edit items inline on the page without taking up any extra real estate on the screen.

CHAPTER 8

Enhancing SharePoint with jQuery

In the previous chapters, we have looked at creating artifacts, such as web parts and application pages. Now let's take a look at how it is possible to manipulate and extend existing functionality. In this chapter, you will learn how you can use jQuery to extend what is available out of the box with SharePoint.

SharePoint Enhancement Considerations when Using jQuery

Making changes to the HTML rendered by SharePoint comes with a few risks. SharePoint 2010 makes use of JavaScript to provide its own functionality, and you need to be careful whenever you are trying to customize that functionality. If you are working with HTML elements that you have not created yourself, you may not be fully aware of how and why they are used on the page, and your customizations could have an untoward effect. You will need to disable your custom JavaScript files before asking for Microsoft support.

If you find that you are making a lot of changes to the existing UI, that could be an indication that you are doing something wrong. Creating a custom master page and applying just the jQuery functionality required to that page is far more sensible than trying to contort the standard master page to fit your requirements. CSS can often be a better solution if styling is all you are trying to do with jQuery.

One of the benefits of using jQuery to enhance SharePoint is that if your jQuery script cannot run for some reason, it will fail over to the standard SharePoint functionality.

Adding Functionality to the SharePoint UI

SharePoint does a lot of really cool things for you out of the box, and jQuery allows you to extend some of its offerings to enhance the user experience. By adding jQuery to a SharePoint page, you can change the behavior of elements that are typically out of your control. Here, we'll explore how to allow users to expand and collapse items in the Quick Launch menu, display graphs from SharePoint list data, use jQuery from the Ribbon, and filter the Quick Launch menu.

Expanding and Collapsing from Quick Launch

The first example we will look at is how to allow end users to collapse and expand items from the Quick Launch menu. As shown in Figure 8-1, with the Quick Launch menu expanded, you can see the categories of the items, such as Libraries, Lists, and Discussions, as well as the items from each of the categories, such as Site Pages, News, and Team Discussion.

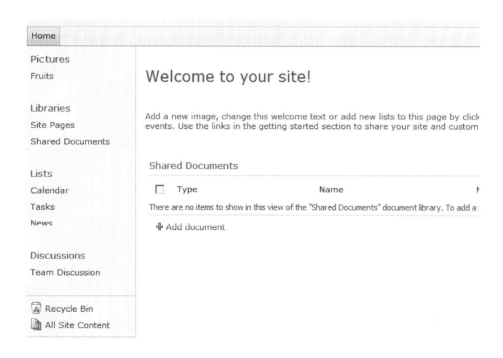

Figure 8-1. *Quick Launch with expanded categories and items*

Creating a Proof of Concept using a JavaScript File in the Layouts Folder

For this example, we are going to try a slightly different way of building the solution than we've used in previous chapters. This method makes it easy to put together a proof of concept before fleshing out a full solution. This approach will work only if you are developing directly on your SharePoint environment (no, not your production server, a development box). If you don't have this option, you can just put the whole code in a Content Editor web part instead of the JavaScript file, as you have seen in previous chapters.

1. Navigate to the SharePoint root: `C:\Program Files\Common Files\Microsoft Shared\Web Server Extensions\14`.

2. Continue to navigate to the `Template\Layouts` folder.

3. Create a new folder called `CustomScripts`.

4. Create a new file called `ExpandCollapse.js`.

5. Open the file in Notepad and add the following code, just so you can make sure it is being used:

```
$(document).ready(function(){
        alert("Hello from Expand & Collapse");
});
```

6. Save the file.

7. Navigate to your SharePoint page where you have a Quick Launch menu with some items in it.

8. Add a Content Editor web part.

9. In the Format Text section of the Ribbon, choose Edit HTML Source, as shown in Figure 8-2.

Figure 8-2. *Editing the HTML source of a Content Editor web part*

10. In the dialog that opens, add the `script` tag to the path to the JavaScript file, as follows:

```
<script src="/_layouts/CustomScripts/ExpandCollapse.js"
type="text/javascript"></script>
```

This means that you can make changes to the `ExpandCollapse.js` file and save it, and those changes will be reflected in the SharePoint page immediately.

11. Once the script link has been added, click OK and exit edit mode. You should be presented with the lovely alert that you added earlier, letting you know that the link to the JavaScript file has been made, as shown in Figure 8-3.

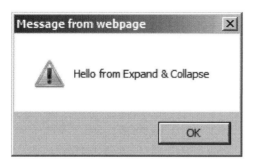

Figure 8-3. Alert to show that the JavaScript file is being read

With the JavaScript now working, it is time to explore how to add the functionality to expand and collapse the menu items.

Getting and Hiding Quick Launch Items

From your experience so far, you should realize that the simplest way of adding the expand/collapse functionality is to show or hide the child elements of the titles. The first question to explore is how, in jQuery, you can get the container of the elements that should be manipulated. This is easy to do with whichever browser tool you are using that allows you to inspect elements in a page. This example uses the Internet Explorer 9 F12 Developer Tools to inspect the elements.

1. Press F12 to open the Developer Tools.

2. Click the Select element by click button, as shown in Figure 8-4.

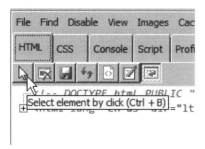

Figure 8-4. Choosing the element-selection function using the F12 Developer Tools

3. Move the cursor over the elements on the page, and you will see that the one that is currently under the cursor is highlighted, as shown in Figure 8-5.

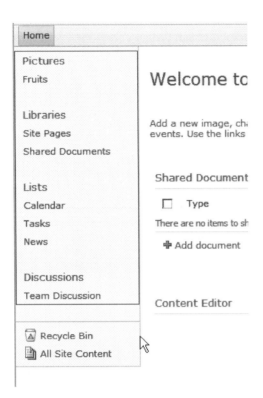

Figure 8-5. The div element has been selected.

4. Once you have found the correct element, left-click, and the corresponding element will be shown in the tool pane. For this example, it makes sense to find the element that has an ID you can use as close to the elements you want to manipulate as possible. In Figure 8-6, you can see that there is a div with an ID of zz17_V4QuickLaunchMenu.

Figure 8-6. Finding the correct element to target in jQuery

5. Looking down the structure of the menu, you will see another child `div`, which you can ignore. Further down, there is an unordered list that contains the categories. Each item contains a header anchor link and also another unordered list that holds the subitems. This sublist is what should be shown or hidden as each category is expanded or collapsed.

6. Now it is time to write some code. Open the `ExpandCollapse.js` file, which is neatly stored in the `CustomScripts` folder.

7. The file will still contain the test script. Remove the alert line but keep the rest.

8. Add the following lines:

```
$(document).ready(function () {

    // Get the quick launch menu items
    var menuItems = $('#zz17_V4QuickLaunchMenu>div>ul>li>ul')

    // Hide the items
    menuItems.hide();
});
```

The first line is a jQuery selector that walks down the path mentioned in step 5, by selecting the outer `div` by using its ID. Looking at it in reverse from right to left, it is selecting all `ul` items that have a parent of a list item that has a parent of another `ul` that has a parent of a `div` that has a parent of the `div` with the ID specified! Oh my! The second line will promptly hide the matching elements (a bit easier to understand).

9. Save the JavaScript file.

10. Refresh your SharePoint page. You will see that the subitems have been hidden, as shown in Figure 8-7.

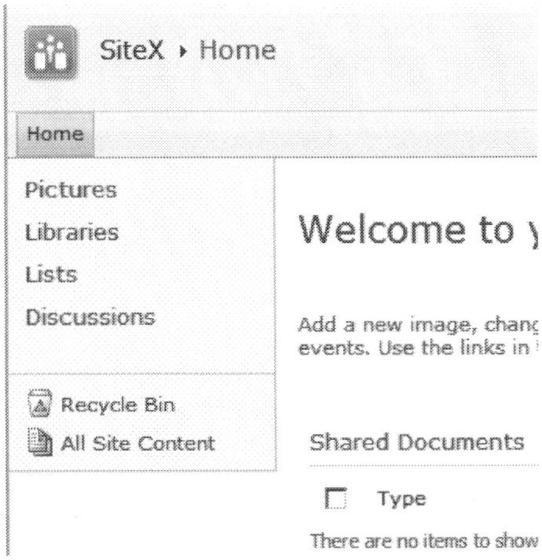

Figure 8-7. *Hiding the Quick Launch subitems*

You may notice that when the page loads, the subitems are there and then they disappear. This occurs because jQuery waits until the whole document has loaded before running the code inside the document.ready event. This can cause some odd-looking behavior. If you're working with your own elements, you are better off with elements starting off hidden and then showing them when required. However, when enhancing elements that you haven't created, you are likely to come across this behavior.

Adding Expand and Collapse Icons

The next step is to allow your end users to expand and collapse the categories. The most common user experience for this is to click a + (expand) or a – (collapse) icon to the left of the element. As you are making use of jQuery, this functionality can be added dynamically by injecting some clever code.

Insert the following code in the ExpandCollapse.js file:

```
$(document).ready(function(){
      // Get the quick launch menu items
    var menuItems = $('#zz17_V4QuickLaunchMenu>div>ul>li>ul')

    // Hide the items
    menuItems.hide();

      // Create element for expand\collapse icon
      // Float left to keep it inline
      // Add expandCollapseMe class to use to add event handler later
      // Use existing SharePoint image as image
      var expandCollapseButtonElement = $('<img style="float:left" style="cursor:hand"↵
class="expandCollapseMe" src="/_layouts/images/TPMax2.gif">');
```

```
    // Add the new button to all menu items from selector query
    menuItems.siblings('a').before(expandCollapseButtonElement);
```

```
});
```

The code creates a new img tag, which contains the expand\collapse image. The img tag has a class that can be used to wire up the click event. The last line finds the header a tag, which is a sibling of the unordered list and inserts the new image before it—all very clever stuff.

Save the file again and refresh the SharePoint page. You will see the new image, as shown in Figure 8-8.

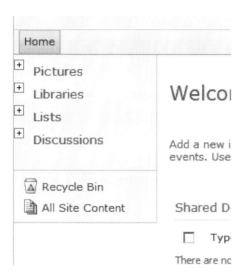

Figure 8-8. *Showing the dynamically added icons*

You could click the expand icon until your finger gets sore, but nothing will happen. That's because you have not told it to do anything when clicked. The next logical step is to wire up the button. When you click the icon, the subitems should appear, and the icon should change to reflect the new state of expanded by showing a collapse icon. When you click a collapse icon, it should do the reverse.

The event handler and code are incredibly simple. Add the following into the document.ready function:

```
// When Element is clicked
// use on() for 1.7 or live() for 1.6
$('.expandCollapseMe').live('click', function () {
    // Get the list containing the subitems
    var subItemMenu = $(this).siblings('ul');

    // Check visibility
    if ($(subItemMenu).is(':visible')) {
```

```
        // Hide all items
        subItemMenu.hide();

        // Update expand\collapse image to expand
        $(this).prop('src', '/_layouts/images/TPMax2.gif');
    } else {

        // Show all items
        subItemMenu.show();

        // Update expand\collapse image to collapse
        $(this).prop('src', '/_layouts/images/TPMin2.gif');
    }
});
```

The code binds the expand\collapse behavior to all current and future elements that match the query selector. The selector here is returning elements with the class of expandCollapseMe. The first line inside the event handler gets the list of the subitems. As with the insertion of the image element, you are able to use the sibling method, as it sits at the same level in the Document Object Model (DOM) tree. Next, the is method can check if the element is visible. If it is visible, then the code hides the subitems list and updates the src property of the a tag to reference the expand image. If the subitem is not visible, then the code shows the items and sets the image to the collapse icon.

Once the changes have been made, the complete code for this task should look like the following.

```
$(document).ready(function(){
        // Get the quick launch menu items
    var menuItems = $('#zz17_V4QuickLaunchMenu>div>ul>li>ul')

    // Hide the Items
    menuItems.hide();

        // create element for expand\collapse icon
        // float left to keep it inline
        // Add expandCollapseMe class to use to add event handler later
        // use existing SharePoint image as image
        var expandCollapseButtonElement = $('<img style="float:left" style="cursor:hand"↵
class="expandCollapseMe" src="/_layouts/images/TPMax2.gif">');

        // Add the new button to all menu items
        menuItems.siblings('a').before(expandCollapseButtonElement);

        // When Element is clicked
    // use on() for 1.7 or live() for 1.6
    $('.expandCollapseMe').live('click', function () {
        // Get the list containing the sub items
        var subItemMenu = $(this).siblings('ul');

        // Check visibility
        if ($(subItemMenu).is(':visible')) {
```

```
                    // Hide all items
                    subItemMenu.hide();

                    // Update expand\collapse image to expand
                    $(this).prop('src', '/_layouts/images/TPMax2.gif');
                } else {

                    // Show all items
                    subItemMenu.show();

                    // Update expand\collapse image to collapse
                    $(this).prop('src', '/_layouts/images/TPMin2.gif');
                }
            });
        });
```

I am sure you will agree that this nifty little piece of functionality is achieved with a fairly simple solution.

If you wanted to apply this as a solution to all your SharePoint pages, you could deploy and activate it in any of the methods used for the main jQuery library itself.

▓ **Tip**   To make sure that jQuery has been deployed, you can always add a Feature activation dependency for the jQuery feature. See `http://msdn.microsoft.com/en-us/library/aa543162.aspx` for details.

This expand\collapse example demonstrates how building a proof of concept using an external JavaScript file can speed up the development process. Remember that this is only for your proof of concepts. Once it is working, you should create your Visual Studio solution. This way, you will be able to activate and deactivate your solutions as features and control their usage.

Next, you'll look at an example that can turn a regular SharePoint list into a visual feast (of sorts).

Showing SharePoint List Data As a Graph

Sometimes users will want to view information differently from what is output by SharePoint by default.

As an example, suppose that you have been tasked with making a list of sales figures more visually appealing in the display. The managers are interested in how the best-selling product is doing and how other products compare. They want to see products doing similar sales (75 percent and above) and products that are way off the mark (25 percent and below) easily, so they don't need to waste time poring over the list data. In this example, you'll use a simple jQuery script to turn numerical information into a graph-like visual representation.

Creating the Custom List

To begin, create the sales figures list for this example.

1. Create a new custom list in SharePoint called Sales Figures.

2. Go to List Settings for the list.

3. Rename the Title column to Product.

4. Add a new column called Units Sold and set the column type as Number.

5. Add a few sample items to the list using the New Item dialog, as shown in Figure 8-9.

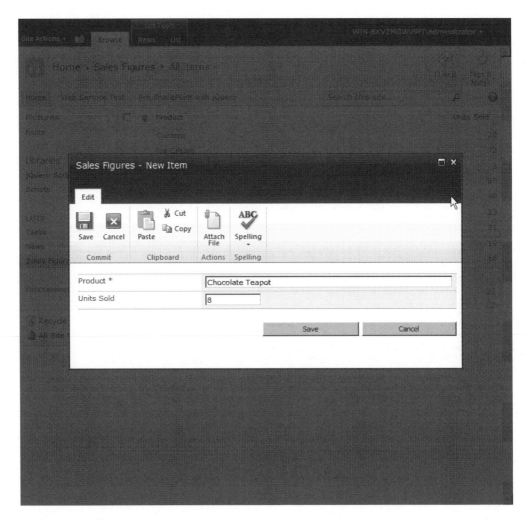

Figure 8-9. Adding items to the list

The complete list for this example with ten sample items is shown in Figure 8-10. Notice that even though the numbers are available, it is not particularly easy to see which are the better-selling products compared to the others.

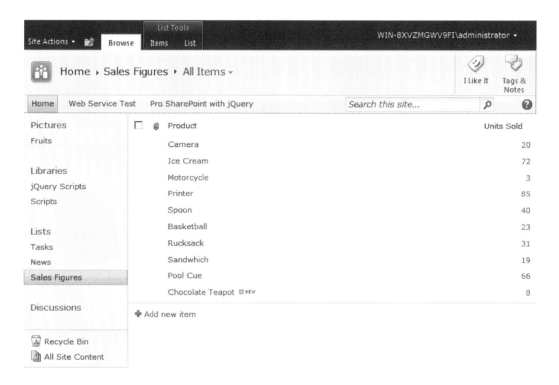

Figure 8-10. *List with ten test items*

Displaying a List Column in Graph Format

To be able to add the jQuery script to just this page, you can add a Content Editor web part to the list page and place the code in there. In Chapter 10, you will see how you can make it easier to reuse such functionality for other lists without needing to repeat a lot of code.

With the Content Editor web part added to the page, navigate to Edit HTML Source from the Format Text section of the Ribbon. Then add the following code into the newly opened window:

```
<script type="text/javascript" >

$(document).ready(function () {
    GraphItems();
});

function GraphItems() {
```

```
// Retrieve the table cells in the 4th column ('Units Sold')
var listItems = $('.ms-listviewtable>tbody>tr.ms-itmhover>td:nth-child(4)');

var count = listItems.length;
var total = 0;
var numbers = [];

// Iterate through each unit sold value
listItems.each(function (index) {
    if ($(this).text() != "") {
        number = parseInt($(this).text())
        numbers.push(number)
    }
});

// Get the most popular product unit count using
// JavaScript method on the numbers array
var largest = Math.max.apply(Math, numbers);

// Iterate through each table cell for item
listItems.each(function (index) {

    // Create a new empty div
    var div = $('<div/>');

    // get the number of the table cell
    number = parseInt($(this).text())

    // Work out the average compared to largest
    // number of units sold
    var average = parseInt(number / largest * 100);

    // Set CSS properties on the new div
    div.css('font-weight', 'bolder');
    div.css('color', 'white');

    // Set width to average % to give
    // div a graph look
    div.css('width', average + '%');

    // Switch to set color based on
    // Comparison to the average
    switch (true) {
        case (average >= 75):
            div.css('background-color', 'green');
            break;
        case (average >= 25):
            div.css('background-color', 'orange');
            break;
        default: div.css('background-color', 'red');
            break;
    }
```

```
        // Wrap the existing contents of the td
        // with the new formatted div
        $(this).wrapInner(div);
    });

}
</script>
```

The script uses a jQuery selector to get the table and the cells required. Using the nth-child, it is easy to select the column to use. Once the columns have been returned to the `listItems` variable from the selector query, several things happen. The first is that each Unit Sold value is retrieved using the each function and stored in an array. `Math.max.apply(Math, numbers)` is a useful method that will return the highest value from the array. This highest number is used as the 100 percent value in the graph, so that all others show as a percentage of that value. With the highest value found, the code iterates through each item again and creates a `div`, which is styled depending on the values. Its width is set as the average, and its color is determined by whether its value is greater than or equal to 75 percent, greater than or equal to 25 percent, or less than 25 percent of the average. The final step is to wrap the contents of the `td` with the new `div`.

Save your changes and exit edit mode. You will now be presented with an easy-to-view representation of the data, as shown in Figure 8-11.

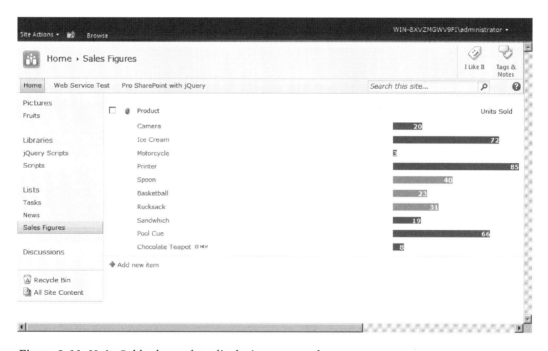

Figure 8-11. Units Sold column data displaying as a graph

This simple example showed how you can read data from the page and, using your own business logic, transform or enhance SharePoint to fit your own business requirements. You may encounter many situations where you can take the data provided by SharePoint and transform it to provide the information that you require. You will need to consider whether it is more suitable to create your own web part and read the SharePoint data from the Client Object Model or web services, or just use jQuery to manipulate the rendered HTML elements. Obviously, the benefits of the latter are that the hard work of the data retrieval has been done for you already.

Using jQuery from the SharePoint 2010 Ribbon

In this example, you will look at how you can call jQuery code from the SharePoint 2010 Ribbon. This simple example will allow the end user to select items and make them highlighted.

Creating a Highlighting Function

Begin by setting up a new project and then adding the JavaScript function to highlight selected items.

1. Open Visual Studio 2010.

2. Create a new Empty SharePoint 2010 project and call it MyjQueryRibbonButton.

3. Deploy the project as a Farm Solution.

4. Add a new SharePoint Layouts mapped folder. This will add the mapped folder and a subfolder based on the project name.

5. Add a .js file to the folder called documenthighlighter.js, as shown in Figure 8-12.

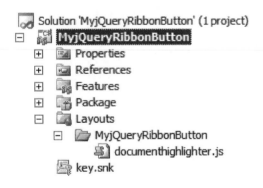

Figure 8-12. Adding the Layouts folder for the script

6. Add the following code to the JavaScript file:

```
function highlightSelected()
{
    // Select items based on if they're checked
    var citems = $('#onetidDoclibViewTbl0>tbody>.ms-itmhover>.ms-vb-
itmcbx>input:checked');

    // Iterate through each checked item
    citems.each(function(index, element)
    {
        // Find the table row
        var tr = $(element).closest('tr');

            // Toggle the highlight class
            tr.toggleClass('ms-rteStyle-Highlight');
    });
}
```

The simple function, called highlightSelected, uses a jQuery selector to find the document table on the page, and then drills down to find all items that have been checked by using the :checked selector. Once the list of elements has been found, it iterates through each of them using the each utility, and uses the element to find the table row to highlight. The toggleClass method means that if the element already has the class, the code will remove it; if it does not exist, the code will add it.

Adding a Ribbon Button

With the JavaScript file added, it is time to add a new Empty Element item from the SharePoint 2010 category to the project, as shown in Figure 8-13. This element will be used to deploy the Ribbon button.

Figure 8-13. Inserting an empty element for the Ribbon button

Open the newly added `Elements` file and replace the contents with the following:

```xml
<?xml version="1.0" encoding="utf-8"?>
<Elements xmlns="http://schemas.microsoft.com/sharepoint/">

  <CustomAction
    ScriptSrc="/_layouts/MyjQueryRibbonButton/documentHighlighter.js"
          Location="ScriptLink"
          Sequence="100">
  </CustomAction>

  <CustomAction
    Id="myjQueryRibbon"
    RegistrationType="List"
    RegistrationId="101"
    Location="CommandUI.Ribbon">
    <CommandUIExtension>
      <CommandUIDefinitions>
        <CommandUIDefinition
         Location="Ribbon.Documents.New.Controls._children">
          <Button
            Id="Ribbon.Documents.New.Controls.myJqueryButton"
            Alt="jQuery Ribbon Button"
            Sequence="10"
            Image32by32="/_layouts/images/OBJECTIV.GIF"
            Command="highlightUsingjQuery"
            LabelText="jQuery Highlight"
            TemplateAlias="o2"/>
        </CommandUIDefinition>
      </CommandUIDefinitions>
      <CommandUIHandlers>
        <CommandUIHandler
         Command="highlightUsingjQuery"
         CommandAction="javascript:highlightSelected()"/>
      </CommandUIHandlers>
    </CommandUIExtension>
  </CustomAction>

</Elements>
```

The first `CustomAction` loads the JavaScript file, which contains the `highlightSelected` method. This method of loading JavaScript to the page is the same as how the jQuery library itself can be loaded. Note that as with the jQuery library, this JavaScript will be loaded every time the Ribbon is loaded where the feature has been activated. If you want to have the code load only at the same time as the Ribbon button, you can put the JavaScript in the `CommandAction` of the Ribbon button's `CustomAction`, as follows:

```
<CommandUIHandlers>
        <CommandUIHandler
         Command="highlightUsingjQuery"
         CommandAction="javascript:

         var example = "I am an example";
         alert(example);

         "/>
</CommandUIHandlers>
```

If you have the JavaScript inline, there is no need for the first custom action.

The second CustomAction contains the necessary XML to load the Ribbon button. This button is targeted to a document library, and the button will be added to the New section. The CommandAction is what will call the highlightSelected method.

▓ **Tip**   You can find more information about Ribbon customization at `http://msdn.microsoft.com/en-us/library/ff630938.aspx`. Also, Chris O'Brien has a fantastic series of articles on Ribbon customization available at `http://www.sharepointnutsandbolts.com/2010/01/customizing-ribbon-part-1-creating-tabs.html`.

With the changes made, you're ready to test the new Ribbon button. Deploy the solution, navigate to a document library that has a few items in it, and select a couple of the items. Then navigate to the Documents tab and find the New section. Click the jQuery Highlight button, and then uncheck the boxes. You should see that the items that were checked now have a highlighting applied to them, as shown in Figure 8-14.

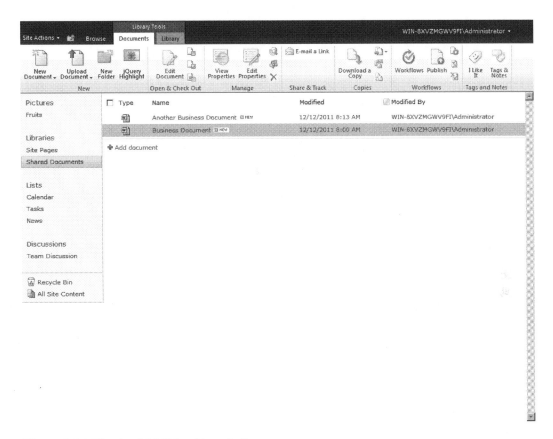

Figure 8-14. Viewing highlighted item in list

This example demonstrates how you can call your jQuery code from the Ribbon. This is a lightweight addition, but by working with the Client Object Model—particularly `SP.ListOperation.Selection` methods (see `http://msdn.microsoft.com/en-us/library/ff407815.aspx`)—you will find that you can really extend the functionality provided. You have also learned how to make functions available globally by adding a `CustomAction` and how to add JavaScript functionality to just a single Ribbon button.

Filtering Quick Launch

The final example in this chapter demonstrates how to easily filter items in the Quick Launch menu by using the `contains` selector.

As an example, suppose that your end users have started complaining that due to the high numbers of lists and libraries on the page, they are having trouble finding the items that they want. The solution you have come up with is a text box that allows end users to type in part of the list or library name, and the Quick Launch menu will be filtered accordingly.

Adding the JavaScript File Link

You will be using the same technique as used earlier in this chapter to allow you to build a proof of concept for this solution.

1. Navigate to the Layouts\CustomScripts folder in the SharePoint root (the same folder that was used in the first couple of examples).

2. Create a new .js file (rename a .txt file) called QuickLaunchFilter.js. Leave it blank for now.

3. Navigate to a SharePoint page that has a few lists and libraries available, such as the page shown in Figure 8-15.

Figure 8-15. Quick Launch with its many items

4. Add a Content Editor web part and enter Edit HTML Source mode.

5. Add the following script tag to read in the JavaScript file that you will be adding to later:

```
<script src="/_layouts/CustomScripts/QuickLaunchFilter.js"
type="text/javascript"></script>
```

6. Click OK and exit edit mode.

Adding a Quick Launch Filter

Next, open the QuickLaunchFilter.js file and add the following document.ready code:

```
$(document).ready(function () {
    QuickLaunchFilter();
});
```

It should be well and truly ingrained into your brain now that this will call the QuickLaunchFilter method once the document (the HTML page) has been completely loaded and has indicated that it is ready.

Add the following function beneath the closing bracket of the ready function:

```
function QuickLaunchFilter() {
    // Select the QuickLaunch div
    var div = $('#zz17_V4QuickLaunchMenu>div');

    // Find all of the subitems in the menu
    var menuItems = div.find('ul>li>ul>li')

    // Create text box to perform the filtering
    var tb = $('<input type="text" name="find" />');

    // Attach handler on the keyup event
    tb.keyup(function () {

        // Read the text box value
        var typedText = $(this).val();

        // Find all of the spans that contain the entered text
        // The 'contains' method is case-sensitive
        var matching = menuItems.find('span.menu-item-text:contains("' + typedText + '")');

        // Hide all of the menu items first
        menuItems.hide();

        // Show the list item for the span that contains
        // the matching text
        matching.closest('li').show();
    });
```

```
    // Add the text box as the first item
    // in the div element
    div.children(':first').before(tb);
}
```

The code is relatively simple. First, the Quick Launch div is retrieved by using its ID, and then the child div is selected. From the div, all submenu items are found and stored in a variable. A text box is then created in memory. The text box has an event handler registered on the keyup event. The keyup event retrieves the current value in the text box, and then using another selector, it finds all of the menu-item-text span elements that contain the value that was entered by the user. All of the submenu items are hidden. Then, using the spans returned from the text-match query, the parent list items of the span elements are shown. The contains selector is case-sensitive, so *T* will find *Tasks*, but not *tasks* or *Sites*. If you need it to be case-insensitive, you can iterate over the items in an each loop and do your own comparison.

Finally, the text box is added before the first child of the div, so it's at the top.

Save the JavaScript file and navigate back to the SharePoint page. You may need to refresh the page if it was already open. You should now see a text box at the top of Quick Launch, as shown in Figure 8-16.

Figure 8-16. Unfiltered Quick Launch menu items

Enter some text into the text box, and the Quick Launch elements will be filtered, as shown in the example in Figure 8-17.

Figure 8-17. Quick Launch menu items filtered by the letter F

In this example, you have seen how to filter elements on the page using jQuery. The text box used does not need to be added dynamically. If this were to be used as a full solution, the text box could be added to the master page, and the JavaScript could be loaded by any of the other means you have learned.

Summary

In this chapter, you have looked at a few of the different ways that SharePoint can be enhanced using jQuery—from expanding and collapsing the Quick Launcher menu to displaying list items in a graph. The examples demonstrated how various the solutions can be.

As mentioned early in the chapter, you should always think about the impact the extra functionality will have on the page. You need to make sure that the functionality is deployed only to the correct scope and will not interfere with any other functionality on the page.

The next chapter covers jQuery plug-ins, which offer a whole new range of enhancement functionality.

CHAPTER 9

Using jQuery Plug-ins
to Enhance SharePoint

Most of the applications and enhancements that you have looked at so far have been created from scratch using the default functionality of jQuery. One of the most valuable and powerful features of jQuery is the plug-in structure, and many incredibly useful and beautiful plug-ins are being added to the list every day.

Most of the plug-ins have not been built with SharePoint specifically in mind, but because of their configurable nature, getting a plug-in to work in a SharePoint environment is just like adding it to any other HTML page. The benefit is that you have the SharePoint API on hand, too, to help work with your data.

The plug-ins available range tremendously in the value they offer. Arguably, the most utilized is jQuery UI, which adds a host of UI enhancements to jQuery. Another example is SPServices, which provides a fantastic jQuery wrapper around the SharePoint web services. There are plenty of other plug-ins that you may find useful.

We all have too much on our plates and precious little time to do it, so it makes sense to use a plug-in rather than reinvent the wheel each time that you want something a bit more than out-of-the box functionality. If, however, like so many of the great folks who have spent time writing these free, open source plug-ins, you want to create your own, the existing plug-ins are a great resource to examine to see how they make jQuery perform such fantastic things.

In this chapter, you will see how powerful these additions can be to the jQuery library and realize the benefits of jQuery plug-ins. The next chapter demonstrates how make your own plug-ins.

Using a jQuery Plug-in

A jQuery plug-in is typically deployed and made available in the same way as the jQuery library itself. The plug-in will extend the jQuery functionality by adding new methods, which you can call on the jQuery objects. For example, if there were a (made-up) plug-in called Chart2000, you would use a jQuery selector, as follows:

```
$('#myElement').Chart2000();
```

This would perform the functionality of the Chart2000 plug-in on the resulting object from the selector.

Also, you can often apply some extra configuration to the plug-in so that it suits your requirements more closely. Parameters, whether optional or not, can be configured like this:

```
$('#myElement').Chart2000({
    chartType: 'Bar',
    column: 10,
    charted: function () {
        alert('You just made a chart!');
    }
});
```

With the basics outlined, we'll get started by looking at jQuery UI, which is a great introduction to the world of jQuery plug-ins.

Working with jQuery UI

jQuery UI, an official plug-in, offers many features that make creating jQuery-based solutions and enhancements much simpler. According to the jQuery home page (`http://jqueryui.com/`):

> *jQuery UI provides abstractions for low-level interaction and animation, advanced effects and high-level, themeable widgets, built on top of the jQuery JavaScript Library, that you can use to build highly interactive web applications*

The jQuery UI plug-in library offers the following features and functionality above and beyond the standard library:

- Interactions
- Widgets
- Utilities
- Effects

You will take a closer look at each of these new features and functions in this chapter. For now, you just need to be aware that the library is designed to make developing a feature-rich UI (which also looks pretty and does cool stuff) a lot easier.

Deploying jQuery UI

The first thing you will need to do is to download the library itself. Head over to `http://jqueryui.com` to get your hands on it. As with the jQuery library, you can tailor the download and choose whether to get the production/minified version or the development version.

For this chapter, you will deploy the jQuery UI plug-in alongside the regular jQuery library; however, by splitting out the feature to load the script on the page, you gain some control over where it is used. Deploying jQuery UI using the same solution as you used for deploying jQuery makes sense here, as even though the library will be placed in the same location, there is another step required to make the script available on the page. However, users can still reference the script if they know its name and location.

Open the Visual Studio jQueryDeploymentProject solution you created in Chapter 2. Once the solution has loaded, locate the jQuery folder, as shown in Figure 9-1.

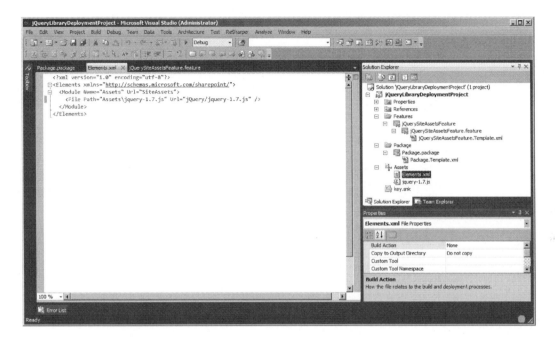

Figure 9-1. *Locating the jQuery folder*

Copy and paste the jQuery UI library from your download location into the folder. When the solution is deployed, the jQuery UI library will be deployed to the same folder as the main jQuery library. But don't deploy just yet, as you will want to include the styling, as described next.

Deploying the jQuery UI Styling

jQuery UI comes with a CSS style sheet as well as its matching images. The styles are very useful to get up and going quickly, but you may wish to create your own to fit in with your SharePoint branding and style. The web site at `http://jqueryui.com/themeroller/` makes it easy to customize a theme for use with jQuery UI. The styling is used on the elements that the plug-in creates for its various widgets, which are described later in this chapter. The CSS files will be deployed to the Layouts directory in your own jQuery folder, alongside the jQuery and jQuery UI JavaScript libraries.

In Visual Studio, locate the jQuery folder again. Then copy and paste the css folder from the extracted zip file of the jQuery UI download into this folder. The structure should look like Figure 9-2.

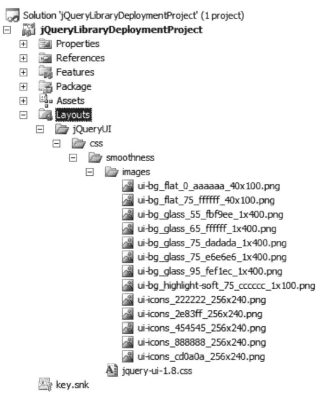

Figure 9-2. *jQuery UI styling added to the solution*

With these changes made, you can deploy the solution. Then jQuery UI will be available in the jQuery folder, as shown in Figure 9-3.

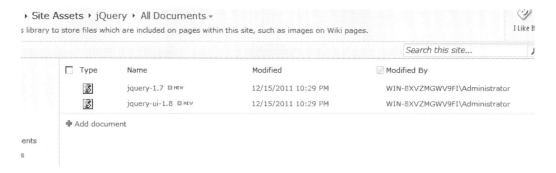

Figure 9-3. *jQuery and jQuery UI libraries deployed to the Layouts folder*

If you navigate to the css folder, you will see that the styling has been deployed, too, as shown in Figure 9-4.

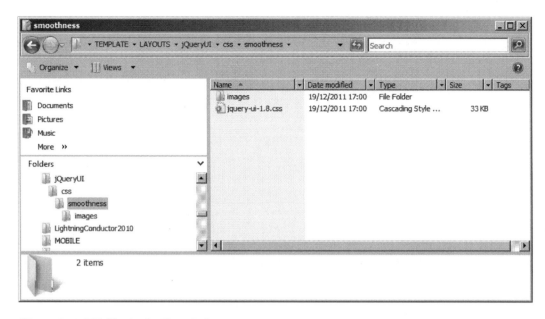

Figure 9-4. *CSS files in the SharePoint root*

Making jQuery UI Available

To make the jQuery UI library available, you can use any method covered in the previous chapter. For simplicity, let's add it to the jQueryCustomActionProject project. You may want to have some locations that can use the jQuery UI plug-in and other places where it's not used. If you want this level of control, you can add a new SharePoint Feature that deploys the jQuery UI library on its own, so it can be activated and deactivated at your discretion.

Open the Visual Studio jQueryCustomActionProject project. Find and open the elements file located in the jQueryCustomActionElement folder. Edit the file to add a new custom action for the jQuery UI library, as follows (the new lines are shown in bold):

```
<?xml version="1.0" encoding="utf-8"?>
<Elements xmlns="http://schemas.microsoft.com/sharepoint/">
  <CustomAction
    ScriptSrc="_layouts/jQuery/jquery-1.7.js"
         Location="ScriptLink"
         Sequence="100">
  </CustomAction>
```

```
<CustomAction
 ScriptSrc="_layouts/jQuery/jquery-ui-1.8.js"
        Location="ScriptLink"
        Sequence="101">
</CustomAction>
</Elements>
```

Here, you are simply adding another custom action that will load the jQuery UI library as well as the default jQuery library.

Once again, deploy the solution. Now it is time to make use of the library. The following examples will get you started with jQuery UI and show you some of its capabilities.

Getting Started with jQuery UI

A simple way to demonstrate what jQuery UI can offer is to create a new application page that shows off some of its features. This example will add some user interactivity to the page.

Creating the Plug-in Application Page

Create a new plug-in project and application page as follows:

1. Create a new Empty SharePoint project called PluginPageProject, and choose to deploy it as a Farm Solution.

2. Add an Application Page item to the project, and name the application page Default.aspx.

3. Rename the application page's folder to PluginPage. The structure should look like Figure 9-5.

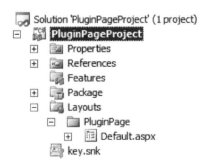

Figure 9-5. Project structure for the plug-in application page

4. Double-click the Default.aspx page to enter edit mode.

5. In the PlaceHolderAdditionalPageHead content placeholder, add the following tag to tell SharePoint to register the jQuery UI CSS file:

```
<asp:Content ID="PageHead" ContentPlaceHolderID="PlaceHolderAdditionalPageHead"↵
 runat="server">
    <SharePoint:CssRegistration Name='<% $SPUrl:/_layouts/jQuery/css/smoothness/↵
jquery-ui-1.8.css%>'
        runat='server' />
</asp:Content>
```

The CSS link tag will be added to the page, and the style sheet will be loaded.

Adding jQuery UI Code

It's time to code against your first jQuery plug-in. Add the following code beneath the CSS registration tag:

```
<asp:Content ID="PageHead" ContentPlaceHolderID="PlaceHolderAdditionalPageHead"↵
 runat="server">
    <SharePoint:CssRegistration Name='<% $SPUrl:/_layouts/jQuery/css/smoothness/↵
jquery-ui-1.8.css%>'
        runat='server' />
    <script type="text/javascript">
        $(document).ready(function () {
            $('#s4-leftpanel').draggable();
        });
    </script>
</asp:Content>
```

The function being used is draggable, which, as the name suggests, adds dragging functionality to the element. It looks like just any other jQuery code, which is great. Being able to drag elements around the page offers a huge range of possibilities, especially if you are thinking about functionality on a touchscreen device. I am sure you'll agree this nifty bit of code is nice and succinct.

The element being used here is the poor Quick Launch-containing left panel, which seems to be getting most of the attention so far in this book. What will it do? Deploy and find out! Don't forget that you will need to navigate to the application page by entering its path, as there is nothing pointing to it. In my setup, the URL is as follows:

```
http://SP2010/_layouts/PluginPage/Default.aspx
```

Once the page has loaded, it all seems ordinary. That's until you click and drag the left panel, and see that it moves. You can drag it anywhere you want, and it will sit where you leave it. All of this is just client-side cleverness, which has been abstracted away by the jQuery and jQuery UI libraries.

You may notice that when the panel is moving around, it remains behind some elements and in front of others. This is where the configuration options come in handy. Let's make a change to introduce using a plug-in option. Change the draggable method from this:

```
$('#s4-leftpanel').draggable();
```

to this:

```
$('#s4-leftpanel').draggable({
        zIndex: 1000
    });
```

Be careful not to leave out the curly braces.

The clever people who wrote this plug-in realized that developers may want to adjust the z-index, so they have exposed an option to change it. Here, you set zIndex to 1000 when you start to drag the panel, so that it hovers above the other elements.

Now deploy the project again and see what happens. This time, you will notice that while the element is being dragged, it sits happily above all other elements, as shown in Figure 9-6. When the mouse is released, however, it just stays where you left it, hovering on the page.

Figure 9-6. Dragged element above other elements

So, how do you get the panel to return to its original location? It's a simple case of setting the revert option to true:

```
$('#s4-leftpanel').draggable({
    zIndex: 1000,
    revert: true
});
```

The options are separated by a comma. As in normal JavaScript, if the value is a string, it needs to be surrounded by quotes. If it is a variable, a number, or true/false, it does not need the quotes.

Deploy the project, and then watch as the panel smoothly returns home after you have dragged the poor thing around your page.

This first example has given you a tiny insight into how the jQuery UI plug-in can be used to create an interactive user experience. Now let's look at some of the other features that are offered by the jQuery UI plug-in.

Using jQuery UI Interactions

The jQuery UI plug-in offers five different interactions you can add to elements:

- Draggable

- Droppable

- Resizable

- Selectable

- Sortable

Let's take a look at how you might use these interactions to enhance your SharePoint solutions.

Draggable and Droppable

As you saw in the preceding example, draggable allows you to click and drag elements around the page. This method is rarely used by itself. Typically, it is used with a droppable-enabled element.

The droppable method is the partner in crime for the draggable method, as it is used to set up an element or elements to receive a dragged item. Consider how moving something to the Recycle Bin works in Windows. It's this kind of interaction you can create with draggable and droppable.

For example, if you wanted to re-create the Task List Viewer application from Chapter 6 for use with a tablet, you could change the interaction from requiring the user to click the arrows to move between states to allowing the user to just drag a task to the desired state, which is much more finger-friendly. Let's do that now.

Open the jQueryTaskViewApplication Visual Studio solution to begin. All of the functionality to allow the end user to drag items between states can be done in the JavaScript file; there is no need to touch the .aspx file. You will be making a small change in the CSS file, but that is to just make the dragging and dropping a little easier.

Open the jQueryTaskViewerScript.js file. At the bottom of the document.ready section, before the closing bracket, add the following snippet of code:

```
// Add droppable to the 'Not Started' list
// Will only accept items from 'In Progress'
$('#notStartedTasksDiv>ul').droppable({
    activeClass: "task-active",
    hoverClass: "task-hover",
    accept: function (d) {
        // Check if item is coming from valid state
        // if it is then accept to drop
        if (d.data('status') == "In Progress") {
            return true;
        }
    },
```

```
      drop: function (ev, ui) {
          // Get the element being dragged
          var taskItem = $(ui.draggable);
          // Update the item
          ChangeStatus(taskItem, direction.Left);
      }
});
```

This code is adding the drop functionality to notStartedTasksDiv and has several options configured. The first two options apply some styling so that it is clear to end users where they are able to drag their task.

The accept option is called when an item is dragged on the page to see if it is able to accept the dragging element. The option can either take a selector, such as $('.task'), or it can use a function, as in this example. The code is using a function because it needs to read the status value from the data property on the element. Recall from the original requirements that items can move only from one state at a time. Here, the code is checking to make sure the element has come from the In Progress state. If so, the code returns true to indicate it can accept the drop.

The last option is drop. This is what happens when an accepted element gets dropped. In this case, its status should be updated to reflect the change. Using the ui parameter, you can get the element that was dropped, and from there, you can pass it to the ChangeStatus method to update the list item.

Add the rest of the methods for the other two columns that will be accepting tasks: the In Progress and Completed columns. The revised version for all three columns looks like this:

```
// DRAG AND DROP SECTION

    // Add droppable to the 'Not Started' list
    // Will only accept items from 'In Progress'
    $('#notStartedTasksDiv>ul').droppable({
        activeClass: "task-active",
        hoverClass: "task-hover",
        accept: function (d) {
            // Check if item is coming from valid state
            // if it is then accept to drop
            if (d.data('status') == "In Progress") {
                return true;
            }
        },
        drop: function (ev, ui) {
            // Get the element being dragged
            var taskItem = $(ui.draggable);
            // Update the item
            ChangeStatus(taskItem, direction.Left);
        }
    });

    // Add droppable to the 'In Progress' list
    // Will accept items which are not 'In Progress'
    $('#inProgressTasksDiv>ul').droppable({
        activeClass: "task-active",
        hoverClass: "task-hover",
```

```
        accept: function (d) {
            if (d.data('status') != "In Progress") {
                return true;
            }
        },
        drop: function (ev, ui) {
            var taskItem = $(ui.draggable);
            if (taskItem.data('status') == "Completed") {
                ChangeStatus(taskItem, direction.Left);
            } else {
                ChangeStatus(taskItem, direction.Right);
            }
        }
    });

    // Add droppable to the 'Completed' list
    // Will only accept items which are 'In Progress'
    $('#completedTasksDiv>ul').droppable({
        activeClass: "task-active",
        hoverClass: "task-hover",
        accept: function (d) {
            if (d.data('status') == "In Progress") {
                return true;
            }
        },
        drop: function (ev, ui) {
            var taskItem = $(ui.draggable);
            ChangeStatus(taskItem, direction.Right);
        }
    });

    // END DRAG AND DROP SECTION
```

You need to make two more changes to get the dropping functionality working. The first is to add the draggable functionality to the tasks as they are created. Locate the addTaskToList function and add the following code (shown in bold):

```
function addTaskToList(list, id, title, description, status) {
    // Create a copy of the <li> template
    var itemTemplate = $('#TemplateListItem').clone();

    // Remove the unnecessary id attribute
    itemTemplate.attr('id', null);

    // Set the title to the task title
    itemTemplate.find('.taskTitle').text(title);

    // Set the description to the task description
    itemTemplate.find('.taskDescription').html(description);

    itemTemplate.data('status', status);
    itemTemplate.data('taskId', id);
```

```
itemTemplate.draggable(
        {
            helper: 'clone'
        });

// Only show possible direction of movement
switch (status) {
    case "Not Started": itemTemplate.find('.moveLeftButton').hide();
        break;
    case "Completed": itemTemplate.find('.moveRightButton').hide();
        break;
}

// Add Task Element created from template
list.append(itemTemplate);
}
```

This example uses a helper so that the element can't just be dragged and left in a random location on the page. If the helper does not get dropped, the page will remain as it was.

One last change in the JavaScript file is needed to slightly modify the behavior of the ChangeStatus method. In the previous version of the application, the first parameter being passed in was the button element of the arrow that moved the task either right or left. To get the task, the ChangeStatus method found the parent list item of the button. Because you are passing in the list item directly, there is no need for this. To get around this in the code, you can use the is() method to determine if the element being passed in is a list item. If it is, then the code can use that. Otherwise, the element must be the button, and the code will need to find the parent list item. Update the method as follows (changes shown in bold):

```
function ChangeStatus(taskElement, moveDirection) {

    taskElement = $(taskElement);
    var taskListItemElement;

    if (taskElement.is('li')) {
        taskListItemElement = taskElement;
    } else {
        taskListItemElement = $(taskElement).parents("li:first");
    }


    // Get the new status based on the existing status
    // and the direction it is moving
    var updatedStatus = GetNewStatus(taskListItemElement, moveDirection);

    // Return if invalid new status
    if (updatedStatus == null) {
        return;
    }
```

```
    // Update the SharePoint task list item with the new status
    updateTaskStatus(taskListItemElement.data('taskId'), updatedStatus);

    // Get the tasks again from the server
    GetTasks();
}
```

Save the JavaScript file.

Next, open `style.css`. There are just a few lines to add here, at the bottom of the CSS file:

```
.task-hover
{
    border: 1px solid #fbcb09;
    background: #fdf5ce;
    min-height: 300px;
}

.task-active
{
    border: 1px solid #b18e01;
    background: #fdf5ce;
    min-height: 300px;
}
```

▓ **Note** In the updated version of the Task List Viewer application, you may find that if you are adding an item to an empty list, it can be tricky to get the item to drop. One of the tricks I use is to set the `min-height` attribute so that it gives me a bit of a runway for landing the element.

With these final changes made, it is time to take this dragging-and-dropping stuff for a test drive, so buckle up! Deploy the application and navigate to the Task List Viewer page. I am imagining cheers about now, as you realize the joy that this newfound drag-and-drop knowledge has given you. Check out Figure 9-7 for a view of the dragging in action.

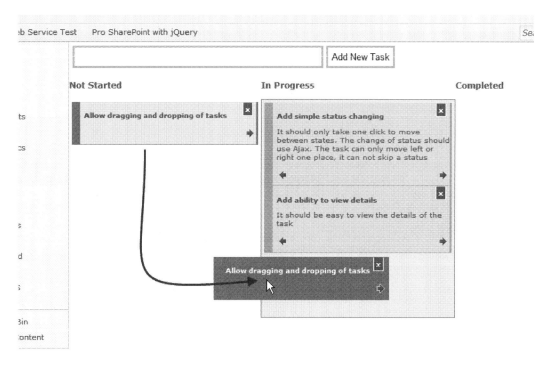

Figure 9-7. Dragging and dropping a task

Resizable and Selectable

Resizing an element dynamically can be really useful. The `resizable` function puts a little handle in the bottom-right side of an element and allows the user to drag to change the size proportions of the element.

Selectable functionality gives the user the ability to select individual elements or use the "lasso" to select multiple elements. This can be used if you want to allow an end user to select some products to add to an order, for example.

Sortable

Sortable functionality allows you to sort elements. It's typically used with a list, but can be applied to any element.

As with most of these interactions, it's worth remembering that all you are doing is manipulating the Document Object Model (DOM) in the user's browser. If the browser is refreshed, it will revert to the original format. You need to make use of the various events available on the methods to persist any data or changes that you want to keep. For example, if you want to update a SharePoint list item's priority depending on its order in an ordered list, you need to call one of its events, such as the following:

```
$( "#MyTasksList" ).sortable({
    update: function(event, ui)
        {

        }
});
```

Let's take a more detailed look at how you could use sorting to update a SharePoint list. This example will allow you to order places that you have visited.

1. Create a new Custom SharePoint list in your SharePoint environment called Places Visited.

2. Rename the Title column to Place Name and add a new number column called Order Visited.

3. Add places and order visited values to your list. It doesn't matter in which order they are added here, as that's what you will be able to update using the application page. Figure 9-8 shows the small list of items I added.

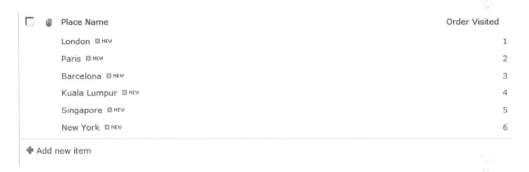

Figure 9-8. Custom Places Visited list

4. In the Main placeholder in the Default.aspx application page, add the following ordered list tag. This will hold the list of places visited.

```
<asp:Content ID="Main" ContentPlaceHolderID="PlaceHolderMain" runat="server">
    <ol id="MyVisitedPlaces" />
</asp:Content>
```

5. All of the prerequisites are now set up, so it's time to add the almighty jQuery. Add an empty document.ready event handler to use later.

```
$(document).ready(function()
{

});
```

6. The first code to add will load the visited places from the list. Add the following function after the previous code you just inserted. It uses the Client Object Model to retrieve the places visited sorted by the order in which they were visited. For each item in the list, it creates a new list item and adds the item to the ordered list.

```
// Global variable to hold places
var places;

function GetPlaces() {
    try {

        // Get the context
        var context = new SP.ClientContext.get_current();

        // Load the web object
        this.web = context.get_web();

        //Get the 'Places Visited' list
        var list = this.web.get_lists().getByTitle('Places Visited');

        // Create new CAML Query
        var camlQuery = new SP.CamlQuery();

        //Set the CAML-Query-XML to sort by Order Visited
        camlQuery.set_viewXml("<Query><OrderBy><FieldRefName='Order_↵
x0020_Visited' /></OrderBy></Query>");

        // Get all the items in the list
        places = list.getItems(camlQuery);

        // Load the web object in the context and retrieve only selected
columns
        context.load(this.places, 'Include(ID, Title,
Order_x0020_Visited)');

        //Make a query call to execute the above statements
        context.executeQueryAsync(Function.createDelegate(this, this.↵
GetPlacesOnSuccess), Function.createDelegate(this, this.GetPlacesOnFailure));
    }
    catch (e) {
        alert("An error occurred while fetching data.");
    }
}
```

```
function GetPlacesOnSuccess() {
    // Get the collection
    var placeCollection = this.places.getEnumerator();

    // Iterate through places
    while (placeCollection.moveNext()) {
        // Get current item
        var place = placeCollection.get_current();

        // Create new element HTML
        var listItemHtml = '<li>' + place.get_item('Title') + '</li>';

        // Create new element using HTML
        var listItem = $(listItemHtml);

        // Set the ID
        listItem.prop('id', "Place_" + place.get_item('ID'));

        // Add order visited data
        listItem.data('listId', place.get_item('ID'));

        // Add item to list
        $('#MyVisitedPlaces').append(listItem);
    }
}

function GetPlacesOnFailure() {
    alert("An error occurred while fetching data.");
}
```

7. With the data-retrieval code written, you can update the document.ready method with the call to this function. As the function is making use of the Client Object Model, which in turn uses the SP object, it needs to make sure the library has been loaded before calling the new function, so you again need to use the execute or delay method.

```
$(document).ready(function () {
    ExecuteOrDelayUntilScriptLoaded(GetPlaces, "sp.js");
});
```

8. Deploy the solution to make sure that the data is being returned, as shown in Figure 9-9.

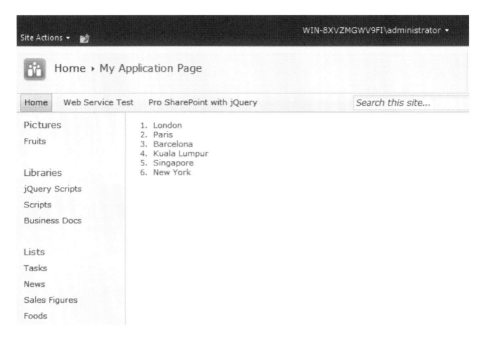

Figure 9-9. *Data being returned from the list successfully*

9. The next step is to use the `sortable` method on the ordered list. Find the `document.ready` method again and add the following snippet, which applies the sorting functionality to the list.

```
$(document).ready(function () {
    ExecuteOrDelayUntilScriptLoaded(GetPlaces, "sp.js");
    $("#MyVisitedPlaces").sortable();
});
```

10. Go ahead and test the solution to make sure you can reorder the items. I am sure it will work fine.

11. As mentioned previously, all this is doing is manipulating the DOM on your own browser. If you want to actually make a change, then you need to do something about it. Add an update option to the `sortable` function, as follows:

```
$(document).ready(function () {
    $("#MyVisitedPlaces").sortable({
        update: function (event, ui) {
            // Retrieves list of item IDs in order
            var placeArray = $(this).sortable('toArray');
```

```
        // Pass the array to update method
        UpdateData(placeArray);
    }
});

    ExecuteOrDelayUntilScriptLoaded(GetPlaces, "sp.js");
});
```

The update method is called when the user has stopped sorting the items, so it is the perfect time to save changes back to the list. The code uses the toArray parameter, which can be passed to the sortable method, which returns an array of all of the IDs of the elements.

12. The next and final step is to update the list items with their new order by finding the element that matches the ID; then reading its listId property, which is stored in the element's data; and then updating the list item's Order Visited value to the index location of the element.

```
function UpdateData(placeArray) {

    // Get the context
    var context = new SP.ClientContext.get_current();

    // Load the web object
    this.web = context.get_web();

    //Get the 'Places Visited' list
    var list = this.web.get_lists().getByTitle('Places Visited');

    // Iterate through each item in the place array
    $.each(placeArray, function (index, element) {
        // Get the list item for the current element using the id
        var placeListId = $("#MyVisitedPlaces").children('#' +↵
element).data('listId');

        // get the List Item using the ID
        var placeItem = list.getItemById(placeListId);

        // Set the Order Visited column to Index + 1
        // Using + 1 so it starts from 1 and not 0
        placeItem.set_item('Order_x0020_Visited', index + 1);

        // Call update on changes
        placeItem.update();
    });
```

```
                // Execute query
                context.executeQueryAsync(Function.createDelegate(this,↵
        this.OnUpdatePlaceOrderSuccess), Function.createDelegate(this,↵
        this.OnUpdatePlaceOrderFailure));
            }

            function OnUpdatePlaceOrderSuccess() {
                console.log("Place order updated successfully.");
            }

            function OnUpdatePlaceOrderFailure() {
                alert("Error occurred while updating place order.");
            }
```

You should be able to do the final test now. Deploy the project, move the items around, and then look at the list itself and see how the Order Visited column has changed. Because the list items are also ordered when retrieved from the list, when you go back to the page, they will appear in the sorted order. Figures 9-10 and 9-11 show an example of the list after some sorting.

Figure 9-10. *Reordered list on application page*

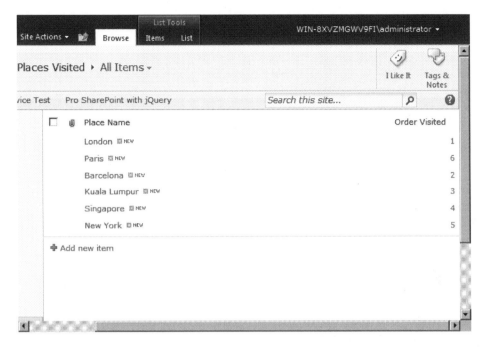

Figure 9-11. *Order Visited values reflected in SharePoint list*

The following is the complete code for the solution.

```
<%@ Assembly Name="$SharePoint.Project.AssemblyFullName$" %>
<%@ Register TagPrefix="SharePoint" Namespace="Microsoft.SharePoint.WebControls"
    Assembly="Microsoft.SharePoint, Version=14.0.0.0, Culture=neutral,↵
PublicKeyToken=71e9bce111e9429c" %>
<%@ Assembly Name="Microsoft.Web.CommandUI, Version=14.0.0.0, Culture=neutral,↵
PublicKeyToken=71e9bce111e9429c" %>

<%@ Page Language="C#" AutoEventWireup="true" CodeBehind="Default.aspx.cs"↵
Inherits="PluginPageProject.Layouts.PluginPageProject.Default"
    DynamicMasterPageFile="~masterurl/default.master" %>

<asp:Content ID="PageHead" ContentPlaceHolderID="PlaceHolderAdditionalPageHead"↵
runat="server">
    <SharePoint:CssRegistration Name='<% $SPUrl:/_layouts/jQuery/css/smoothness/↵
jquery-ui-1.8.css%>'
        runat='server' />
    <script type="text/javascript">
```

```
$(document).ready(function () {
    $("#MyVisitedPlaces").sortable({
        update: function (event, ui) {
            // Retrieves list of item IDs in order
            var placeArray = $(this).sortable('toArray');

            // Pass the array to update method
            UpdateData(placeArray);
        }
    });

    ExecuteOrDelayUntilScriptLoaded(GetPlaces, "sp.js");
});

// Global variable to hold places
var places;

function GetPlaces() {
    try {

        // Get the context
        var context = new SP.ClientContext.get_current();

        // Load the web object
        this.web = context.get_web();

        //Get the 'Places Visited' list
        var list = this.web.get_lists().getByTitle('Places Visited');

        // Create new CAML Query
        var camlQuery = new SP.CamlQuery();

        //Set the CAML-Query-XML to sort by Order Visited
        camlQuery.set_viewXml("<Query><OrderBy><FieldRef Name='Order_x0020_Visited'↵
/></OrderBy></Query>");

        // Get all the items in the list
        places = list.getItems(camlQuery);

        // Load the web object in the context and retrieve only selected columns
        context.load(this.places, 'Include(ID, Title, Order_x0020_Visited)');

        //Make a query call to execute the above statements
        context.executeQueryAsync(Function.createDelegate(this,↵
this.GetPlacesOnSuccess), Function.createDelegate(this, this.GetPlacesOnFailure));
    }
    catch (e) {
        alert("An error occurred while fetching data.");
    }
}
```

```
function GetPlacesOnSuccess() {
    // Get the collection
    var placeCollection = this.places.getEnumerator();

    // Iterate through places
    while (placeCollection.moveNext()) {
        // Get current item
        var place = placeCollection.get_current();

        // Create new element HTML
        var listItemHtml = '<li>' + place.get_item('Title') + '</li>';

        // Create new element using HTML
        var listItem = $(listItemHtml);

        // Set the ID
        listItem.prop('id', "Place_" + place.get_item('ID'));

        // Add order visited data
        listItem.data('listId', place.get_item('ID'));

        // Add item to list
        $('#MyVisitedPlaces').append(listItem);
    }
}

function GetPlacesOnFailure() {
    alert("An error occurred while fetching data.");
}

function UpdateData(placeArray) {

    // Get the context
    var context = new SP.ClientContext.get_current();

    // Load the web object
    this.web = context.get_web();

    //Get the 'Places Visited' list
    var list = this.web.get_lists().getByTitle('Places Visited');

    // Iterate through each item in the place array
    $.each(placeArray, function (index, element) {
        // Get the list item for the current element using the id
        var placeListId = $("#MyVisitedPlaces").children('#' +↵
element).data('listId');
```

```
            // get the list item using the ID
            var placeItem = list.getItemById(placeListId);

            // Set the order visited column to index + 1
            // Using + 1 so it starts from 1 and not 0
            placeItem.set_item('Order_x0020_Visited', index + 1);

            // Call update on changes
            placeItem.update();
        });

        // Execute query
        context.executeQueryAsync(Function.createDelegate(this,↩
this.OnUpdatePlaceOrderSuccess), Function.createDelegate(this,↩
this.OnUpdatePlaceOrderFailure));
    }

    function OnUpdatePlaceOrderSuccess() {
        console.log("Place order updated successfully.");
    }

    function OnUpdatePlaceOrderFailure() {
        alert("Error occurred while updating place order.");
    }
    </script>
</asp:Content>
<asp:Content ID="Main" ContentPlaceHolderID="PlaceHolderMain" runat="server">
    <ol id="MyVisitedPlaces" />
</asp:Content>
<asp:Content ID="PageTitle" ContentPlaceHolderID="PlaceHolderPageTitle" runat="server">
    My Plugin Page
</asp:Content>
<asp:Content ID="PageTitleInTitleArea" ContentPlaceHolderID="PlaceHolderPageTitleInTitleArea"
    runat="server">
    My Plugin Page
</asp:Content>
```

This example demonstrates how you can use the sortable interaction. You have seen how being able to supply your own function for when an element has been changed provides a way to hook in to update any necessary SharePoint data that requires it.

```
$("#MySelector").sortable({
            update: function (event, ui) {
                // Do own updating code
            }
        });
```

Adding jQuery UI Widgets

Widgets are a very powerful component of jQuery UI. They offer an intuitive set of controls to make displaying and working with data a lot easier. The following are the widgets in the current version of jQuery UI:

- Accordion
- Autocomplete
- Button
- Datepicker
- Dialog
- Progressbar
- Slider
- Tabs

As with the interaction functions, you have a great level of granular control of these widgets to tailor them to fit your own requirements. One of their useful features is that they use the CSS styles that come with the jQuery UI download. So, they look very impressive out of the box, and if you require them to suit your own branding, you have a great template to start from.

Let's take a look at what these widgets can offer you and SharePoint.

Accordion

The accordion is a useful way to have data on a page and show more content only when required. In Chapter 5, you created a News application that retrieved data from a news list and showed that in an accordion-type manner. This time, we will look at the same functionality and see how using a plug-in can simplify the task. This example will also use the Client Object Model.

The accordion expects the elements on which it is applied to be in a specific syntax, as mentioned on the jQuery UI web site:

The markup of your accordion container needs pairs of headers and content panels:

```
<div id="accordion">
    <h3><a href="#">First header</a></h3>
    <div>First content</div>
    <h3><a href="#">Second header</a></h3>
    <div>Second content</div>
</div>
```

With this in mind, we'll get cracking on the updated News application.

1. Add a new application page called NewsAccordion.aspx to the Visual Studio project. Make sure you add it to the PluginPage folder, as shown in Figure 9-12.

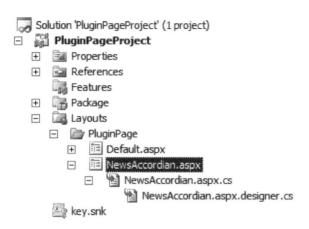

Figure 9-12. Adding a NewsAccordion application page

2. Open the NewsAccordion.aspx page and edit the PageHead section with the required basics: the CSS link and a document.ready function.

```
<asp:Content ID="PageHead" ContentPlaceHolderID="PlaceHolderAdditionalPageHead"↵
 runat="server">

    <!-- Register jQuery UI CSS -->
    <SharePoint:CssRegistration Name='<% $SPUrl:/_layouts/jQuery/css/smoothness/↵
jquery-ui-1.8.css%>' runat='server' />

    <script type="text/javascript">

        $(document).ready(function () {

        });

    </script>
</asp:Content>
```

3. Add a div into the Main content placeholder, which will be the container for the accordion. The div will need to have an ID so that it can be easily selected using a jQuery selector.

```
    <!-- News Story Accordion -->
    <div id="NewsAccordion" />
```

4. Add the following code to the PageHead section. The code is pretty much identical to what you used for getting the places in the previous example. The difference is that this time it is loading from the News list and retrieving just the Title and Body data.

```
<script type="text/javascript">

        $(document).ready(function () {
            ExecuteOrDelayUntilScriptLoaded(GetNews, "sp.js");
        });

        var newsItems;

        function GetNews() {
            try {

                // Get the context
                var context = new SP.ClientContext.get_current();

                // Load the web object
                this.web = context.get_web();

                // Get the 'News' list
                var list = this.web.get_lists().getByTitle('News');

                // Get all the items in the list
                newsItems = list.getItems('');

                // Load the web object in the context and retrieve only selected
columns
                context.load(this.newsItems, 'Include(Title, Body)');

                //Make a query call to execute the above statements
                context.executeQueryAsync(Function.createDelegate(this,↵
    this.GetNewsOnSuccess), Function.createDelegate(this, this.GetNewsOnFailure));
                }
            catch (e) {
                alert("An error occurred while fetching data.");
            }
        }

        function GetNewsOnSuccess() {
            // Get the collection
            var newsCollection = this.newsItems.getEnumerator();
```

```
                    // Iterate through news articles
                    while (newsCollection.moveNext()) {
                        // Get current item
                        var newsItem = newsCollection.get_current();

                        // Create new element HTML for section
                        var newsItemSectionHeaderHtml = '<h3><a>' + newsItem.get_↵
            item('Title') + '</a></h3>';
                        // Create new element
                        var newsItemSectionHeader = $(newsItemSectionHeaderHtml);

                        // Body comes wrapped in a Div so no
                        // need to add the tag
                        var newsItemBodyHtml = newsItem.get_item('Body');

                        // Create new element
                        var newsItemBody = $(newsItemBodyHtml);

                        // Add item to list
                        $('#NewsAccordion').append(newsItemSectionHeader);
                        $('#NewsAccordion').append(newsItemBody);
                    }
                }

                function GetNewsOnFailure() {
                    alert("An error occurred while fetching data.");
                }

        </script>
```

5. Deploy this solution now. You will see the news coming back in its "natural"
    form, as shown in Figure 9-13.

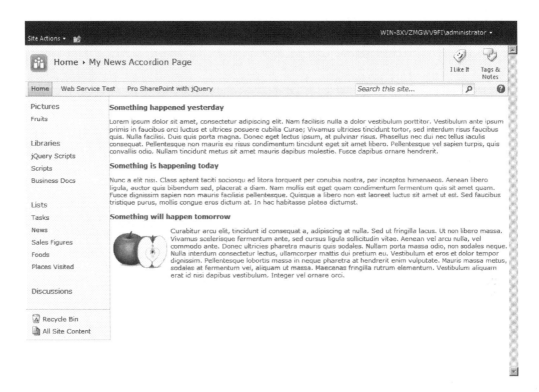

Figure 9-13. News articles without the accordion applied

6. To apply the accordion, you just need to add one line to the bottom of the GetNewsOnSuccess method. The entire GetNewsOnSuccess method should look like this:

```
function GetNewsOnSuccess() {
    // Get the collection
    var newsCollection = this.newsItems.getEnumerator();

    // Iterate through news articles
    while (newsCollection.moveNext()) {
        // Get current item
        var newsItem = newsCollection.get_current();

        // Create new element HTML for section
        var newsItemSectionHeaderHtml = '<h3><a>' + newsItem.get_↵
item('Title') + '</a></h3>';
        // Create new element
        var newsItemSectionHeader = $(newsItemSectionHeaderHtml);
```

```
                            // Body comes wrapped in a Div so no
                            // need to add the tag
                            var newsItemBodyHtml = newsItem.get_item('Body');

                            // Create new element
                            var newsItemBody = $(newsItemBodyHtml);

                            // Add item to list
                            $('#NewsAccordion').append(newsItemSectionHeader);
                            $('#NewsAccordion').append(newsItemBody);
                        }

                    $('#NewsAccordion').accordion();
                }
```

7. Deploy the solution to reveal the accordion in all its glory, as shown in Figure 9-14.

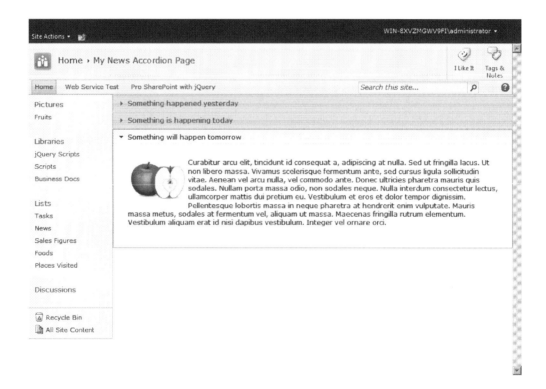

Figure 9-14. *News accordion in full swing*

You can also use configuration options to make the accordion behave exactly as you wish, but the default functionality is a great weapon to have in your arsenal.

Tabs

Tabs offer a similar functionality to accordions; however, they tend to work in a horizontal space, whereas the accordion is usually vertical. Figure 9-15 shows an example of a page with tabs.

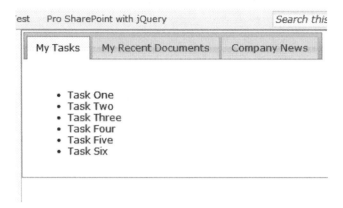

Figure 9-15. Tabs showing information

The code to make an easy-to-use tabbed interface is simple: just call `$('#tabs').tabs();`. The following is the complete code for the example shown in Figure 9-15. Make sure you put the code into the correct content placeholders.

```
<asp:Content ID="PageHead" ContentPlaceHolderID="PlaceHolderAdditionalPageHead" ↵
 runat="SharePoint">
    <SharePoint:CssRegistration ID="CssRegistration1" Name=●
'<% $SPUrl:/_layouts/jQuery/css/smoothness/jquery-ui-1.8.css%>'
        runat='server' />
    <script type="text/javascript">

        $(document).ready(function () {
            $('#tabs').tabs();
        });
    </script>
</asp:Content>
<asp:Content ID="Main" ContentPlaceHolderID="PlaceHolderMain" runat="server">
    <div id="tabs">
        <ul style="overflow: hidden">
            <li><a href="#tasksTab">My Tasks</a></li>
            <li><a href="#recentDocumentsTab">My Recent Documents</a></li>
            <li><a href="#companyNewsTab">Company News</a></li>
        </ul>
        <div id="tasksTab">
                <ul>
                    <li>Task One</li>
                    <li>Task Two</li>
```

```
                    <li>Task Three</li>
                    <li>Task Four</li>
                    <li>Task Five</li>
                    <li>Task Six</li>
                </ul>
        </div>
        <div id="recentDocumentsTab">
            <p>
                Recent Documents</p>
        </div>
        <div id="companyNewsTab">
            <p>
                Company News</p>
        </div>
    </div>
</asp:Content>
```

■ **Note**   The <ul style="overflow: hidden"> is a work-around for using the tabs. Otherwise, the code doesn't render correctly.

Autocomplete

Autocomplete functionality is everywhere now, and it is a real asset to have a plug-in that can make this task so much easier.

For an example, you'll add a few bits and pieces to the Places Visited example from the "Sortable" section earlier in the chapter. The code will populate the list of sources for the autocomplete box with the place names, and when a selection is made, it will highlight the item in the list—magic.

1. Open the Default.aspx page.

2. In the Main content placeholder, add an input with an ID of placeNames:

   ```
   <asp:Content ID="Main" ContentPlaceHolderID="PlaceHolderMain" runat="server">
       <input id="placeNames" />
       <ol id="MyVisitedPlaces" />
   </asp:Content>
   ```

   This is simply the text box in which users will enter their selection choice. It is all you need in terms of creating elements on the page for this example to work.

3. The next step is to create a global array that can hold the place names as they are returned from the Client Object Model call. Add a global variable declaration to create the array just before the GetPlaces function:

   ```
   var placeNames = new Array();
   ```

4. Populating this array with the place names is just a case of pushing the items onto the placeNames array as they are enumerated in the GetPlacesOnSuccess method. Once the place names have been added, then the autocomplete method can be called on the text box to give it superpowers (of sorts). The following is the completed GetPlacesOnSuccess method.

```
function GetPlacesOnSuccess() {
    // Get the collection
    var placeCollection = this.places.getEnumerator();

    // Iterate through places
    while (placeCollection.moveNext()) {
        // Get current item
        var place = placeCollection.get_current();

        // Create new element HTML
        var listItemHtml = '<li>' + place.get_item('Title') + '</li>';

        // Add place names to the array
        placeNames.push(place.get_item('Title'));

        // Create new element using HTML
        var listItem = $(listItemHtml);

        // Set the ID
        listItem.prop('id', "Place_" + place.get_item('ID'));

        // Add Order Visited data
        listItem.data('listId', place.get_item('ID'));

        // Add Item to list
        $('#MyVisitedPlaces').append(listItem);
    }

    $("#placeNames").autocomplete({
        source: placeNames,
        select: function (event, ui) {
            // Get the selected value
            var selectedValue = ui.item.value;

            // Remove highlight class from all elements
            $('#MyVisitedPlaces>li').removeClass('ms-rteStyle-Highlight');

            // Add highlight class for matching element
            $('#MyVisitedPlaces>li:contains(' + selectedValue +
')').addClass↵
('ms-rteStyle-Highlight');
        }
    });
}
```

The source option is using the array that you created and populated. The select is the event that is fired once the user has typed text in the text box and chosen an item. Using the ui.item.value property, you can get the selected value. Using a jQuery selector with the contains filter, you can find the matching element and apply the highlight class to it.

5. Deploy the solution to see it in action. In Figure 9-16, you can see the list of autocompletion items as text is entered. Figure 9-17 shows the selected item has been highlighted.

Figure 9-16. Selecting an item using autocomplete

Figure 9-17. Selected item highlighted

You can do a lot more with the autocomplete widget, such as using a remote data source to populate the drop-down list. This small example should give you an idea of what you can achieve. Another point worth noting is that you can apply the autocomplete functionality to an existing SharePoint element to enhance it.

Button, Datepicker, Progressbar, and Slider

The button, datepicker, progressbar, and slider widgets provide controls to enhance standard form elements to make them easier to use. You will probably find a use for them while creating your own solutions.

Create a new application page called Widgets.aspx, and make the following changes to the Head and Main sections to get an idea of what these four widgets bring to the table:

```
<asp:Content ID="PageHead" ContentPlaceHolderID="PlaceHolderAdditionalPageHead"↵
 runat="server">
    <SharePoint:CssRegistration ID="CssRegistration1" Name=↵
'<% $SPUrl:/_layouts/jQuery/css/smoothness/jquery-ui-1.8.css%>'
        runat='server' />
    <script type="text/javascript">
        $(document).ready(function () {
            $('#myButton').button();
            $('#myProgressbar').progressbar({
                value: 84
            });
            $('#mySlider').slider();
            $('#myDatePicker').datepicker();
        });
    </script>
</asp:Content>
<asp:Content ID="Main" ContentPlaceHolderID="PlaceHolderMain" runat="server">
    <div>
        <h3>
            Button</h3>
        <div>
            <a id="myButton">Anchor Button</a></div>
        <h3>
            Progress Bar</h3>
        <div>
            <div id="myProgressbar">
            </div>
        </div>
        <h3>
            Slider</h3>
        <div>
            <div id="mySlider">
            </div>
        </div>
        <h3>
            Date Picker</h3>
        <div>
            <input type="text" id="myDatePicker" /></div>
    </div>
</asp:Content>
```

This code will produce the page shown in Figure 9-18.

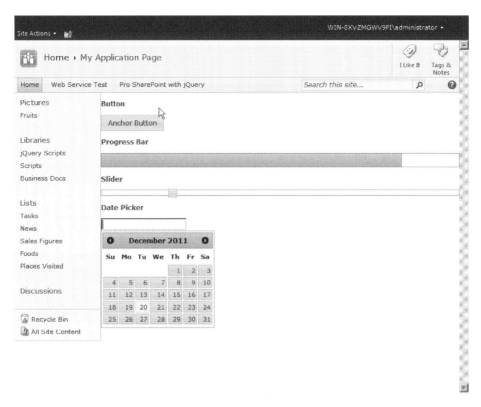

Figure 9-18. Displaying some of the useful jQuery UI widgets

Dialog

With the SharePoint 2010 modal dialog (http://msdn.microsoft.com/en-us/library/ff410058.aspx) being such a big part of SharePoint 2010, there is not much of a need to work with the jQuery UI dialog. However, if you are still working with SharePoint 2007, you can make great use of the dialogs to show users extra information without making them navigate away from the page.

With a simple dialog call, you can make your floating window appear, and all other elements on the page are blocked until it has been dismissed, as follows:

```
$("#dialog").dialog();
```

As with the other jQuery elements, the dialog can be configured to suit your needs.

Adding jQuery UI Effects

Effects are another area where you can enhance the user experience. For example, you might add menus that can be pulled in from one side to reveal a whole new set of options, or have a new item fading in from nowhere as it loads. Many of the third-party plug-ins use such effects to create a pleasant visual experience for the end user.

The following effects are currently available with jQuery UI:

- Blind
- Bounce
- Clip
- Drop
- Explode
- Fold
- Highlight
- Puff
- Pulsate
- Scale
- Shake
- Size
- Slide
- Transfer

To get a sample of some of these effects, create another application page called Effects.aspx and add the following into the Main content placeholder, replacing the existing code. This is just a bunch of divs that contain the effect that will be used as their ID and also serve as the element on which that effect will be applied.

```
<asp:Content ID="Main" ContentPlaceHolderID="PlaceHolderMain" runat="server">
    <div class="effectDiv" id="blind">
        Blind
    </div>
    <div class="effectDiv" id="bounce">
        Bounce
    </div>
    <div class="effectDiv" id="clip">
        Clip
    </div>
    <div class="effectDiv" id="drop">
        Drop
    </div>
    <div class="effectDiv" id="explode">
        Explode
    </div>
    <div class="effectDiv" id="fade">
        Fade
    </div>
```

```
    <div class="effectDiv" id="fold">
        Fold
    </div>
    <div class="effectDiv" id="highlight">
        Highlight
    </div>
    <div class="effectDiv" id="puff">
        Puff
    </div>
    <div class="effectDiv" id="pulsate">
        Pulsate
    </div>
    <div class="effectDiv" id="shake">
        Shake
    </div>
    <div class="effectDiv" id="slide">
        Slide
    </div>
</asp:Content>
```

Next, add this code into the PageHead section, making sure that you remove the previous code:

```
<asp:Content ID="PageHead" ContentPlaceHolderID="PlaceHolderAdditionalPageHead"↵
 runat="server">
    <!-- Register jQuery UI CSS -->
    <SharePoint:CssRegistration ID="CssRegistration1" Name=●
'<% $SPUrl:/_layouts/jQuery/css/smoothness/jquery-ui-1.8.css%>'
        runat='server' />
    <!-- Styling the Div -->
    <style type="text/css">
        .effectDiv
        {
            height: 50px;
            width: 50px;
            border: crimson 4px solid;
            margin: 10px;
            padding: 0.3em;
            position: relative;
        }
    </style>
    <script type="text/javascript">

        $(document).ready(function () {
            // Attach click event handler
            $('.effectDiv').click(function () {

                // Get the effect name from the id
                var currentEffect = $(this).prop('id');
```

```
            // Apply the effect for 500 ms
            $(this).effect(currentEffect, 500);
        });
    });

    </script>
</asp:Content>
```

Deploy this solution, and you will have something that looks like Figure 9-19 available on the page. Clicking a div will make it perform its effect. Some effects end up hiding the element; other effects perform an animation and return the element to its original state.

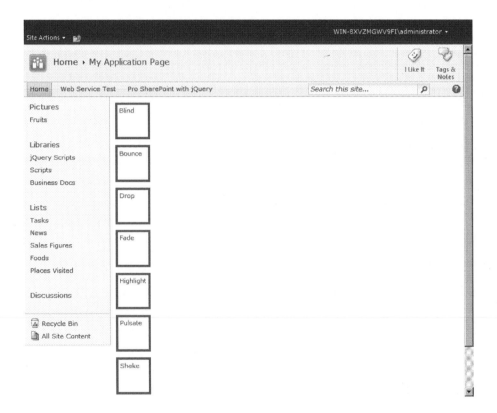

Figure 9-19. Divs with effects readied!

This concludes a semi-whistle-stop tour of the jQuery UI plug-in. I hope you agree it is a very powerful set of tools to have when tackling a browser-based application. With the jQuery and jQuery UI libraries, you can achieve a lot. Both are in constant development, so there are many exciting opportunities arising all the time.

■ **Note**   It is wise to keep checking on compatibility between the jQuery library and the UI library, just to make sure that updating one of them does not immediately wipe out all of your lovely hard work. And definitely make sure you test your project on your development and staging environments before moving it to production!

Next, we are going to look at some of the plug-ins made available by other companies and developers in the community.

Third-Party Plug-ins

Along with plug-ins designed just to make things look fancy, you can also find some fantastic utilities to make a developer's life magnitudes easier. Some are SharePoint-specific; others are general jQuery plug-ins that pack a punch. Here, we'll look at some useful third-party plug-ins you can use with SharePoint.

SPServices

One of the long-running and successful plug-ins designed specifically for SharePoint is SPServices (http://spservices.codeplex.com/). The SPServices home page describes the plug-in as follows:

This is a jQuery library which abstracts SharePoint's Web Services and makes them easier to use. It also includes functions which use the various Web Service operations to provide more useful (and cool) capabilities. It works entirely client side and requires no server install.

The really neat thing about this plug-in is that it works for both SharePoint 2007 and SharePoint 2010. The documentation is very complete and up-to-date (very important and generally common in the jQuery plug-in community), which is a lifesaver when you just want something to work, rather than needing to spend weeks trying to get it right.

The following is an example of SPServices in action. You can see information being pulled from an Announcements list and populating an unordered list.

```
<script type="text/javascript" src="filelink/jquery-1.6.1.min.js"></script>
<script type="text/javascript" src="filelink/jquery.SPServices-0.6.2.min.js"></script>
<script language="javascript" type="text/javascript">

$(document).ready(function() {
  $().SPServices({
    operation: "GetListItems",
    async: false,
    listName: "Announcements",
    CAMLViewFields: "<ViewFields><FieldRef Name='Title' /></ViewFields>",
```

```
    completefunc: function (xData, Status) {
      $(xData.responseXML).SPFilterNode("z:row").each(function() {
        var liHtml = "<li>" + $(this).attr("ows_Title") + "</li>";
        $("#tasksUL").append(liHtml);
      });
    }
  });
});
</script>
<ul id="tasksUL"/>
```

For more information about SPServices, you can check its CodePlex page or follow the project on twitter: @jQSPWS.

Content Slider

Many image carousel and slider plug-ins are available for jQuery. Each has its own take on how content should be presented. This is fantastic for developers, who can choose from a plethora of options. You can find plug-ins that support text only, images only, images and captions, videos, or even iframes, so there is a good chance that one will suit your requirements. And even if a plug-in isn't quite right, it probably exposes some options to enable you to turn it into the solution you need.

One content slider plug-in for jQuery is Awkward Showcase, available from http://www.awkwardgroup.com/sandbox/awkward-showcase-a-jquery-plugin/. As an example, you will use this plug-in to display the fruit images from the Fruits picture library created in Chapter 5 (or you can use another picture library). One of the useful features of this particular plug-in is that it has an easy way to display captions with an image. I have added an extra field to my library called Information, which will be used as the caption text.

Once you have downloaded and extracted the plug-in zip file, open the Visual Studio PluginPageProject project and add a new folder called Plugins underneath the PluginPage folder within the Layouts folder. Then copy the jquery.aw-showcase folder into the new folder, as shown in Figure 9-20.

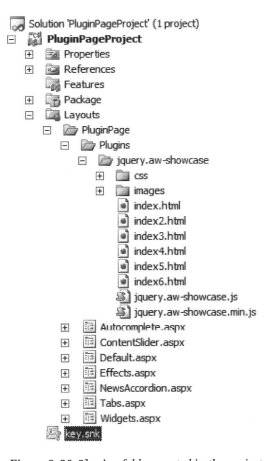

Figure 9-20. *Plugins folder created in the project*

The plug-in includes some files that you do not need for this example. Remove all but the `jquery.aw-showcase.min.js` files (don't delete the folders).

You need to make a slight change to the CSS style sheet to make sure it doesn't interfere with SharePoint's styling. Expand the `css` folder, remove all but the `style.css` file, and then open the `style.css` file. Remove the first section of the CSS all the way down to this comment (in my version, I deleted up to line 56):

```
/* Showcase
------------*/
```

The plug-in web site gives a good example of what the layout of the elements should look like in order for the plug-in to work correctly:

```
<!-- Container Div for the plugin -->
    <div id="showcase" class="showcase">
        <!-- Each child div in #showcase represents a slide -->
        <div class="showcase-slide">
            <!-- Put the slide content in a div with the class .showcase-content -->
            <div class="showcase-content">
                <!-- If the slide contains multiple elements you should wrap them in a↵
 div with the class
                .showcase-content-wrapper. We usually wrap even if there is only one element,
                because it looks better. -->
                <div class="showcase-content-wrapper">
                    <img src="" alt="" />
                </div>
            </div>
            <!-- Put the caption content in a div with the class .showcase-caption -->
            <div class="showcase-caption">
                The Caption
            </div>
        </div>
    </div>
```

This shows the structure. Now, how can this work if the slides are going to be generated automatically? A sensible way is to put the elements into a template, as demonstrated in the task viewer application in chapter 6.

Create a new application page called ContentSlider.aspx. In the Main content placeholder, add the following code:

```
<asp:Content ID="Main" ContentPlaceHolderID="PlaceHolderMain" runat="server">
    <!-- Content Slider Container -->
    <div id="showcase" class="showcase">
    </div>

    <!-- Content Slide Template -->
    <div id="slideTemplate" class="showcase-slide">
        <div class="showcase-content">
            <div class="showcase-content-wrapper">
                <img class='myImage' src="" alt="" />
            </div>
        </div>
        <div class="showcase-caption">
        </div>
    </div>
</asp:Content>
```

You will see that the outer div with the ID of showcase, which is the main container for the plug-in, has had its contents abstracted out to a template. An id has been added to the template of a slide, and a class has been added to the image to make it easier to select in a jQuery selector.

Just inside the PageHead section, add the following CSS and script tag to load the plug-in and its styling:

```
<link href="Plugins/jquery.aw-showcase/css/style.css" rel="stylesheet" type="text/css" />
<script src="Plugins/jquery.aw-showcase/jquery.aw-showcase.min.js"↩
 type="text/javascript"></script>
```

The first line hides the template from view, and the second line will call the GetFruits method once the sp.js script has finished loading.

The following shows the code that is required. Go ahead and use it to replace the whole PageHead section.

```
<asp:Content ID="PageHead" ContentPlaceHolderID="PlaceHolderAdditionalPageHead"↩
 runat="server">
    <link href="/_Layouts/PluginPage/Plugins/jquery.aw-showcase/css/style.css"
rel="stylesheet"↩
 type="text/css" />
    <script src="/_Layouts/PluginPage/Plugins/jquery.aw-showcase/jquery.aw-showcase.min.js"↩
 type="text/javascript"></script>
    <script type="text/javascript">

        $(document).ready(function () {
            $('#slideTemplate').hide();
            ExecuteOrDelayUntilScriptLoaded(GetFruits, "sp.js");
        });

        var fruits;

        function GetFruits() {
            try {

                // Get the context
                var context = new SP.ClientContext.get_current();

                // Load the web object
                this.web = context.get_web();

                //Get the 'Fruits' list
                var list = this.web.get_lists().getByTitle('Fruits');

                // Get all the items in the list
                fruits = list.getItems('');

                // Load the web object in the context and retrieve only selected columns
                context.load(this.fruits, 'Include(FileRef,Information)');

                //Make a query call to execute the above statements
                context.executeQueryAsync(Function.createDelegate(this,↩
 this.GetFruitsOnSuccess), Function.createDelegate(this, this.GetFruitsOnFailure));
            }
```

```
        catch (e) {
            alert("An error occurred while fetching data.");
        }
    }

    function GetFruitsOnSuccess() {
        // Get the collection
        var fruitCollection = this.fruits.getEnumerator();

        // Iterate through the fruits
        while (fruitCollection.moveNext()) {
            // Get current item
            var fruit = fruitCollection.get_current();

            // Clone the content slide template
            var newSlide = $('#slideTemplate').clone();

            // Remove the id
            $(newSlide).prop('id', null);

            // Set the image source to the fruit image FileRef
            $(newSlide).find('.myImage').prop('src', fruit.get_item('FileRef'));

            // Set the caption text
            $(newSlide).children('.showcase-caption').text(fruit.get_item('Information'));

            // Show the element as template is hidden
            $(newSlide).show();

            // Add the content slide to the content slider
            $('#showcase').append(newSlide);
        }

        // Call the plugin on the content slider
        $("#showcase").awShowcase({
            content_width: 700,
            content_height: 470
        });
    }

    function GetFruitsOnFailure() {
        alert("An error occurred while fetching data.");
    }

</script>
</asp:Content>
```

You've seen the majority of this code before, as it uses the Client Object Model to get data from a list. In this example, the Client Object Model code is querying the Fruits list and is getting the FileRef (the path to the image) and the Information field for each picture. For each fruit it finds in the list, it creates a new clone of the Content Slide template and populates the data. Once all of the items have been processed, the awShowcase method on the content slider div calls the method to turn this normal div into a content slider.

Deploy the solution and navigate to the page. You will see that the fruits and their information are loaded into the content slider. By clicking the arrows or pressing the arrow keys, you can cycle through the items. Lovely job! Figure 9-21 shows the content slider in action.

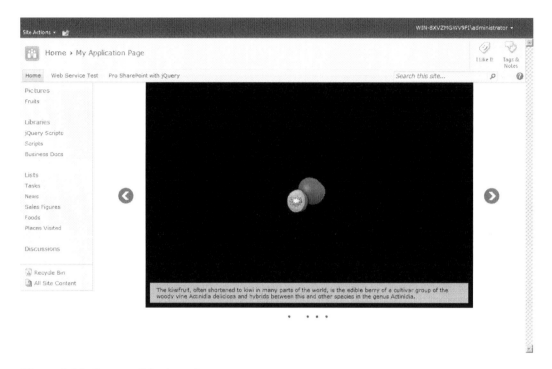

Figure 9-21. *Content slider in action*

This example uses an application page, but being able to create a web part with this level of interaction is very exciting when you consider the possibilities.

Lightbox

A lightbox is a neat way to be able to view an image from a thumbnail without needing to navigate away from the page. A lot of plug-ins offer a similar experience where, from a thumbnail or holding image, a click will open a dialog with the main content—whether this is a full-size image, a movie, or even an iframe. We'll take a look at using the jQuery lightBox plug-in, available from http://leandrovieira.com/projects/jquery/lightbox/.

Download the zip file and extract it to your SharePoint environment. Then, in the PluginPageProject project, add a new folder in the Plugins folder called Lightbox.

Copy the css, images, and js folders from the extracted jQuery lightBox plug-in into the Lightbox folder in the project. Then create a new application page called Lightbox.aspx.

This time, rather than using the Client Object Model to get the images, you will just put in the path manually. Add the following HTML to the Main content placeholder of the .aspx file (you may need to update the image values if your own names are different):

```
<asp:Content ID="Main" ContentPlaceHolderID="PlaceHolderMain" runat="server">
    <div id="FruitGallery">
        <div>
            <a href="/Fruits/apple_large.png">
                <img src="/Fruits/apple_small.png" width="72" height="72" alt="" /></a></div>
        <div>
            <a href="/Fruits/kiwi_large.png">
                <img src="/Fruits/kiwi_small.png" width="72" height="72" alt="" /></a></div>
        <div>
            <a href="/Fruits/lemon_large.png">
                <img src="/Fruits/lemon_small.png" width="72" height="72" alt="" /></a></div>
        <div>
            <a href="/Fruits/pear_large.png">
                <img src="/Fruits/pear_small.png" width="72" height="72" alt="" /></a></div>
        <div>
            <a href="/Fruits/watermelon_large.png">
                <img src="/Fruits/watermelon_small.png" width="72" height="72" alt=""●
 /></a></div>
    </div>
</asp:Content>
```

All you are doing here is creating a wrapper div called FruitGallery, and then adding the individual thumbnails, which the end user will click to open the lightbox.

In the PageHead section, add a reference to the CSS and the JavaScript file. You can also add the plug-in method to add the lightbox functionality to all of the anchor links, which are descendants of the FruitGallery div. The following is the completed code.

```
<%@ Assembly Name="$SharePoint.Project.AssemblyFullName$" %>
<%@ Assembly Name="Microsoft.Web.CommandUI, Version=14.0.0.0, Culture=neutral,↵
 PublicKeyToken=71e9bce111e9429c" %>

<%@ Page Language="C#" AutoEventWireup="true" CodeBehind="Lightbox.aspx.cs"↵
 Inherits="PluginPageProject.Layouts.PluginPage.Lightbox"
    DynamicMasterPageFile="~masterurl/default.master" %>

<asp:Content ID="PageHead" ContentPlaceHolderID="PlaceHolderAdditionalPageHead"↵
 runat="server">
    <link href="/_Layouts/PluginPage/Plugins/Lightbox/css/jquery.lightbox-0.5.css"
rel="stylesheet"↵
 type="text/css" />
    <script src="/_Layouts/PluginPage/Plugins/Lightbox/js/jquery.lightbox-0.5.min.js"↵
 type="text/javascript"></script>
    <script type="text/javascript">
        $(document).ready(function () {
```

```
                $('#FruitGallery a').lightBox(); // Select all links in object with↵
    FruitGallery ID

        });
    </script>
</asp:Content>
<asp:Content ID="Main" ContentPlaceHolderID="PlaceHolderMain" runat="server">
    <div id="FruitGallery">
        <div>
            <a href="/Fruits/apple_large.png">
                <img src="/Fruits/apple_small.png" width="72" height="72" alt="" /></a></div>
        <div>
            <a href="/Fruits/kiwi_large.png">
                <img src="/Fruits/kiwi_small.png" width="72" height="72" alt="" /></a></div>
        <div>
            <a href="/Fruits/lemon_large.png">
                <img src="/Fruits/lemon_small.png" width="72" height="72" alt="" /></a></div>
        <div>
            <a href="/Fruits/pear_large.png">
                <img src="/Fruits/pear_small.png" width="72" height="72" alt="" /></a></div>
        <div>
            <a href="/Fruits/watermelon_large.png">
                <img src="/Fruits/watermelon_small.png" width="72" height="72" alt=""↵
 /></a></div>
    </div>
</asp:Content>
<asp:Content ID="PageTitle" ContentPlaceHolderID="PlaceHolderPageTitle" runat="server">
    Fruit Lightbox Page
</asp:Content>
<asp:Content ID="PageTitleInTitleArea" ContentPlaceHolderID="PlaceHolderPageTitleInTitleArea"
    runat="server">
    My Fruit Lightbox Page
</asp:Content>
```

Deploy the solution, and then click one of the images. You will see the lightbox display with the large version, as shown in Figure 9-22. You can easily scroll through the other items, or close the dialog and return to the normal view.

Figure 9-22. Image being shown in a lightbox

Lightboxes are a great way to initially show users that there is something that may be of interest to them, such as a thumbnail, and allow them to click it to maximize the item and see the full content. The beauty of this is that you don't have a large element that pushes all other elements out of the way, which could be the case if it was just on the page.

jQuery Mobile

The jQuery mobile framework, available from http://jquerymobile.com/, is a fairly new offering to the scene. It offers a great possibility to create solutions that have SharePoint as the host but can run on most mobile devices. Here's how it's described on its home page:

> *jQuery mobile framework takes the "write less, do more" mantra to the next level: Instead of writing unique apps for each mobile device or OS, the jQuery mobile framework will allow you to design a single highly branded and customized web application that will work on all popular smartphone and tablet platforms.*

This offers a great alternative to the mobile view for your SharePoint solutions if you have a specific device-centric solution in mind.

Other Plug-in Types

You can choose from a wide range of plug-ins when developing your jQuery application or SharePoint enhancement. The following are some of the different types available:

- Form validation

- Tool tip

- Ajax helper

- Table sorter

- Layout

- Graphing

- Mapping

- Video player

- Animation

- Face recognition

Summary

This chapter introduced the incredibly powerful and flexible jQuery UI library, which is packed full of features to help streamline your application. We also looked at some of the third-party plug-ins available.

You'll find great community support for jQuery plug-ins. It seems that they're all in competition with each other to create the best and funkiest solution. If you think someone else has encountered the problem you're facing, then you can bet your bottom dollar there is a plug-in out there waiting for your attention.

The next chapter explores creating your own plug-in. If it's a good one (I am sure it will be), then maybe you can release it into the wild for others to enjoy, too!

CHAPTER 10

Extending jQuery

This chapter will give you the knowledge required to write plug-ins for jQuery. One of the really powerful features of jQuery is that you can add extra functionality easily using its plug-in framework. If you have some code that you are using frequently in your jQuery solutions, then it may be time to look at turning it into a plug-in and expose some options to allow it to suit a variety of scenarios. You are probably familiar with the Don't Repeat Yourself (DRY) coding practice, and plug-ins can help by making sure that repeatable code is put into a plug-in where it makes sense. The other thing to consider is that plug-ins can be used to do a huge range of really useful things. In fact, plug-ins can be used to do anything that jQuery can do, such as visual effects, utilities, DOM manipulation, and a whole lot more.

Writing plug-ins can be a tricky concept to learn, but in this chapter, you will learn how to create a working plug-in. Instead of just learning theory, you will be working through lots of hands-on examples to build your first plug-in.

Creating Your First Highlighter Plug-in

The first plug-in you will create will simply highlight elements that match the jQuery selector. This will be a nice introduction to writing plug-ins and a good way to learn the basics before moving onto some of the more complicated components. The plug-in file is a JavaScript file, but as you will see, there is some different coding needed to create the plug-in.

To develop this plug-in, we will use a Visual Studio solution that will deploy and activate the plug-in. You can use this method to deploy your own plug-ins or third-party plug-ins.

Follow these steps:

1. Open Visual Studio 2010 and use the Empty SharePoint Project template to create a project called MyjQueryPlugins. Select "Deploy as a farm solution." By deploying it as a farm solution, you are making it available across the farm, and there will be only one copy of the plug-in's JavaScript file.

2. Add a SharePoint Layouts mapped folder, as in Figure 10-1.x

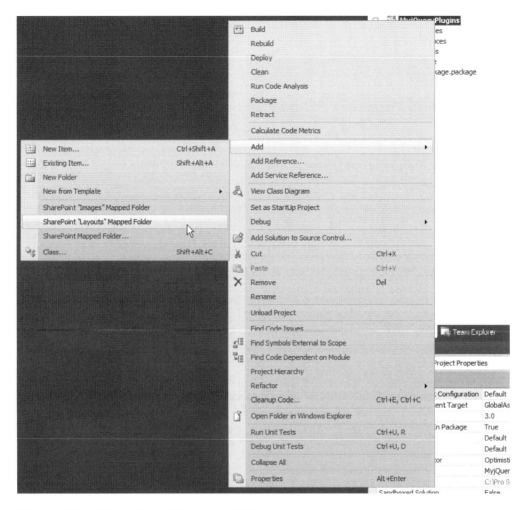

Figure 10-1. Adding a SharePoint mapped folder

3. Add a new Jscript file from the Web category, and name it `MyHighlighter.js`. As you might guess, this file will contain the plug-in code. Before we get started writing the code, we will add the element that will make this plug-in available.

4. Add a new `EmptyElement` to the project called `MyjQueryPluginsElement` and then add a custom action that will load the script:

```xml
<?xml version="1.0" encoding="utf-8"?>
<Elements xmlns="http://schemas.microsoft.com/sharepoint/">
  <CustomAction ScriptSrc="/_layouts/MyjQueryPlugins/MyHighlighter.js"
          Location="ScriptLink"
          Sequence="100">
  </CustomAction>
</Elements>
```

5. With the deployment and activation done, it is time to check that it works.
    Open the `MyHighlighter.js` file and add the following code that will let you
    know that it works:

```javascript
$(document).ready(function () {
    alert("Hello My Plug-in");
});
```

6. Deploy by pressing F5; Visual Studio will open the browser for you, read the
    alert, do a little dance, and close the browser. With the simple stuff working, it
    is time to look at the first parts of a jQuery plug-in. Delete all the contents of
    the JavaScript file.

7. There are a couple of issues to be concerned with right off the bat when writing
    a plug-in, but there are some recommended best practices to deal with them. I
    will show the two alternatives and explain why we won't be using them. The
    first is as follows:

```javascript
jQuery.fn.myHighlighter = function() {

  // Plugin goodness

};
```

And the second is as follows:

```javascript
(function($) {
  $.fn.myHighlighter = function() {

      // Plugin goodness

  };
})(jQuery);
```

Let's break the first example down: `jQuery.fn` is a shortcut for `jQuery.prototype`, and every jQuery
object will inherit the prototype methods. A prototype property, which we have here, allows you to add
other properties and methods to an object; basically, it gives you the ability to add your own custom
plug-in methods to jQuery. The part after that, `jQuery.fn.myHighlighter`, is the plug-in name and will be
the name used when calling the plug-in, in other words, `$('.important').myHighlighter();`. It is
important to name your plug-in appropriately so that it is unlikely to clash with another plug-in; it is also
highly recommended that you use only one namespace per plug-in. An example of how *not* to do it is
shown next. The reason cited by the jQuery web site is that it clutters up the `jQuery.fn` namespace;
however, it can also increase the chances of naming a function the same as another plug-in.

```
jQuery.fn.myHighlighterOn = function() {

  // Turn on Highlighing (BAD EXAMPLE)

};

jQuery.fn.myHighlighterOff = function() {

  // Turn off Highlighing (BAD EXAMPLE)

};
```

The right way to do it is to have just one namespace that will perform the different actions depending on values passed in to the method:

```
jQuery.fn.myHighlighter = function(method) {

  // Read from paramter to turn on or off highlighting (GOOD EXAMPLE)

};
```

Now that you have seen the prototype and the plug-in name, you should see that what is left is the assignment of the function that runs when the plug-in is called. Those are the very basics of creating a plug-in. Earlier, I said there were several different ways to write this. We have this:

```
jQuery.fn.myHighlighter = function() {

  // Plugin goodness

};
```

This is using the named jQuery object; some people use $ because they're used to it from coding with jQuery:

```
$.fn.myHighlighter = function() {

  // Plug-in goodness

};
```

This, however, could cause issues if $ has been commandeered by other JavaScript code to no longer refer to jQuery. So, it is not recommended. If you do want to use $ instead of writing jQuery each time, you can put it in a self-executing function or closure, which will ensure that $ can be used and, unless you change it, that $ will refer to jQuery. To write the plug-in outline in the best-practice form, you can write it like this:

```
(function($) {
  $.fn.myHighlighter = function() {

    // Plug-in goodness

  };
})(jQuery);
```

So, that's some of the theory. We will add a very simple alert now to see whether the plug-in is doing its job.

1. In the JavaScript file, add this code:

    ```
    (function ($) {
        $.fn.myHighlighter = function () {
            alert("I am the My Highlighter plug-in");
        };
    })(jQuery);
    ```

    We are using another alert to make sure that the plug-in is working as a plug-in before we test to see whether jQuery loaded. Deploy the solution, but don't expect to see the alert just yet; it won't show up, because nothing is calling this plug-in.

2. With the plug-in deployed, add a Content Editor web part to the page and enter HTML Source mode. In the HTML Source window, add a `script` tag, with an empty jQuery selector with a call to the plug-in:

    ```
    <script type="text/javascript">
    $().myHighlighter();
    </script>
    ```

3. Save the contents and refresh the page. If the alert doesn't show straightaway, you will be presented with the alert shown in Figure 10-2.

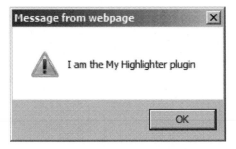

Figure 10-1. Alert showing plug-in loaded

4. It's working because the plug-in is being called; however, for a plug-in called My Highlighter, it is doing a very poor job. Open the JavaScript file again. Remove the alert so we have a clean plug-in.

5. Next we will look at how we can work with the elements that are having the plug-in called on them:

    ```
    $(.important).myHighlighter()
    ```

We want to run the plug-in against each element with the important class. This can be done using the this keyword in the plug-in code. You saw this being used earlier in the book. For instance, when working with a click event, you can use $(this) to get the element that was clicked. When working with the this keyword in your plug-in, there is no need to wrap it like $(this) because it will already be a jQuery object and you will just be wrapping it unnecessarily. It is also recommended you use the each function to iterate through all elements that have been returned by the selector. With some CSS styling being applied to each important element, the plug-in's code will look like this:

```
(function ($) {
    $.fn.myHighlighter = function () {

        // 'this' does not need to be wrapped here
        this.each(function () {

            // 'this' now refers to the element and needs
            // to be wrapped as a jQuery object
            var $this = $(this);

            // Add some highlighting css
            $this.css('border', 'solid 1px red');
            $this.css('color', 'red');
            $this.css('padding', '0.3em');
        });
    };
})(jQuery);
```

You can see that the this in this.each is not wrapped; however, because the elements are being iterated, each element will need to be wrapped in order to use the jQuery methods. The styling will add a border, turn the text red, and add some padding...just so you'll know it's important!

6. Deploy the solution again; you will need to edit the HTML source of the Content Editor web part so that it contains some elements that can be marked as important. The script in the web part will also need to have the selector entered so that it selects the elements. Update the contents with the following:

```
<script type="text/javascript">
    $(document).ready(function()
    {
        $(.important).myHighlighter();
    });
</script>
<div>
    <h3>Shopping List</h3>
    <ul>
        <li class="important">Milk</li>
        <li>Newspaper</li>
        <li>Chocolate</li>
        <li class="important">Dog Food</li>
        <li>Lottery Ticket</li>
    </ul>
```

```
<h3>Reminders</h3>

<p>Pick up dry cleaning</p>
<p class="important">Pay in cheque</p>
</div>
```

In the `script` tag, you will see that the `class` selector is used to select all of the elements with the `important` class. The call to the plug-in is inside `document.ready` because we need to ensure the HTML elements have been rendered. The rest of the code is just the HTML rendering an unordered list and a couple of paragraphs. Only a couple of the elements have the class on them, so only those will have the highlighting applied. With all of the changes made, save and refresh the page. If you're impatient, you've probably already done this; it will look like Figure 10-3.

Content Editor ▾

Shopping List

- Milk
- Newspaper
- Chocolate
- Dog Food
- Lottery Ticket

Reminders

Pick up dry cleaning

Pay in cheque

Figure 10-2. *The elements are highlighted.*

This is working well so far, but let's try chaining a click method to our plug-in.

7. Open the HTML Source code view and update the plug-in call with the following code, which should show an alert when an item is clicked:

```
$(document).ready(function () {
    $('.important').myHighlighter().click(function () {
        // Get the current items text
        var text = $(this).text();
        // Show an alert for the text
        alert(text);
    });
});
```

Here the click event is being chained so that it should be being applied to each element from the query after it has passed through the My Highlighter plug-in. One of the great features of jQuery is the ability to chain methods, so with this change made, it is time to see whether you can click the important tasks to see their text in an alert.

8. Clicking an important element will not show anything because there is a problem. If you turn on the debugger, you will see that an error that occurs, as in Figure 10-4.

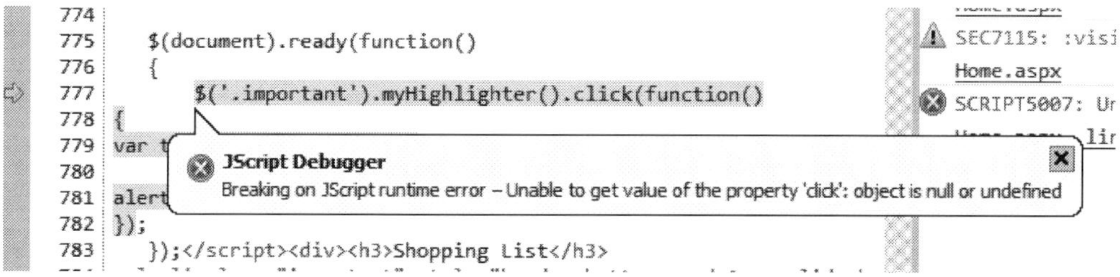

Figure 10-3. Error chaining methods after custom plug-in

The debugger is complaining that click is null or undefined. Why is that? It is because the plug-in that we have written so far is like a void method: it doesn't return anything. This means that click is being called on a null object; we want it to work on the same jQuery-wrapped elements as were passed into the My Highlighter plug-in. This is easily remedied.

9. Open the MyHighlighter.js JavaScript file and add a return in front of this.each. The whole method will look like this:

```
(function ($) {
    $.fn.myHighlighter = function () {

        // 'this' does not need to be wrapped here
        // return collection after
        return this.each(function () {

            // 'this' now refers to the element and needs
            // to be wrapped as a jQuery object
            var $this = $(this);

            // Add some highlighting css
            $this.css('border', 'solid 1px red');
            $this.css('color', 'red');
            $this.css('padding', '0.3em');
        });
    };
})(jQuery);
```

This code is simple to explain; we want to return the same objects that were passed in. We are doing some manipulation of those elements as part of the plug-in code, but because we are returning the jQuery objects, another method can chain on after the plug-in. If you wanted, your plug-in could just return a subset or even more jQuery objects. Deploy and see whether you can now click an important element. Figure 10-5 shows the alert in action.

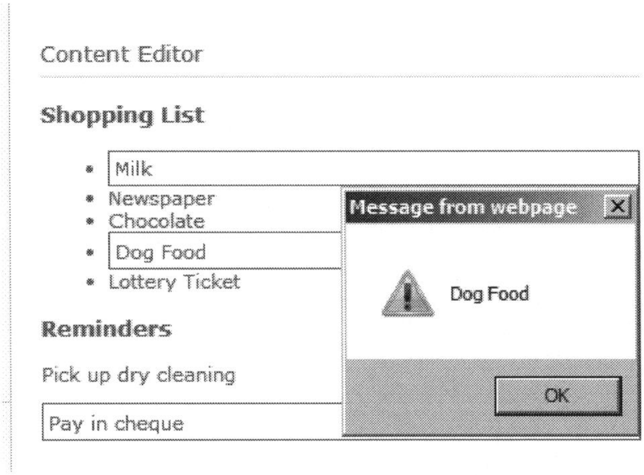

Figure 10-4. *Returning the jQuery object allows the click to work.*

With the alerts showing, that concludes the introduction to creating simple jQuery plug-ins.

Now that you have written a basic plug-in, you can look at adding some parameters to allow a consumer of the plug-in to tailor it to suit their requirements.

Creating a More Complex Plug-in with Parameters

Allowing consumers to customize a plug-in is a great way to allow the plug-in to be reused in many situations without rewriting it. We will look at a slightly more complex plug-in this time. The next plug-in will provide the graphing-type functionality used to show sales figures in Chapter 8. Previously with the jQuery function, we had the following code:

```
function GraphItems() {

    // Retrieve the Table Cells in the 4th column (Units Sold)
    var listItems = $(.ms-listviewtable>tbody>tr.ms-itmhover>td:nth-child(4));

    var count = listItems.length;
    var total = 0;
    var numbers = [];
```

```
    // Iterate through each unit sold value
    listItems.each(function (index) {
        if ($(this).text() != "") {
            number = parseInt($(this).text())
            numbers.push(number)
        }
    });

    // Get the most popular product unit count using
    // JavaScript method on the numbers array
    var largest = Math.max.apply(Math, numbers);

    // Iterate through each Table Cell for item
    listItems.each(function (index) {

        // Create a new empty div
        var div = $('<div/>');

        // get the number of the table cell
        number = parseInt($(this).text())

        // Work out the average compared to largest
        // number of units sold
        var average = parseInt(number / largest * 100);

        // Set CSS properties on the new div
        div.css('font-weight', 'bolder');
        div.css('color', 'white');

        // Set width to average % to give
        // div a graph look
        div.css('width', average + '%');

        // Switch to set color based on
        // Comparison to the average
        switch (true) {
            case (average >= 75):
                div.css('background-color', 'green');
                break;
            case (average >= 25):
                div.css('background-color', 'orange');
                break;
            default: div.css('background-color', 'red');
                break;
        }

        // Wrap the existing contents of the td
        // with the new formatted div
        $(this).wrapInner(div);
    });
```

We can change this code in a few places to make sure that we can run this plug-in against other lists to show this same graphing. The options we will expose to allow the end user to configure the plug-in are as follows:

- Font color

- Above-average, average, and below-average graph bar colors

Previously in the code, the fourth column was used to find the elements that contained the values to graph. In this plug-in, we will need the consumer to supply the column using a jQuery selector; we will use that to find the values to graph. The colors will be a simple visual way to see that the plug-in is working. Follow these steps:

1. Open the MyjQueryPlugin Visual Studio solution and add a new JavaScript file to the MyjQueryPlugins folder in the Layouts mapped folder. Call the new file MyGrapher.js, as in Figure 10-6.

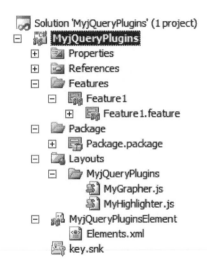

Figure 10-5. Adding a MyGrapher JavaScript file

2. In these steps, we take a look at the code we will be using and at the end of the exercise you will see the full code to use. We will be using the recommended outline for the plug-in, as you saw at the start of this chapter:

```
(function ($) {
    $.fn.myGrapher = function () {

    };
})(jQuery);
```

3. This time, however, we are getting options from the user, so we will need to be adding an options parameter to the function method:

```
$.fn.myGrapher = function (options)
```

4. The next thing we will be adding to the plug-in is the default options to use if the consumer wants to use the plug-in without supplying their own details. Here is the code that will set the default values for each parameter we want to allow the consumer to edit:

```
(function ($) {
    $.fn.myGrapher = function (options) {
        options = $.extend({}, $.fn.watermark.defaultOptions, options);
    };

    // Extend myGrapher with default options
    $.fn.myGrapher.defaultOptions = {
        belowAverageColor: red,
        averageColor: orange,
        aboveAverageColor: green,
        fontColor: white
    };
})(jQuery);
```

The `$.extend({}, $.fn.watermark.defaultOptions, options);` code will merge the contents of the default options and those supplied by the consumer.

We are using a separate property on the myGrapher plug-in function called `defaultOptions` to store the default values. By exposing the properties like this, a consumer could write code like the following to override the value that we have set:

`$.fn.myGrapher.defaultOptions = "black";`

They can also use the default behavior of setting the value, as you will see shortly.

With the options being merged into a variable called `options`, it will allow us to get the values by just calling the property. For example, to get the font color, you can use `options.fontColor`.

5. To make sure that the consumer of the plug-in provides a column that should be used to create the graph, we could add an option; however, the value is not optional, so the thing to do is to add another parameter to the plug-in that takes the column name as follows:

`$.fn.myGrapher = function (`**`columnName,`**` options)`

6. Next we need to find a way to get the column we want using a jQuery selector and the column name that the consumer will be providing. If you use an element selector like the one provided by Internet Explorer Developer Tools, you can find that near the column name in the SharePoint list is a `div` where the display name is stored in an attribute. You can see it in Figure 10-7.

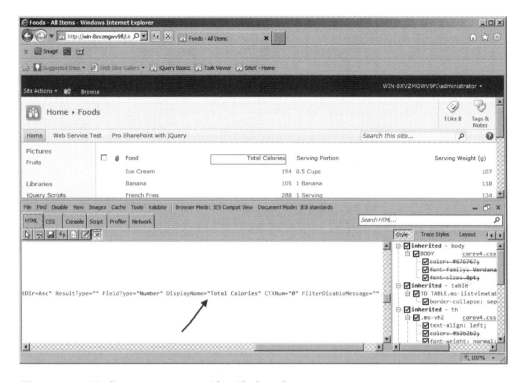

Figure 10-6. Finding an easy way to identify the column

This is good news because it means we can use the attribute selector to help find this column. In our code, we will just be using this to find the column index.

7. This code will get the column index we want; it is finding a div with a DisplayName attribute that matches the one provided as the plug-in's first parameter.

```
var columnIndex = this.find(div[DisplayName=" + columnName + ").parent().index();
```

Remember that this refers to the element that is being used with the plug-in. Looking at the HTML of the SharePoint list, you can see that the div that we are selecting in this query has a parent of a TH. This is great because we can use .parent().index() to get the selected column's position.

8. There is another adaption from the previous code: now we can provide the name of the column required to allow us to get the table cell elements that contain the numbers we want to process as well as add our graph bars to. Here we are adding 1 to the index returned from the last query to make sure it is correct for when using the nth-child filter, which is 1-based rather than 0-based:

239

```
// Change from zero based index to 1
// for use with nth-child
var columnNumber = columnIndex + 1;

// Get all of the Table Cells in the requested column by index
var listItems = this.find(tr.ms-itmhover>td:nth-child( + columnNumber + ));
```

9. The final changes made are to use the configuration options provided by the consumer or the default values for the properties that we exposed as being configurable. Setting the color to white for the div is an example of how the code can be updated:

```
div.css('color', 'white');
```

This can now be changed to the following:

```
div.css('color', options.fontColor);
```

The other location where you will need to update the color is in the switch statement where the code is checking its value to see whether it is above, under, or in the same range as the average.

10. This simple change will mean that the correct values are picked up. These are the only changes we need to make. The entire code for the plug-in is as follows:

```
(function ($) {
    $.fn.myGrapher = function (columnName, options) {

        // Merge user entered options with default options
        options = $.extend({}, $.fn.myGrapher.defaultOptions, options);

        // Get the column based onthe fact the SharePoint stores the name in a
Display Name
        // Attribute. Use Parent Index to get the column number
        var columnIndex = this.find('div[DisplayName="' + columnName +
'"').parent()↵
.index();

        // Change from zero based index to 1
        // for use with nth-child
        var columnNumber = columnIndex + 1;

        // Get all of the Table Cells in the requested column by index
        var listItems = this.find('tr.ms-itmhover>td:nth-child(' + columnNumber +
')');

        // Array to help work out the average value
        var numbers = [];

        // Iterate through each unit sold value
        listItems.each(function () {
            if ($(this).text() != "") {
                var number = parseInt($(this).text());
                numbers.push(number);
```

```
    }
});

    // Get the most popular product unit count using
    // JavaScript method on the numbers array
    var largest = Math.max.apply(Math, numbers);

    // Iterate through each Table Cell for item
    listItems.each(function () {

        // Create a new empty div
        var div = $('<div/>');

        // get the number of the table cell
        var number = parseInt($(this).text());

        // Work out the average compared to largest
        // number of units sold
        var average = parseInt(number / largest * 100);

        // Set CSS properties on the new div
        div.css('font-weight', 'bolder');
        div.css('color', options.fontColor);

        // Set width to average % to give
        // div a graph look
        div.css('width', average + '%');

        // Switch to set color based on
        // Comparison to the average
        switch (true) {
            case (average >= 75):
                div.css('background-color', options.aboveAverageColor);
                break;
            case (average >= 25):
                div.css('background-color', options.averageColor);
                break;
            default: div.css('background-color', options.belowAverageColor);
                break;
        }

        // Wrap the existing contents of the td
        // with the new formatted div
        $(this).wrapInner(div);
    });

};

// Extend myGrapher with default options
$.fn.myGrapher.defaultOptions = {
    belowAverageColor: 'red',
    averageColor: 'orange',
```

```
        aboveAverageColor: 'green',
        fontColor: 'white'
    };
})(jQuery);
```

11. Deploy and navigate to a list where you have a column of values. I am using a food list (Figure 10-8) that is similar, but not identical, to the one we used in Chapter 8, and the column I am working with is the Total Calories field.

Figure 10-7. *Food list with a Total Calories column that can be graphed*

12. Add a new Content Editor web part and add the following code. The first part is a `script` tag to reference to the plug-in's JavaScript file; the second part is the code you use to call the plug-in.

```
<script src="/_Layouts/MyjQueryPlugins/MyGrapher.js"
type="text/javascript"></script>

<script type="text/javascript">

$(document).ready(function () {
    $('.ms-listviewtable').myGrapher('Total Calories');
});

</script>
```

13. Save the contents and refresh the page. The Total Calories data should display in graphical form, just like Figure 10-9.

Food	Total Calories	Serving Portion
Ice Cream	194	0.5 Cups
Banana	105	1 Banana
French Fries	288	1 Serving
Eclair	233	1 Eclair
Pizza	384	1 Serving
Burger	421	1 Hamburger
Doughnut	224	1 Doughnut
Caesar Salad	228	1 Salad
Pie	339	1 Serving
Cake	277	1 Serving

Figure 10-8. The calorie data is being graphed.

When you run the example yourself, you may notice that the default coloring of the bar chart is that items with low values are in red, and the green items are the ones with the highest value. If only there were some options that we could set in the plug-in to change the aboveAverageColor and the belowAverageColor...

14. To sort out the colors, enter the Edit HTML Source mode of the Content Editor and add some options; you don't need to specify a value for each option, because if it is not supplied, then the default value will be used. This is how you should update the code:

```
<script src="/_Layouts/MyjQueryPlugins/MyGrapher.js"
type="text/javascript"></script>
<script type="text/javascript">
    $(document).ready(function () {
        $('.ms-listviewtable').myGrapher('Total Calories',
        {
            aboveAverageColor: "red",
            belowAverageColor: "green"
        });
    });
</script>
```

15. Save and refresh the page; on your screen you will see that the colors are more suitable now (Figure 10-10).

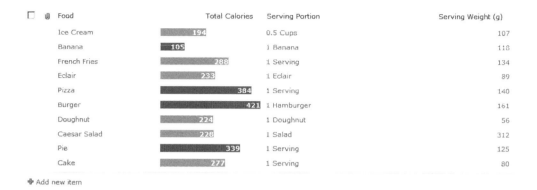

		Food	Total Calories	Serving Portion	Serving Weight (g)
		Ice Cream	194	0.5 Cups	107
		Banana	105	1 Banana	118
		French Fries	388	1 Serving	134
		Eclair	293	1 Eclair	89
		Pizza	384	1 Serving	140
		Burger	421	1 Hamburger	161
		Doughnut	224	1 Doughnut	56
		Caesar Salad	228	1 Salad	312
		Pie	339	1 Serving	125
		Cake	277	1 Serving	80

✦ Add new item

Figure 10-9. Using options, we have updated the colors.

That's your second plug-in complete—a plug-in that allows the consumer to configure the options. Now that we have looked at how to create a plug-in that typically works with elements, we will look at how to create jQuery functions. You can use functions with the jQuery object to perform specific actions such as validation, data retrieval, and so on. A function does not allow you to chain methods like you can with a plug-in.

Creating a jQuery Function

The signature of a jQuery function is slightly different from when you created a plug-in; the outline looks like the following this time:

```
(function($){

    // Extends the jQuery object to peform function
    $.doSomething = function()
    {
        // code here
    };

})(jQuery);
```

This function can be used by calling this:

```
$.doSomething()
```

Writing the Latest List Function

We'll look at an example that will simplify getting the most recent items from a SharePoint list. This example will also show you how to handle callbacks from your plug-in code.

1. Open the Visual Studio MyjQueryPlugins solution and add a new JavaScript file to the MyjQueryPlugins folder. Call this new file MyLatestListData.js.

2. We'll look at the whole code initially and then break it down into its different components:

```
(function ($) {

    $.latestListData = function (listName, options) {

        // Merge user entered options with default options
        this.userOptions = $.extend({}, $.latestListData.defaultOptions, options);

        // Get the current context
        this.context = new SP.ClientContext.get_current();

        // Load the web object
        this.web = this.context.get_web();

        // Get the list
        this.list = this.web.get_lists().getByTitle(listName);

        // Get the latest created items but limit to user provided
        // row count
        var query = '<View>' +
                    '<RowLimit>' + this.userOptions.rowCount + '</RowLimit>' +
                    '<Query>' +
                        '<OrderBy>' +
                            '<FieldRef Name="Created" Ascending="False" />' +
                        '</OrderBy>' +
                    '</Query>' +
                    '</View>';

        // Build Caml Query
        var camlQuery = new SP.CamlQuery();
        camlQuery.set_viewXml(query);

        // Get all the items in the list matching query
        this.listItems = this.list.getItems(camlQuery);

        // Load items but only get columns supplied by user
        this.context.load(this.listItems, 'Include(' + this.userOptions.↵
fieldNames.join(',') + ')');

        var success = Function.createDelegate(this, getLoadListItemsSuccess);
        var failure = Function.createDelegate(this, this.userOptions.onError);

        //Make a query call to execute the above statements
        // On success go to private method, otherwise call passed in function
        this.context.executeQueryAsync(success, failure);
    };

    // Callback from Client Object Model
    function getLoadListItemsSuccess() {
        var base = this;
```

```javascript
            // Variable for list data
            var data = [];

            // Get the collection
            var itemCollection = this.listItems.getEnumerator();

            // Iterate through items
            while (itemCollection.moveNext()) {

                // Load the current item in iteration
                var item = itemCollection.get_current();

                // Create new object to hold item information
                var newItem = {};

                // Iterate through each user defined field
                $(base.userOptions.fieldNames).each(function () {
                    // Set property of item based on list item
                    newItem[this] = item.get_item(this);
                });

                // Add Item to the data array
                data.push(newItem);

            }

        // Call the users function passing in retrieved data
        base.userOptions.onSuccess.call(this, data);
    }

// Create Default Success Method
$.latestListData.onGetItemsSuccess = function (data) {
    var base = this;

    var listInformation = "";

    // Iterate through each item to build a list
    // of items in the SharePoint List
    $(data).each(function () {

        var item = this;

        // Iterate through each user defined field
        $(base.userOptions.fieldNames).each(function () {
            // Set property of item based on list item
            listInformation += this + ": " + item[this] + "\n";
        });
        listInformation += "\n";
    });
```

```
            alert(listInformation);
        };

        // Error handler
        $.latestListData.onGetItemsFailed = function (sender, args) {
            alert('Request failed. ' + args.get_message() + '\n' +
    args.get_stackTrace());
        };

        // Define default values for the plugin
        $.latestListData.defaultOptions = {
            rowCount: 3,
            fieldNames: ['Title'],
            onSuccess: $.latestListData.onGetItemsSuccess,
            onError: $.latestListData.onGetItemsFailed
        };

    })(jQuery);
```

The first function is getting the settings provided by the user and merging them with the default settings, just like with the plug-in code.

Next we are using the Client Object Model to obtain the SharePoint list, based on the user's supplied list name, and then building a query to retrieve the data. The user can optionally supply how many list items to return and also which fields to return; the defaults are three and the Title column, respectively.

Previously, when we used similar code to get data from SharePoint, the executeQueryAsyc method called either a success or fail function in the same code to handle either event. This time, if the list item retrieval is successful, then we are going to call our own function to do some further processing. If the call fails, then it will either call the user-supplied error-handling function or use the default function provided. This is the code that is handling what to do here:

```
var success = Function.createDelegate(this, getLoadListItemsSuccess);
var failure = Function.createDelegate(this, this.userOptions.onError);

//Make a query call to execute the above statements
// On success go to private method, otherwise call passed in function
this.context.executeQueryAsync(success, failure);
```

3. The getLoadListItemsSuccess method takes some of the legwork out of the calling code by processing the list items and putting them into objects. For example, if we had requested to get the Title and Name fields from a list, then in our code we can use it like item.Title or item.Name to retrieve the value. It still uses the same Client Object Model method of extracting the list data in the function's code, but the user doesn't need to worry about this. The following is the code that does this bit of magic; you'll notice that for each list item, it then iterates through each field, which the user has specified to return to build the object and properties:

```
// Callback from Client Object Model
function getLoadListItemsSuccess() {
    var base = this;

    // Variable for list data
    var data = [];

    // Get the collection
    var itemCollection = this.listItems.getEnumerator();

    // Iterate through items
    while (itemCollection.moveNext()) {

        // Load the current item in iteration
        var item = itemCollection.get_current();

        // Create new object to hold item information
        var newItem = {};

        // Iterate through each user defined field
        $(base.userOptions.fieldNames).each(function () {
            // Set property of item based on list item
            newItem[this] = item.get_item(this);
        });

        // Add Item to the data array
        data.push(newItem);

    }

    // Call the users function passing in retrieved data
    base.userOptions.onSuccess.call(this, data);
}
```

As mentioned, this means that this wrapping makes it easy to work with the data. This is how it can be handled, nice and simple:

```
$(data).each(function () {
    var title = $('<h3>' + this.Title + '</h3>');
    $('#myTopItems').append(title);
});
```

4. The next two parts of the code are the default functions for handling either the success or the failure of the "get list items" call. If a user chooses not to supply any options, then they will be presented with the items' details in an alert. If they want to show them in their own way, then they would need to provide their own success handling function. The code is fairly straightforward:

```
// Create Default Success Method
$.latestListData.onGetItemsSuccess = function (data) {
    var base = this;

    var listInformation = "";

    // Iterate through each item to build a list
    // of items in the SharePoint List
    $(data).each(function () {

        var item = this;

        // Iterate through each user defined field
        $(base.userOptions.fieldNames).each(function () {
            // Set property of item based on list item
            listInformation += this + ": " + item[this] + "\n";
        });
        listInformation += "\n";
    });

    alert(listInformation);
};

// Error handler
$.latestListData.onGetItemsFailed = function (sender, args) {
    alert('Request failed. ' + args.get_message() + '\n' + args.get_stackTrace());
};
```

5. At the bottom of the code there are the default options that we have seen before. If the default options are before where the success- or fail-handling functions are, then the default values for onSuccess and onError will be undefined, because this file is processed sequentially, and therefore those functions would not have been instantiated before setting the default values. The field name option is using an array to work with the field name values:

```
// Define default values for the plug-in
$.latestListData.defaultOptions = {
    rowCount: 3,
    fieldNames: ['Title'],
    onSuccess: $.latestListData.onGetItemsSuccess,
    onError: $.latestListData.onGetItemsFailed
};
```

6. Deploy the solution and add a Content Editor web part to a page and prime yourself by opening the HTML source pane.

7. Enter the following code, which will reference the plug-in and also ensure that SP.js has loaded before calling the function because it makes use of the Client Object Model, which needs the SP.js library.

```
<script src="/_Layouts/MyjQueryPlugins/MyLatestListData
.js" type="text/javascript"></script><script type="text/javascript">

$(document).ready(function () {
    // Wait until SP.JS has loaded before calling GetLatestItems
    ExecuteOrDelayUntilScriptLoaded(GetLatestItems, "sp.js");
});

function GetLatestItems() {
        // Call function with list name, I am using my 'Foods' list
    $.latestListData('Foods');

}

</script>
```

8. With the code primed, you are ready to take it for a test-drive. Save the web part and check to see whether you get an alert. The alert should appear because we haven't specified any options, so the default function will be used.

Figure 10-10. Alert showing latest list data

The alert (Figure 10-11) appears with the list data. At this point, you should be able to appreciate that although it may take some time to create a generic function to work with SharePoint data, once it has been created, there are huge gains to be had from only needing to write a couple of lines to return data. This is the only code that was needed:

```
$.latestListData('Foods');
```

9. Now we will take a look at how we can use the function's options to do more with the data being returned from the list. If we take a look at the list, we can see some of the information we can return. We need to remember that the Client Object Model needs the internal field name for the column, so we should make sure we get the right names. Figure 10-12 shows the data in the list that we want to see the top items from.

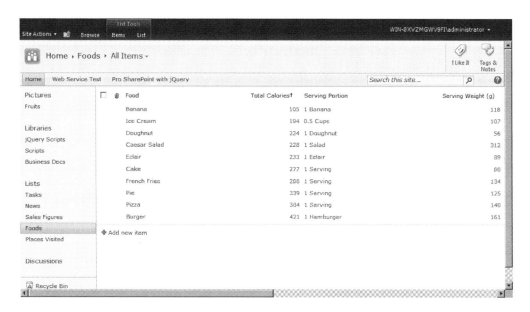

Figure 10-11. List showing foods to use with the jQUery function

10. We'll return all of the columns for this next example of using the function with the options. The column named Food is the Title column, so this can be retrieved using Title. Total Calories is named Total_x0020_Calories, Serving Portion is Serving_x0020_Size, and finally Serving Weight is Serving_x0020_Weight. The simple trick I used to find these internal names is to sort by the field and then look for the SortField query string parameter, as in Figure 10-13. You can see how the names can be different by looking at the Serving Portion column, which actually has an internal name of Serving Size because Service Size was its name when the column was created.

Figure 10-12. Using sorting to find the internal field name from the query string

11. With the field names retrieved, we can add the options to the function call to get the function to do what we want. Replace the Content Editor web part's HTML with this code:

```
<script src="/_Layouts/MyjQueryPlugins/MyLatestListData.js"
type="text/javascript"></script>
<script type="text/javascript">
```

```
$(document).ready(function () {
    // Wait until SP.JS has loaded before calling GetLatestItems
    ExecuteOrDelayUntilScriptLoaded(GetLatestItems, "sp.js");
});

function GetLatestItems() {
    // Call function with list name, I am using my 'Foods' list
    $.latestListData('Foods',
        {
            rowCount: 5,
            fieldNames: ['Title',
                                'Total_x0020_Calories',
                                'Serving_x0020_Size',
                                'Serving_x0020_Weight'],
            onSuccess: GetLatestItemsSuccess
    });
}

function GetLatestItemsSuccess(data) {
    $(data).each(function () {
        var foodInformation = $('<p> The food ' + this.Title + ' has ' +↵
 this.Total_x0020_Calories + ' calories and is usually served as ' +
                this.Serving_x0020_Size + ', which would weigh about ' +
this.Serving_x0020_Weight_x0020__x002 ı 'g </p>');

        $('#LatestFood').append(foodInformation);
    });
}
</script>

<div id="LatestFood" />
```

We are now making use of the options; the first is increasing the number of
elements being returned from the default 3 to 5. The field names are being
entered as an array using their internal names, and finally onSuccess is being
passed in the name of the function we want to use to render the list items to
the page. The GetLatestItemsSuccess function has a parameter called Data,
which will contain the formatted JavaScript objects. The function then iterates
through each item and extracts its values; it outputs them into a sentence,
creates a paragraph tag, and then appends the paragraph to a div with the ID
of LatestFood.

12. Save and check to see whether you have the five latest items coming back.
Figure 10-14 shows how it looks for me.

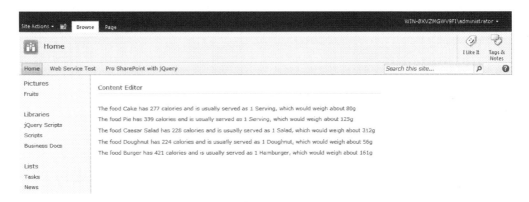

Figure 10-14. Content Editor showing the top five items in our chosen format

13. Adding a new item to the list should mean that it will be added when we come back to look at this page. I have added a steak, and sure enough, it is at the top of this list, as shown in Figure 10-15.

The food Steak has 379 calories and is usually served as 1 Steak, which would weigh about 182g

The food Cake has 277 calories and is usually served as 1 Serving, which would weigh about 80g

The food Pie has 339 calories and is usually served as 1 Serving, which would weigh about 125g

The food Caesar Salad has 228 calories and is usually served as 1 Salad, which would weigh about 312g

The food Doughnut has 224 calories and is usually served as 1 Doughnut, which would weigh about 56g

Figure 10-15. New items will appear at the top of the list.

In conclusion, functions are a fantastic way to be able to abstract away data retrieval tasks when working with SharePoint. Simple functions can be written, too, that can do things such as checking whether an e-mail address is valid or that a user-entered date is within a certain range; many times such functions have already been written, and you just need to find one and adapt it to suit your needs.

Summary

You should now be able to write a jQuery plug-in or function, allowing the consumers to supply their own options, maintaining chainability to make sure the buck doesn't stop with your plug-in, providing default functions for both plug-ins and jQuery functions, and allowing end users to provide their own if desired.

Good job for making it to the end of the book! You should now be comfortable bringing your SharePoint and jQuery solutions to life. I will look forward to seeing your SharePoint jQuery plug-ins appearing in the wild and would love to hear what you create.

Index

Printed in Great Britain
by Amazon.co.uk, Ltd.,
Marston Gate.